Legality and Illegality

Critic of Institutions

Roberta Kevelson
General Editor

Vol. 3

PETER LANG
New York • Washington, D.C./Baltimore • San Francisco
Bern • Frankfurt am Main • Berlin • Vienna • Paris

Legality and Illegality

Semiotics, Postmodernism and Law

Edited by
W. Richard Janikowski
& Dragan Milovanovic

PETER LANG
New York • Washington, D.C./Baltimore • San Francisco
Bern • Frankfurt am Main • Berlin • Vienna • Paris

Library of Congress Cataloging-in-Publication Data

Legality and illegality: semiotics, postmodernism and law / edited by W. Richard Janikowski & Dragan Milovanovic.
p. cm. — (Critic of institutions; vol. 3)
Includes bibliographical references and index.
1. Law—Philosophy. 2. Critical legal studies. 3. Postmodernism. 4. Semiotics (Law). I. Janikowski, W. Richard. II. Milovanovic, Dragan. III. Kevelson, Roberta. IV. Series.
K235.L44 340'.1—dc20 94-44888
ISBN 0-8204-2512-5 (hardcover) CIP
ISSN 1068-4689

Die Deutsche Bibliothek-CIP-Einheitsaufnahme

Legality and illegality: semiotics, postmodernism and law / ed. by W. Richard Janikowski, ... - New York; Washington, D.C./Baltimore; San Francisco; Bern; Frankfurt am Main; Berlin; Vienna; Paris: Lang.
(Critic of institutions; vol. 3)
ISBN 0-8204-2512-5
NE: Janikowski, W. Richard [Hrsg.]; GT

Cover design by Nona Reuter.

The paper in this book meets the guidelines for permanence and durability of the Committee on Production Guidelines for Book Longevity of the Council on Library Resources.

Printed in the United States of America.

DEDICATION

To my mother, Anna, who taught me to love books and the written word, and to my wife, Phyllis, whose love, support and encouragement allows me to pursue my true interests. *WRJ*

To Brian Burdekin, Human Rights Commissioner of Australia, for his relentless efforts to make a difference. *DM*

ACKNOWLEDGEMENTS

We gratefully acknowledge the support of the University of Memphis and of Northeastern Illinois University during our work on this manuscript. We especially wish to thank the Department of Criminology and Criminal Justice and the University Honors Program at the University of Memphis for their unqualified assistance during this project.

A special thanks to Dr. Jerry Sparger for his support during the duration of this project. Special thanks to Nancy Wilson and Jean Petrick for their untiring work and assistance in preparing this manuscript for publication.

We also wish to express our appreciation to the Center for Semiotic Research in Law, Government and Economics at Penn State University whose annual sponsorship of the Round Table on Law and Semiotics provided, and continues to provide, the intellectual inspiration for projects such as this one.

TABLE OF CONTENTS

Part I - Legality

Part II - Illegality

Chapter I

INTRODUCTION: SEMIOTICS, POSTMODERNISM AND LAW-QUESTIONS OF LEGALITY AND ILLEGALITY

W. Richard Janikowski and Dragan Milovanovic

The general topic of this anthology is the question of legality and illegality. The articles address a variety of issues in semiotics and postmodernism.

We find ourselves in an age of rapid change, and a semiotic analysis to phenomena, including law, provides us some critical tools of inquiry into the conditions of humankind. No longer a modernist society, we have entered the postmodernist society, a society marked by optimism and skepticism, hope and despair, openness and rigidity, hyper-real (simulacrum) and real, all at the same time. We look toward recent revolutionary changes in Eastern Europe and the former U.S.S.R. and can see firsthand the reconstitution of the semiotic field. Old signifiers are being filled in with new signified; "new" signifiers, on occasion with old signifieds (consider the resurgence of old communists in new party clothes). Closer to home, we see new, more subtle forms of social control developing. Alternative discursive fields are rapidly taking form within which novel constructions of reality may take place. Semioticians are especially well-suited in deconstructing ideologies claiming to be enlightening, and even better suited for contributing to reconstruction.

In Part I we include articles concerned primarily with legality. Part II is concerned more with the question of illegality. With these thoughts we move onto the chapters included here that look toward the postmodern society with a healthy degree of skepticism as to what it may provide.

Part I included five articles. Chapter two by Peter K. Manning, entitled "Postmodernism and Law," shows how a postmodernist perspective challenges conventional wisdom as to legal decision-making. From there, Manning provides an application of the deconstructive method by the application to rape and rape law.

Bruce A. Arrigo authors "Feminist Jurisprudence and Imaginative Discourse: Toward Praxis and Critique," our third chapter. Arrigo indicates how a postmodernist analysis could be brought to bear on the development of feminist jurisprudence. The key here is for establishing how precisely an *ecriture feminine* may be established. After examining the nature and potential for this discourse, Arrigo applies a feminist jurisprudential analysis to rape. His analysis compliments Peter Manning's. Arrigo, drawing out some possible, tentative implications for an *ecriture feminine*, concludes by informing us that this discourse must be grounded in an experiential feminism.

In our fourth chapter, Dragan Milovanovic in "Inscribing the Body with a Sign" provides some insights as to an alternative paradigm that is posed as better capturing the nature of the desiring subject. Accordingly, he draws from chaos theory as to alternative notions of cause, recent insights from cosmologists/physicists as to the nature of space (of greater than three-space dimensions), and psychoanalytic semiotics as to how desire is inscribed (mapped, *territorialized*) on the body. He concludes by showing how postmodern society often discovers the disciplinary mechanisms that produce docile bodies of utility.

The fifth chapter written by David S. Caudill, entitled "Two Ideological Monsters: The Subject of the Bar and the Object of Desire in *Bleak House*," is an application of a critically informed psychoanalytic semiotics to literature and law. He indicates the usefulness of these tools in the examination of hidden ideological structures.

Maarten Henket, in his chapter "Witness Under Cover," examines limits and precautions imposed on the use of testimonial evidence in the United States and the Netherlands. Exploring the cross-fertilization of concepts between the two legal systems--common law and civil law - he discerns future directions in each system regarding criminal procedure and individual rights.

Our final article in Part One is by Dion Dennis, entitled "License and Commodification: The Birth of an Information Oligarchy." He offers us the idea that the nature of pedagogy and management practices can be analyzed from a common critical framework. Dennis has undergone an archaeological dig, as in Foucault, to discover new forms of power that are based on information gathering, storing, and releasing. Cultural practices and social fields, he tells us, are being reconfigured. Market logics extend their force to all aspects of human existence and relations.

In sum, Part Two indicates that there are some potentially exciting lines of inquiry to be developed which would consider the first five articles together in examining the nature of the postmodern society. This is one of the challenges ahead for each of these theorists.

Part Two is focused on illegalities. This section includes articles which further examine the relationship of semiotics to law but specifically look at crime and its control.

Chapter eight, by Martin D. Schwartz and David O. Friedrichs entitled "The Value of Postmodern Theory to Critical Criminology: Violence Against Women and Corporate Violence," provide a critical overview of postmodernism as it has so far been applied to criminology. They then apply their understanding of postmodernism to violence against women and to corporate violence. They conclude with some thoughts as to what further can be done with a postmodernist analysis in criminology.

Jody Miller, in chapter nine, provides a discursive analysis of delinquent girls in her article "The Discursive Construction of 'Delinquent' Girls: Race, Class, Sexuality and Generation in Probation Investigation Reports." She is especially concerned with how race and class intersect with gender in the production of formal narratives and texts in the criminal justice system. Her case study focuses on probation workers and how they go about constructing texts in the presentence investigative reports which are used at sentencing/disposition time by the judge. Miller shows how particular discursive frameworks develop that reflect not only class biases, but also race and gender biases. They intersect, she informs us. She suggests that scholars be more sensitive to discursive constructions and how they often reflect hegemonic group's ideologies.

Our tenth chapter by Michael J. Lynch, Richard A. Lynch and Dragan Milovanovic, entitled "Deconstruction and Radical Criminology: An Analysis of Post-Modernism and its Possible Uses in Criminology," offers suggestions as to how deconstruction can be applied in critical criminology. They note how deconstructive techniques have not as of yet been embraced by critical criminologists. Marxism is compared with deconstruction to draw out some of the tools each may offer in an integrated critical framework. In the end, the authors offer some suggestions for a critically informed, materialistically based deconstruction in criminology.

In his chapter "'Good Faith', 'Bad Faith': Rhetoric, Ideology and the United States Supreme Court," W. Richard Janikowski explores the fluidity of our concepts of the legal and illegal. Focusing on U.S. Supreme Court decisions he investigates rhetorical techniques used to construct concepts within the law. He concludes by suggesting the opinions reflect tensions between modernist understandings of the law and the influences of postmodern thought.

Our final chapter is by Dragan Milovanovic, entitled "Moral Philosophy, Social Justice and the Question of Punishment in a Just Society." Milovanovic applies a critically informed psychoanalytic semiotics to the question of how to define social justice. He briefly reviews some dominant conceptions of justice, particularly on how "first principles" can be established. He then explores Jeffrey Reiman's recent offering of a "labor theory of moral values." He concludes with a postmodernist analysis--incorporating Lacan's psychoanalytic semiotics, chaos theory, and constitutive theory in law -- which is offered in order to examine the wherewithal of principles of justice in a just order. Five specific, but somewhat preliminary validity claims are offered for the development of a more holistic approach in establishing just principles in a just order.

In sum, the included chapters offer much provocative material that can, no doubt, be applied to not only a better deconstructive practice, but also to a reconstruction of the political economy and discursive practices in which the desiring subject can more adequately express her/himself in social encounters and better develop in the spirit of community.

Chapter II

POSTMODERNISM AND THE LAW*

P. K. Manning**

There is currently considerable interest in the social sciences in challenges to traditional, case-based, socio-legal analysis and in the postmodernist perspective. This paper first outlines a view of case-based legal decision-making that is challenged by the postmodern perspective. This analysis then provides a background for a discussion of deconstruction as a method for socio-legal analysis. A final section includes an example of the deconstruction of "rape" and rape law.

THE TRADITIONAL CASE LAW METHOD

A rather narrow "individualistic" perspective dominates socio-legal approaches to decision-making. Several of the most salient features of this perspective are: a) It assumes that legal decision-makers are isolated individuals who are unanchored by social ties, group obligations or interactional context. They are neutral and objective persons whose social values are either irrelevant or are consciously set-aside for the decision. b) It imagines that these decision-makers weigh carefully a known set of options in a given instance, case, or event. c) The deciders scrutinize all the relevant available (and non-problematic) facts and e) compare and contrast this data with other potentially relevant data. f) They will then weigh a limited number of options, and g) compare this (forthcoming) decision with other similar past (precedent-setting) or analogous decisions in order to produce a decision. h) These decisions are seen as typically, if not exclusively, having binary (yes/no, guilty/innocent) outcomes. i) The outcomes or decisions are assumed to meet clear and unambiguous organizational goals and objectives. Finally, j) these decisions will be so cast that they are in line with the relevant constraints and legal rules. Given this model, case outcomes, usually binary, such as "arrest" or "non-arrest," "guilty" or "innocent," "prison sentence" or "parole" can be correlated with selected "variables" to characterize or "predict" patterns of decisions made by courts, juries, prosecutors, or police officers.

The individualistic-case law model is complemented in socio-legal research by attitude-based survey research that aggregates individual views or attitudes as renditions of collective lines of action or working institutions and uses these as surrogates for patterns of deciding. This type of research can be seen in studies of legal discretion. A recent example may be of use. The author argues that structural attributes of counties and of judges can be taken as representative of the decision-making context in which judges make decisions about drug law violations. These attributes are correlated with length of sentence without an interpretation of the links (recognized or not) between these variables and the measured outcomes. After an elaborate statistical analysis, the author concludes, "...differential treatment by race depended simultaneously on both the offense and the political and social climate [unmeasured of analytically characterized in the article-PKM] during which sentencing occurred" (Myers, 1989: 312).

Typically, the case law approach, because of the above foci on the "rational case decider," omits several relevant matters. First, it glosses the *field* in which a decision is taken. These are the social forces, objective and subjective that shape the decision (Bourdieu, 1977). Second, it omits the process of framing the facts of the case and the associative paradigms and cognitive domains within which it is understood. Third, it omits the *context*, assumptions, values, ideologies, and social norms brought to the deciding process by the decision-maker(s). Finally, the *surround*, or the larger political environment of deciding, is unexplicated. Legal doctrine, legal rules, and prior decisions cannot account for these matters, and thus a perspective on deciding that permits a deconstruction of legal decision-making is useful.

The postmodern perspective, developed later in the paper, illuminates the case-law focus. The postmodern perspective questions the validity of all forms of authoritative deciding under formal, especially juridical, rules and procedures.

A CHALLENGE TO THE CASE-LAW METHOD: POSTMODERNISM

Postmodernism is a product of modern life and a perspective on modern social life. It undercuts many of the basic assumptions of the case-law method. Let us review some of the relevant features of postmodernism.

Postmodernism seeks to situate understandings in the complex world of signs, to eschew simple referential statements about the "real world," and to reject metanarratives that have long been associated with the powerful, the males, the whites, and members of developed societies. It grows directly from developments based on semiotics called "structuralism," and "post structuralism." It is heavily influenced by semiotics, or the science of signs, and uses this language to examine the central features of modern life. Postmodernism focuses on the role of the signifier, or the *simulacra*, as an unconnected and arbitrary point in a field of meaning that is often fragmented and disconnected from experience.

Images of events, media-generated scenarios, and second and third hand notions about life increasingly dominate experience. Two features of human beings emphasized in postmodernism are symbolic and they are linked: their capacity to freely use symbols (mainly language) and their ability to deceive themselves and others. As a *simulacrum* or image is widely reproduced, reified, especially by the mass media, it becomes a commodity. An image no longer is tied to experienced reality or the reality of everyday life, it becomes a reality to itself,"...the media provides the public with the illusion of reality and actuality" (Denzin, 1986: 196). What is true is that which can be reproduced.

The reality to which imagery refers is the reality created by imagery (other images) and the *hyperreality* (signs about signs taken as objective or universal opinion or truth) it produces and reproduces (Poster, 1989). Ironically, even as trust becomes more essential because of the distant and media-based nature of experience, *trust* in communication must increase. Intimacy and certainty decline. The centrality of imagery in guiding social life escalates. People share fewer close, intimate relations governed by known and agreed-upon values, standards and moral codes (or rules for interpretation). As the role of ordering assumptions and rhetorics, law, religion, science and even social science itself, are undercut, visual experience and media produced images gain in power and credibility.

Law, religion and science decline in their legitimacy. The hierarchy of credibility - the truth attributed to different socially valued sources of knowledge - of communicational forms (science, music, history, religion) is now blurred.

Time collapses. The present is seen as containing the past and the future; various forms and kinds of communication are used in different settings.

Authoritative versions of events are questioned and the legitimacy of the private/public distinction, along with distinctions between "true" and "false," are set aside.

Changes in the nature of social relations in postmodern societies have important implications for the nature, functions and quality of socio-legal studies. Facts and information become problematic.

Information overload becomes common, and the level of socially unwanted communication, noise, increases as well. Ambiguity is reflected and amplified even as variety is reduced. The possibilities for marking social relations unambiguously decreases.

Ambiguity and uncertainty in communication is assumed and taken for granted especially in interactions with strangers and mere acquaintances. Anxiety attends information overload. The marking of social relations, the differentiation of groups, the cultural and social ranking and individuation resultant within groups, and the quality of the transmission of information and expression ("culture") are now being fundamentally altered.

Public communication, especially among strangers, is not likely to be embedded in known premises, use-shared vocabularies and manifest similar symbolic repertoires (sets of symbols such as cliches, slang, framing remarks, and rituals that introduce them). Ambiguity and equivocality increase. Meanings and boundaries of categories used to establish the correct, suitable and proper, are messy and not well understood; moral categories and rules are not shared, or if shared in the abstract, not interpreted in shared ways. Furthermore, communication is less likely to entail corrective negative feedback, thus leaving much to ambiguity and clarification via authoritative or "marked" communicational channels or sources e.g. law and government. "Meaning" is not established when a message intended by a sender is received. For example, even within organizations, if communication is thought of as "strategic," then the management of the appearance of understanding is as important as clear and unambiguous communication.

Modern communication, not based entirely on shared values, edges along the lines of seeking a mere "working consensus," and the appearance of agreement is sought. The preoccupation is with achieving surface agreement rather than agreement on basic value premises. Language should be adequate to situational exigencies and should guide and outline action choices rather than a means for communicating absolutes in generalized forms of authoritative communication. Language will surely and truly fail to fully represent the layers of untruth, and so can be used best to play with the "unrepresentable" or unspeakable (Denzin, 1986: 202).

Even authoritative forms of communication have changed in nature and function in modern and post-modern societies. As Niklas Luhmann (1985) suggests, the relative autonomy of the law is being modified. It's legitimacy is based more on communicational mechanisms than upon tight social consensus. No longer can speculation about what a "rational and reasonable man" might do capture the range of intentions and actions in postmodern society. Words are used as tokens that cue a sense of order and continuity, and change in function from coherent expressive and instrumental aims embedded in shared contexts to shabby instruments. Simulation remains.

The ellision of immediate images, media images, and the decline of standardized formats for framing information yields new uncertainty and undecidability not only in texts, but in everyday life. In this sense, the law is embedded in social worlds and contexts that are not previously sedimented in decisions, especially common law doctrine assembled primarily in the last century. These ideas, now in rapid flux, are the "non-contractual elements of contract" so vividly illustrated by Durkheim and later elaborated skillfully by Stuart Macauley (1961).

The law is one of the "metanarratives" or grand schema for maintaining control over disparate meanings, fragmented values and perceptions, and a multiplicity of interpretations. Like science (Cf. Lyotard, 1981), law has been widely criticized. Derrida (1976) has provided, in the form of deconstruction, an approach to reconstituting hegemonic discourse. The implications of the work of writers such as Derrida and Lyotard, like critical legal studies in the United States, is to urge scholars to reconstitute the law. This may involve critically examining assumptions that render law inappropriate for modern socio-legal analysis. It is useful in this next section, then, to interweave a critique of the socio-legal case method with a discussion of deconstruction.

DECONSTRUCTION AND SOCIO-LEGAL STUDIES

Deconstruction

The most prominent exponent of deconstruction, Jacques Derrida, asserts emphatically that deconstruction cannot be reduced to mere "technique." He associates "technique" or even method with reification and the reduction and impoverishment of an imaginative approach to social and literary criticism. Deconstruction questions the ontology of being and the philosophic means by which reality is constituted.

Deconstruction is a carefully guided systematic critical activity or process that rejects notions of a standard method or set of techniques and preconceived approaches to texts or materials. Based on the semiotic analogy, deconstruction rejects binary oppositions and deductive logic, elevates the importance of overlapping meanings, mixed metaphors and volatile tropes, and seeks to identify traces of past meaning now sedimented into language. It envisions works on several levels at once, and often produces contradictory messages at different levels. Rather than seeing the system of signification as closed, it sees all texts as open to interpretation. The purpose of deconstructive analysis is to inspect and clarify the potential of various perspectives, narrative points of view, metaphors, and ideologies found in a rich mix in any text. Deconstruction asserts that systems of signification, once surfaced, provide the basis for undercutting their own features. That is, language is not a "mirror of reality" (Rorty, 1979), but the primary problematic. The imagined line between "society" and "discourse" is erased and society becomes a kind of text (Brown, 1990).

Deconstruction employs a model of texts, or writing more generally, that modifies the assumptions of semiotics. It is concerned with what is symbolized or represented in texts, not with explaining social life, choices, or individual behaviours. Language is both its data and source of inspiration. Like semiotic analysis, deconstruction can reveal *how* language contains contradiction, omissions, suppressed meanings, and can conceal disruptions and anomalies. Contradictions in communication at the surface and other levels work by tropes and modes of figurative language: lies, rhetorical style, ironies, oxymorons, framing and re-framing. Any placement of an idea in a given context risks containing self-contradictory features. As *Webster's* (Ninth New Collegiate Dictionary: 461) notes, figurative language "expresses one thing in terms normally denoting another with which it may be regarded as analogous." For example, both Umberto Eco (1979) and Jonathan Culler (1981) argue persuasively that the figurative properties of literary language are its defining features. Furthermore, if the devices of literature define it, an ironic conception of literature is possible: it displays in abundance the ultimately perverse, diverse, converse and reverse of all apparent meanings. Literary figures and literary analysis can be applied as well to legal texts and decisions as to any other form of written expression (Jackson, 1986).

The great forms of reasoning, law, literature, and philosophy, and even the social sciences, are dependent upon the communicative constraints of language (McCloskey, 1989). Such constraints, such as the ambiguity of metaphor and rhetoric, resist final, complete analysis and total understanding. All texts are open to endless debate, exegesis, and reinterpretation. Changes in levels and gaps in meaning produce a "supplement," or traces in association that emerge from the "undecidability" or openness of texts. Analysis of this internal potential for contradiction, in turn, produces yet another paradox, for the critical language (or the poetics) used to reveal the assumption of a single authoritative reading itself "works according to the principles being contested" (Culler, 1981: 41). Any critique is itself subject to the same internal critique. A spiral of interpretations and counter interpretations can result. The cognitive and informative features of language, its poetics and politics, cannot be easily wrenched from the metaphoric and figurative, and they are densely interwoven to convey the drama of social life.

Deconstruction is a profoundly powerful attack on logocentrism. One of the basic presuppositions of modern philosophy is the idea that a person, the intentional speaking subject, is the determinant of meaning. Logocentricism contains a false metaphysics of presence: the idea that a single reality is apprehended by a speaking subject. Notions summarized by the idea of *cogito ergo sum*, the claim that I think [speak], therefore I am are questioned. Western philosophy has built on the idea of a continuous presence of individuals and the idea of clear transcendental, shared meanings of words. Deconstruction rejects the superiority of speech over writing, e.g. the idea that different words all refer to the "same thing," while existing in spite of misleading speech. Derrida calls "the ruling illusion of Western Metaphysics" the belief that reason can somehow dispense with the complexities and productive vagaries of language and create a pure self-authenticating truth or method, and that there exists a reality "out there" that can be precisely mirrored in science and philosophy.

Deconstruction rejects the notion that communication works solely by means of patterns of binary opposition. All signifiers potentially contain their opposites. An X contains a Y within it; signs supplement and partially express each other. In the process of deconstruction, only *differences* remain. Signs produce difference and deterrence (described by Derrida in a french neologism, *différance*). This means signs express through difference (distinction) and delay what is not immediately obvious in the appearance of the signifier. Nevertheless, such omissions are central to analysis because they are critical to explication of a full range of the functions of signs. Uncertainty is implicit in the unfolding aspects of communication, and establishing single, unified and stable readings of texts is impossible. Furthermore, this suggests the relevance of spatial and temporal aspects of changes in meaning. A deconstructive move extracts the interplay of structure, meaning and uncertainty.

Deconstruction implies wrestling with the internal contradictions produced by any text. It seeks a dynamic, dialectic dialogue with given texts. A dialectic method places text and alternative readings or counter-text in tension and seeks to identify the conditions of thought that such reasoning imposes. If attends to that which it [logocentrism] seeks to repress. It has been called a means for analyzing the "war of the text," or the text as a "battleground of meanings." It eschews seeking to uncover the essential integrity of texts. All texts contain paradoxes; their own self-defeating contradictory or paradoxical elements that are suppressed or being repressed in the text.

The surplus meanings revealed by an analysis of the "absent differences" mentioned above, are one focus of Derrida's analysis of "writing." Writing is produced by the overlap of the written text and other deconstructed meanings. "Writing" is the product of examining the differences between the text and the critique. Much taken with the early Freud, and with the indeterminacy of action, and the effervescence of meaning, it plays with the tensions between the center of dominant structure of a text and the allusions, metaphors, slips, and "suppressed" or absent meanings marginal to an established reading of any social phenomenon or text. Thus, general explanations are not sought; deconstruction enables one to analyze that which in writing and texts resists or exceeds any such general summary and undercuts its utility. Some themes are repressed, yet available. In particular, any text will order reality in a specific fashion, and omit other aspects that a text might capture. All writing produces a subtle repression of potential meanings. The not-present leaves traces, supplements, or meanings not captured directly but suppressed or implicit in the writing. Let us now consider some of the implications of these philosophic ideas for the analysis of legal texts.

THE SOCIAL ORGANIZATION OF THE LAW AND DECONSTRUCTION

The case law method in fact draws on a number of assumptions that might be called the social organization of legal life. To reveal these is to make possible further exploration of the tacit and unrevealed work of deciding.

Deconstruction suggests that one first examine the institutional structures that freeze meaning. The institutional structures of law (and the legal system itself) provide a sanctioned basis for screening, framing and re-reframing social and cultural realities, as well as precisely delimiting the internal cognitive forms of knowledge that will be used to transact informational exchanges within legal setting. These institutionalized cognitive foci serve to direct attention away from extraneous and non-juridical facts standing outside the institutional boundary. Deconstruction draws attention to them. While the institutional focus will be on the facts of the case, interpolated into legal decisions and dogma, as initially presented by legal actors, other facts are suppressed by rule and tradition. Think, for example, of the rules of evidence that govern what is admissible in court in Anglo American criminal law, or the topics on which a witness is permitted to speak.

Rules powerfully omit from consideration facts that are not either/or, for these "facts of the case" will be used to determine the court's decisions. The cognitive blinder, omitting from view what is not "legal," "institutionalized misrecognition" (Bourdieu, 1977: 171) is a powerful conservative force. It operates to stabilize facts and to sustain and protect them from change, erosion, or extinction. Rules, said to be the heart of the legal institution, are embedded within institutional assumptions about the context within which these rules will be seen as relevant. Rules are both indices of patterns and pattern-setting devices within legal institutions. The internal structure of the social world of the law is also maintained by characteristic patterns of legal reasoning.

Conceptual fictions, such as "the reasonable man," stabilize the internal relations, as do legal discourse, interpretations of rules, and interpretations of interpretations. These latter are what H.L.A. Hart (1961) terms "secondary rules." By seeing these as constructions used to close the legal system and sustain its legitimacy in spite of the counter-factual character of its operation, deconstruction opens a closed world of texts having a sanctioned reality and limited interpretation. That is, it highlights how the law operates to reassert repeatedly the priority of its constructions over the everyday and routine putative law-breaking behaviour of defendants and litigants.

Moral actions with legal consequences are glossed by the label, "legal." The legal institution, as Luhmann points out, screens and controls " case-input" and the validity of the invocation of the law. This work of reasserting the precarious legal template takes place in spite of miscellaneous delicts, crimes, torts, violations of contracts, and human failures to observe the ordering rules embedded in law. A world of sustained and reified binary oppositions, "good" and "evil," each having identifiable legal consequences, is seen to cohere and be firmly lodged within the institutional structure. This moral world is itself sustained by the context of deciding. Thus, deconstruction would draw attention to the context that sustains the umbrella, "legal" and show that it overlaps with the ambiguous and murky social world of differences and ambiguities.

Decision-making is the core of the legal institution, but to "see" the nature of that core, one must explore the context within which a decision is taken. A (legal) context is all that is brought to a decision by the relevant parties, including all those expectations, rights and duties, and some conception of the nature of the process for the negotiation of claims amongst parties in instances where tacit agreement is not acknowledged by at least one of the parties.

In other words, the *legal context* sets and dramatizes the relevant "expectations about expectations" (Luhmann, 1986) that participants must adopt in order to operate within the legal institution. They must be prepared to accept a decision as either "yes" or "no," accept defeat (or victory) in those terms, and accept this particular conversion of morally messy matters into binary decisions. Legal cases must be carried across the line or boundary between everyday life and the legal system, and crossing this analytic boundary redefines a matter as something about which the participants are prepared to accept only a binary outcome. If one pulls back from these assumptions to deconstruct legal context, one could see that withdrawal of legitimacy, for example by religious groups such as Seventh Day Adventists, or Anti-Abortion groups, strips away context and sets in motion other expectations. The domain of God and that of "man" come into secular conflict.

The social organization of legal life includes more that the rules and mechanisms constitutive of the formal legal institution. It also includes the cognitive and social underpinnings which are necessary, if not sufficient, to sustain that differentiated socio-legal world. From this basis can be understood the specific transformations of meanings that occur within the formal legal institution, especially those taking place as a result of framing, keying, and re-keying. The focal point of legal decision-making, the case, is variously framed (See Hawkins and Manning, forthcoming).

Deconstruction would of course immediately see the relevant forces, field, or *champ* (Lemert, 1981) as determining outcomes. The individualistic perspective noted above focuses almost entirely on the presumed immediate cognitive focus or frame ostensively employed by lawyers. This cognitive isolation of an event is the process by which the rules or principles governing "what is going on here" may be surfaced. Any such frame, although a sharply drawn boundary around a set of activities, will also be found to exist within a field of activities. Deconstruction would allow reframing, or seeing an event as neither one thing or the other.

Clearly focusing exclusively upon the cognitive framing operations omits the influence of the field defined as the horizon of facts (social cues) within which a decision about that event is located by the deciders. The field may include a foreground of relatively salient facts or social cues (what happened as reported by various witnesses, for example) and a background of less salient or tacit knowledge against which the "foregrounded" cues are defined. Deconstruction transforms background and foreground.

Once decisions are named, or accounted for in some fashion publicly, they are sorted out by arbitrary organizational standards. For example, until recently, rape was considered a "sexual" crime, but has now been redefined as a crime of violence not of "sex" or "passion." Of course, it is neither one nor the other, but plays on the difference that it suggests exists between these two complex ideas.

Once made, decisions do not stand alone, for they are units or tokens that fit within a set of types of organizational decisions. They are associated within paradigms of ideas, e.g. operational decisions, programmatic decisions, financial decisions, sentencing decisions. A cluster of justifications are employed to rationalize decisions, and decisions can be classified further into domains or cognitive divisions found within a paradigm.

What might be called the *surround*, the broad political and economic developments within which decisions are cast and rationalized, embeds any frame set within a given decision field. Deconstruction, for example, would point out that the *surround* for legal decisions on abortion and rape was radically altered as a result of the women's movement, womens' employment, and economic power.

AN EXAMPLE OF DECONSTRUCTION: TWO CASES OF RAPE

Having seen some examples of how deconstruction might approach socio-legal analysis of decisions, we are prepared to examine more closely a legal example. Kim Lane Scheppele, in a masterful review (1987) of lawyer Susan Estrich's *Real Rape* (1987), provides an example of deconstruction of a legal concept, rape. It is a dense, well-argued essay consistent with the argument of this paper. Semiotic analysis is used to elaborate several of Scheppele's points.

Rape is a *signifier*, part of a sign with unclear or ambiguous referents. The *signifiers* of "rape" are unclear until analysis is undertaken. The sign, "rape", is an index of assumptions, or more generally, points to what one assumes others assume: "culture." In an important sense, the sign coexists in two social worlds. It has meaning within the common-sense world of the individual and in the social world of the law.

Scheppele, a sociologist, argues, following Estrich, that cases labelled with the term "rape," or those defined by the criminal charge, "rape," present what Scheppele calls "an interesting tension." On the one hand, "rape" cases are dismissed frequently by prosecutors for lack of evidence, willing witnesses or a credible victim. These cases typically manifest a high rate of attrition (they are dropped by the victim or the prosecutor, or dismissed in court) as they move through the criminal justice system. On the other hand, "rape" is considered a very serious crime, perhaps the most serious other than incest and first degree murder. Those convicted of rape are given very long prison sentences and treated with moral opprobrium in the press. Why these two kinds of outcomes?

The problem can be clarified by deconstructing the term. It is possible that the term "rape" indexes, or refers to, more than one phenomenon. Perhaps it refers not to a single concept, but rather to a "family of concepts" (Wittgenstein, 1953). If one thinks of the signifier-signified link in the first instance as one of denotative meaning, then "rape" has several important denotations. The denotations, or what might be called the "first-level signifiers", or the term "rape", can be assembled or clustered into two paradigms. The first paradigm is called "real rape." The second, no less real to the victims, is called "technical or simple rape" (Scheppele, p. 1100).

These two linguistic paradigms, associative contexts within which ideas cohere and have meaning, permit a closer analysis of "rape." Any given case can be considered a token of one of the two types. These two paradigms highlight the similarities necessary to unravel the differences between the two kinds of denotations.

The field of events in which the case arises differ. Let us further deconstruct the events, the social circumstances or *field of activities*, from which the report of the rape arises.

The first type of rape is *real rape*. In the situation that is subsequently called "real rape," the event involves a woman who is either accosted by stranger(s) with force or with weapons or by multiple rapists. The reported race of the defendant(s) and the accused differ. This is especially salient if the victim is white and the putative assailants are black. This set of elements or denotations combine within the real rape paradigm. They now are clustered as elements or having connotative meaning. The facts are framed as instances of "real rape." The victim will be treated sympathetically by the criminal justice agencies. A decision may be reversed at the appellate level if additional facts are not perceived as present.

If it takes place, an appellate review can be seen as a kind of "deconstruction" of the event labelled "real rape." The facts of the case, or the elements assembled within the paradigm, are isolated from other potentially relevant facts, *the field*, when the first decision was taken. Appellate courts may reverse the field and the ground. Facts that normally remain as background may become focal in an appellant review. These facts are such matters as whether the woman resisted the attacker, whether she had prior knowledge of the person, and whether her behaviour is seen as blameless. These constitute a new, deconstructed field that sets aside some facts seen as constituting the case before appeal and highlights others. This new field is now the pertinent field within which the case lies. In a sense, the appellate court "deconstructs" the facts of the "real rape" thus transforming it into a "simple rape."

A second type of rape is the *simple rape*. Cases seen as "simple" rapes have a high probability of being refused by prosecutors or subsequently dismissed. These cases lie in a field of facts that include as salient facts: female victims who know, however fleetingly, their assailants, force or weapons are absent, and the accused rapist acts alone. The victim of simple rape produces dubious sympathetic value. The field in this case reflects an event constituted from reports of that are read off as indicating that the victim had prior knowledge of her assailant, use "poor judgement," and failed to resist. The facts are framed differently. As a result, the victim is blamed. This transformation of facts means that the case is now placed in the paradigm or associative context of "simple rape."

As a result of this mental encoding and decoding of facts, framing of the event within a field, the notion that two types of rape, each with quite different action potential and institutional consequences, is sustained. Scheppele, following Estrich, believes that revisions in rape laws, such as changes in evidentiary rules, and in the nature of resistance required of the victim to prove herself innocent, did not, and perhaps will not in future, alter the processing of rape cases by the courts. The cases were still placed into one of the two extant paradigms. The mental constructs used within the criminal justice system to make sense of rape cases are rather durable.

The paradigmatic ordering of the facts into "real" and "simple" and the resultant legal decisions were little altered in spite of diligent attempts and some successes in legal reform of-state rape laws in the 1970's. As Estrich points out (1987), these reforms simply added new screens or "filters" that sorted out facts in the case used to frame "real rapes" and "simple rapes." The courts deal formally primarily with "real rape" cases.

There are several reasons why reform did not work to provide greater protection for victims. The case as constituted by police and prosecutors is cognitively framed as it was before. It is slotted into one or the other of these two paradigms. The social construction of facts and evidence is shaped by these matters of context and framing, what is brought to the facts. The framing serves to suppress as legal evidence relevant differences in the perceptions of men and women of such key ideas as "force," "touch" and "caressing." For example, if force is defined using what Scheppele calls "boys' rules" -- those governing playground fights -- one paradigm, then physical touching, even an unwanted caress, for wome, is a source of anger and potentially a crime, while in another paradigm, "courting" or "dating," they are just moves in a "game," not serious violence. Thus, an encounter can be defined into two quite different ways by participants. Consistent with the deconstructionist position, words and what is said are but an index of "something else." It is not a question of whether the woman says "no," but the way she frames it and the paradigm within which she construes the gestures, postures and words exchanged in the encounter.

These matters of context and paradigmatic thinking unfold in a socially constructed narrative in court. It will omit certain facts, perceptions and interpretations, and will make others legally relevant. Scheppele writes, "*Women and Men do* [italics in the original] have very different perceptions of experience, but in the context of law one set of perceptions is hidden...What remains - the perceptions acknowledged, recognized, *seen* in law - is the socially constructed 'objective' point of view against which both men's and women's actions are judged by both men and women. That point of view is the law. But it is not the point of view of all." (Scheppele, 1987:1112-1113). Scheppele has managed to deconstruct the accepted facts in law and add a relevant context, framing, and field to her analysis. This analysis is augmented by her explication of the *surround* or horizon which changed between the late seventies and the present. The womens' movement, changing legal procedures, police investigative training and sensitivity, including using more female detectives as interviewers in allegations of rape, have altered the *surround*. Alterations in legal rules and laws governing case-decisions have also occurred.

However, a full analysis of rape decisions would require a refined conceptual framework derived from semiotics. It would require an explication of the paradigms into which actual cases are cast. Fieldwork should focus on the extent to which "real rape" and "simple rape" paradigms work to shape legal deciding at critical points in the criminal justice system (Cf. Hawkins and Manning, forthcoming).

In Scheppele's analysis, the notion that an objective narrative containing legal facts that captures a single core notion found in the law is questioned. The socially arbitrary character of legal thought is highlighted. It is not far from this critique to a more detailed postmodernist critique of law. Such a critique is unfortunately beyond the scope of this paper.

COMMENT

This paper hints at the utility of deconstruction and analyses of case law shaped in part by postmodernism. However, it is quite clear that whatever the hegemonic power of legal thinking and individualistic case-law analyses, many challenges to it exist. These challenges are represented broadly by phenomenological analyses of deciding and discretion, feminist jurisprudence, critical legal studies and the re-vision of law generally.

* *Presented in a session, "Postmodernism and the Law" at the annual meetings of the Law and Society Association, Berkeley, CA. 30 May 1990.*

** *Peter K. Manning is Professor of Sociology and Criminal Justice at Michigan State University.*

REFERENCES

Bourdieu, P. 1977. *An Outline of a Theory of Practice* Cambridge: CUP.

Brown, R. H. 1990. "Rhetoric, Texuality, and the Postmodern turn in Sociological Theory" *Sociological Theory* 8 : 188-197.

Culler, J. 1981. *Deconstruction* Ithaca: Cornell University Press.

Denzin, N. 1986. "Postmodern Social Theory." *Sociological Theory* 4:194-204.

Derrida, J. *Grammatology* trans. with an introduction by G. C. Spivak. Baltimore: Johns Hopkins University Press.

Eco, U. 1979. *A Theory of Semiotics* Bloomington: Indiana University Press.

Estrich, S. 1987. *Real Rape*. Harvard University Press.

Hart, H. L. A. *The Concept of Law*. Oxford: OUP.

Hawkins, K. and P. K. Manning, *Legal Decision-Making*, OUP, forthcoming

Jackson, G. 1986. *Semiotics and Legal Theory*, London: Routledge, Kegal Paul.

Lemert, C. 1981. "Introduction:" to C. Lemert (ed.) *French Sociology* New York: Columbia University Press.

Luhmann, N. 1986 *Sociology of Law* Routledge, Kegan Paul, London.

Lyotard, J. F. 1981. *The Postmodern Condition*. Minneapolis: University of Minnesota Press.

Macauley, S. 1961. "Non-contractual relations in Business" *American Sociological Review* 28:55-67.

McCloskey, R. *The Rhetoric of Economics*. Madison: University of Wisconsin Press.

Manning, P. K. 1987. *Semiotics and Fieldwork*. Newbury Park, CA: Sage.

____. 1992. *Organizational Communication*. Hawthorne, NY: Aldine.

Myers, M. 1989. "Symbolic Policy and the Sentencing of Drug Offenders" *Law and Society Review* 23.

Poster, M. (ed.) 1989. *Jean Baudrillard*. Stanford University Press.

Rorty, R. 1979. *Philosophy and the Mirror of Nature* Princeton: Princeton University Press.

Scheppele, K. L. 1987. "The Revisioning of Rape Law," *University of Chicago Law Review* 54:3, 1095-1116.

Wittgenstein, L. 1953. *Philosophical Investigations*. Trans. G.E.M. Anscombe. Oxford: Blackwell.

Chapter III

FEMINIST JURISPRUDENCE AND IMAGINATIVE DISCOURSE: TOWARD PRAXIS AND CRITIQUE[*]

Bruce A. Arrigo[**]

From a postmodern and semiotically-conceived feminist perspective, the phenomenal countours of legality and illegality need to be reconfigurated. Not only does the juridico-linguistic communicative market (i.e., the phallocentric market) cleanse the juridic subject's multiaccentual (oppositional/alternative) discourse, but the intrapsychic and intersubjective dimensions of feminine desire are denied affirmative codification in the domain of legal "male speak". The result is that commodity production (i.e., discourse construction) of feminist ways of knowing is minimized and this juridico-linguistic cirrculation is denied. Put another way, the postmodern, semiotically-informed feminist point of view is typically relegated to the realm of linguistic banality and, when applied to legal dogmatics or jurisprudence, intellectual absurdity. The question that must be addressed, therefore, is whether any criticially conceived feminist thought can prevent itself from the dangers of disappearing into a mysogynous sea of silence. If so, the issue then is what contributions would such a language portend for the sociology of law. Situated within the more recent trend of "second wave" feminist scholarship is the debate concerning the establishment of a feminist jurisprudence. A pivotal, although understated, theme addressed by legal commentators is whether it is even possible to render an *écriture féminine* (an uncultivated discourse for and about women) (e.g., Littleton 1987; MacKinnon 1983; Thorton 1986; Bottomley 1987).[1] Alternatively expressed, in the communicative market of law and justice the question is whether it is even conceivable to fashion a language of jurisprudence freed from the misogynous trappings of our culture (Arrigo 1992). Thus far the current climate of evolving consciousness for women suggests that the insights of Marx and conflict theory (MacKinnon 1989; 1983;

Cain 1979; Smart 1984), Foucault and the postmodern critique (Bell 1991; Diamond and Quinby 1988; Taylor 1986; Smart 1989), Lacan and psychoanalytic discourse (Duchen 1986; Grosz 1990; Sellers 1991; Ragland-Sullivan 1986) while indeed controversial are, nonetheless, heuristic avenues that inform the dialogue.

Not surprisingly, this diversity of analytical approaches has spawned some rather remarkable speculation on the question of an *écriture féminine*. Related to this intriguing theoretical work, however, is the pragmatic skepticism of some who question the wholesale "quest for a feminist jurisprudence" (Smart 1989, p. v). Others have commented on how "grand theorizing" tends to ignore any reference to the material world or social order (Gilligan 1982; Gilligan, Lyons and Hanmer 1990). In addition, still other feminist legal critics suggest that any form of global analysis is itself within the logic of masculine reasoning (Lahey 1985). This particular position embraces a psychoanalytic reading of thought structures and language patterns. For those who reject the role of theory as a necessary condition for establishing an *écriture féminine*, context is irrelevant to unconscious intent. The unconscious intent of totalizing analysis is understood as signifying "phallogocentric" interests. These interests induce oppositional and conflictual thought processes linked to "the allocation of power, domination, oppression and exploitation [of women] (Lahey 1985, p. 538). This oppositional and conflictual discourse is designed to eliminate or invalidate ambiguities and contradictions (crucial moments of knowing within a feminist praxis) because they are considered imperfections. This analytical approach is precisely what atheoretical feminists claim is the cornerstone of the masculine linguistic code and it is also why they contend that it is thoroughly dangerous. In short, the preceding analysis is anathema to the feminist agenda because it is predicated on male thought, reproduces power relations and, consequently, subtends any alternative discourse such as an uncultivated linguistic market for and about women.

In recognition of the various contributions and the assorted criticisms from feminist scholars on the issue of establishing an *écriture féminine*, the aim of this work will be to attempt a theory of feminist jurisprudence and to demonstrate its paradigmatic utility by considering the specific issue of rape. Elsewhere, I have referred to this theory as "experiential feminism" (Arrigo 1992). Not unlike any evolving analytical paradigm, the abstract dimension of the theory can benefit from some refinement. Following in the tradition of Foucault (1970; 1972; 1980), Lacan (1977; 1978; 1982), Irigaray (1985), Ricoeur (1973; 1975), Kristeva (1980; 1984), Lyotard (1984) and other postmodern critics, there is a resonating *leitmotif* in this scholarship which suggests that all language is essentially figurative. This realization has prompted Murray (1986) and Dews (1987) to argue that situating oneself in the realm of imaginative discourse renders possible the establishment of a freer, more liberating dimension of desire. In other words, establishing alternative communicative markets (like the language system of a feminist jurisprudence) is possible to the extent that it requires one to be re-situated in and to return to the imagination.

The theoretical outline of experiential feminism will explore the important issue of the imagination and its role in fashioning an uncultivated discourse on jurisprudence for and about women. This outline will briefly include a recent historical presentation of important critical thought on the subject, followed by a more defined assessment of experiential feminism's constitutive elements. Moreover, this work will address the question of whether establishing an *écriture féminine*, understood as experiential feminism, is or is not itself an inherently "essentialist" (and therefore phallocentric) endeavor. Some position on this issue, in the domain of jurisprudence, will also be taken.

In addition to sketching experiential feminism's conceptual framework and addressing the framework's potential for phallocratic essentialism, this paper will move toward the level of praxis. Praxis is important to the feminist agenda because experience (practice) has always been a starting point from which to examine the material world, step back and construct a methodology and discover a general theory or an evolving truth (Smart 1989).

This article will move to the level of praxis by exploring the question of rape. With regard to this issue, feminist observers and the intellectual camp to which they claim allegiance are quite divided. The insights of Foucault (1979), Lacan (1982), Irigaray (1985), Plaza, (1980), MacKinnon, (1987; 1989) and other notable theoreticians have provided a powerful backdrop for applied research on the topic of rape (e.g., Bell 1991; Tempkin 1987; Scully and Morolla 1984; Rowland 1986; Adler 1987). The full scope of this scholarship will not be canvassed in this paper. However, the deconstructive analysis which many of these commentators have done (especially the decoding of rape understood as signifying power, violence and sexuality) will be examined.

In the last section of this piece some provisional statements about the philosophical underpinnings of experiential feminism will be offered. As tentative propositions (i.e., as a critique of the theory), they point out where future research on the theory, in its corresponding relationship to the law, must be targeted. Thus, these final comments are nothing more than textual departures signifying the incompleteness of the project and the importance of their refinement and resolution to the overall task.

EXPERIENTIAL FEMINISM: SOME RECENT HISTORICAL ANALYSES

The idea of experiential feminism embraces the centrality of the imagination in constituting and re-constituting reality. Modern studies on the imagination's capacity to fashion the world of everyday experience largely borrow from philosophical investigations (e.g., Husserl 1983; Heidegger 1962; Sartre 1979; Ricoeur 1975; Murray 1986; Dews 1987). A pivotal issue addressed in these and similar studies is the strategy of metaphorical discourse to "shatter and increase our sense of reality by shattering and increasing our language" (Ricoeur 1973, p. 111). Ricoeur's reference to language as metaphorical anticipates the more general activity of living imaginatively (i.e, dwelling in the communicative market of paradox, ambiguity, contradiction, etc.) (Murray 1986). More importantly for feminism, however, Ricoeur's reference leaves open the possibility of announcing the articulation of an *écriture féminine*. That is to say, a woman's "authentic" reality finds expression through language. The word "authentic" is used here in the existential-phenomenological sense and includes the possibility of revealing the stream of meaning embedded in one's discourse construction and the intersubjective validity of this grammar through concernful reflexivity (Diamond and Quinby 1988; Husserl 1983; Heidegger 1962).

"Stepping back" from language and examining each morphemic element of discourse is precisely the methodological approach that Irigaray (1985) offers us in her deconstructive psycholinguistics. The focus of Irigaray's psycholinguistic analysis is a critical examination of language, linked to sexuality, and the absence (repression) of a grammar that authentically represents a woman's experiences. Irigaray's point is that an *écriture féminine* must begin by displacing the "phallic economy of sameness." The phallic economy of sameness is an unconscious and reductive mechanism that privileges "male speak" and, by necessity, invalidates and oppresses--within broader political economic dimensions (Kristeva 1980; 1984)-- alternative communicative markets, especially the feminine code. For Irigaray, *contra* the phallic economy of sameness, feminine consciousness is not phallogocentric but polymorphous. In order to resist the discursive phallomorphic mechanism operating in discourse, Irigaray calls for a close re-reading (deconstruction) of the "grammar of each [languaged thought], "its syntactic requirements, its imaginary configurations, its metaphoric networks and...its silences" (p. 75).

In part, Irigaray's disruption of language can be seen as borrowing from Foucault (1970; 1972; 1979; 1980) and Lacan (1977; 1978; 1982). The full body of Foucault's work was a deliberate effort to *resist* power/knowledge discursive formations (Merquior 1982; O'Farrell 1989). In other words, Foucault found modern society to be constituted by certain truths (knowledges) which functioned as the form of the expression of power. He argued that these power/knowledge formations (technological advances in psychology, forensics, criminology, epidemiology and so forth) were designed to "de-pathologize and normalize" the deviant or regulate the behavior of the uninitiated (Lemert and Gillan 1985). Foucault concluded that these technologies, as disciplinary systems, linguistically (and therefore socially) *privileged* only certain truths while dismissing others. This logic is compatible with Irigaray and other psycholinguistic feminists who posit that the discursive formation of sexuality, viz., male speak, phallomorphically invalidates the discourse of women.

While Irigaray's (1985) postmodern rejection of male-dominated thought and language structures includes a condemnation of Jacques Lacan's phallocentric Symbolic Order, Lacan (1982; 1978; 1977), too, can be seen as partially informing Irigaray's project of discovering an *écriture féminine*. A close reading of Lacan's work from the early to mid 1970s indicates some profound statements regarding the exclusion of women in the Symbolic Order, founded on the Father's Law (Milovanovic 1992). The argument hinges on the notion of Freud's (1949) theory of sexuality. Specifically for Lacan, and those feminists who claim allegiance to the Lacanian psychoanalytic school, the Oedipal phase is a way of understanding the process by which women enter the Symbolic Order, conceived of as male (Grosz 1990; Sellers 1991).

Lacan, however, does not end his commentary on the Symbolic Order here. He also contends that women have access to an "supplementary *jouissance*" (Lacan 1982, p. 144). This more liberating, sexual identity (excess) for women is the key to a vastly different (alternative) discourse, an *écriture féminine*. Moreover, for Lacan (1982) the locus of this *jouissance* is myth and narrativity (the unfolding of one's life story). Thus, like Foucault, Lacan also informs Irigaray's postmodern critique of female sexuality, psychoanalytic thought, and discourse construction by recognizing that the birth (rediscovery) of an uncultivated communicative market for and about women requires a return to narrativity and myth.

EXPERIENTIAL FEMINISM: ASSESSMENT OF A DEVELOPING THEORY OF JURISPRUDENCE

Following in the tradition of postmodern feminist analysis, experiential feminism identifies the imagination as the locus of establishing an *écriture féminine* (Arrigo 1992). The constitutive elements of experiential feminism include the place of metaphor, symbol and myth in altering prevailing social reality. Each of these elements is examined in this section. Their link to establishing a feminist jurisprudence is also addressed.

Metaphor - Earlier the suggestion was made that metaphorical discourse possesses the capacity to alter prevailing subjectivity (reality) in that the coordinates of a linguistic system can be shattered and increased. This preliminary interpretation of metaphorical language has important implications for legal semiotics (Robertshaw 1980; 1984; Tiefenbrun 1986) or sign system analysis (Foucault 1972). Exploring the full dimension of either theory in its relationship to metaphorical discourse is too substantial a digression for purposes of this article. In part, though, the point being made is that linguistic coordinate systems "select out" what phenomena will be identified as events and what phenomena will be identified as non-events (Milovanovic 1986; 1988). The more Marxist-based semiotics of Goodrich (1984; 1987), for example, pursues this theme by examining the structure of legal discourse. He claims that the juridico-linguistic communicative market is the argot of "elite or professionalized power; it is the language of authority [and patriarchy], which takes the discursive form of monologue, distance (temporal and hierarchical), and specialization" (Goodrich 1984:187). Thus, for Goodrich, legal discourse "selects out" what communicative structure will represent its own phallogocentric interests.

The importance of metaphor is that it communicates in ways that defy traditional understanding and resists the phallogocentric (reductive) process of selecting out. The metaphorical in language re-situates our experiences in ambiguity, multiplicity, uncertainty and contradiction (crucial moments of knowing for a feminist praxis). Metaphorical discourse is "as a lie that tells the truth, a confusion that clarifies, a detour that puts one directly on the road, a blindness that enables one to see all the better" (Murray 1975, p. 281). The relationship between legal semiotics and metaphorical discourse signifies how profoundly linguistic systems (e.g., law) can be disrupted (shattered and increased). In other words, the metaphor possesses the capacity to disassemble and reassemble reality in countless different ways, like a collage that signifies multiple meanings. Thus, the metaphor refuses the privilege-based and normalizing (Foucault 1980) limitations of uniaccentual (one meaning) (Volosinov 1986) male-speak.

This resistance to one meaning, this multi-accentuality, is significant for experiential feminism in its rendering of a feminist jurisprudence. As experiential feminism uncovers metaphorical expressions that more authentically describe the feminine in consciousness (Irigaray's resistance to the phallic economy of sameness), a more meaningfully lived account of one's story will unfold. This unfolding, then, functions as an oppositional or insurgent discourse (Milovanovic 1986) that repudiates linguistically privileged (male-dominated) conceptions of law, justice, rights, freedoms, equities and the like.

Symbols - Susan Langer (1951) describes the two symbolic modes that ground our human responses to experience as constructive and active. One idea of symbols is their ability to express the logical as a function of scientific knowledge and certainty. The other notion attends to the world of emotion, fantasy and dreams. This latter reference to symbolism characterizes the human subject's experiences in the *lebenswelt*: the realm that is beset by plurisignification, multiple meanings and ambiguity rather than the antiseptic, calculating, dispassionate realm of logic.

Wheelwright (1968) elaborates upon the symbolic as lived world. He unpacks the various levels upon which the symbol can be discerned, revealing five such grades. One of the more interesting symbolic levels is the cultural where images extend to an entire community or people. Here they possess the capacity to instantly reveal and touch the traditions of a society and its individuals, while, at the same, they can effect a transformation of both (Murray 1986, p. 129). This transformation is like a rebirth, rooted in our imagination and its ability to contextualize experience in ways that more intimately announce our own life stories.

Symbols function as "indexical" signs (Peirce, 1958). They point to (signify) something more, or something other, than what is presented. Experiential feminism, as a method for announcing an *écriture féminine*, must resist those phallocratic images that reductively define the feminine in consciousness. Linear depictions of woman as "the homemaker", "the wife", "the career woman", "the mother" and other comparable examples, are selecting out processes that dismiss the possibility for symbolic characterizations that would otherwise identify the feminine as *multiplicity* (Arrigo 1992). *All* women are identified as either homemakers, wives, professionals, mothers or, some combination, without more (or other) reference to what these indexical phrases signify. Returning, as does Irigaray (1985), to a critique of Freud's (1949) theory of sexuality also illuminates how this masculine reductionistic imperative prevails. A woman's sexual pleasure does not reside *either* in clitoral activity *or* vaginal passivity, as Freud maintained. Female eroticism is diversified. The symbolic characterizations of the feminine mentioned above privilege form, unity, identity, sameness and so forth. These are the constituents of masculine logic. Dismissed in the process is any alternative reading, any alternative discourse. The project of experiential feminism through symbols is to displace, to dismantle, phallogocentric imagery, making way for those symbols that speak the grammar of an uncultivated feminine discourse.

Applying this interpretation of symbols to a feminist jurisprudence is a three-step process. First, legal icons (patriarchal symbols), and the discourse used to codify their meaning, must be shown to invalidate (oppress) the place of feminine consciousness. Second, these misogynous characterizations (images) of juridical truth, justice, liberty, interests and the like, must be sufficiently de-centered and/or de-stabilized through active linguistic and social resistance to their unitary and normalizing power. Third, alternative juridical symbols communicating themes of multiplicity, contradiction, paradox, ambiguity, inconsistency, plurisignification, etc. (the linguistic coordinates of a feminist praxis), must be identified and articulated.

Myth - Like metaphor and symbol, myth and myth-making are critical ingredients in the imaginative discourse process. Through myth, a world is established where the customs, beliefs and even institutions of a culture are mirrored (Murray 1986, pp. 159-163). In this way, myth is linked to ritual; the two manifest a delicate interdependence illuminated by language where the spoken narrative is transformed into lived action. The myth, then, announces a particular style of language or a unique understanding of a people's thought, just as much as ritual enacts that language or thought. This wording returns us to the symbolic and metaphorical order that, in turn, informs our culture's choice of mythology and/or myth-making.

Because the myth is always and already of a language, the form that it takes is that of the narrative (Murray 1986, p.169). Stories are imbued with a sense of character, situation and time, describe the unfolding and enduring drama of one's existence, and point to the dissonance and ambiguity of one's decisions. We are forever living our stories with all their incompletenesses, inconsistencies and inevitabilities. We touch and are touched by those of others because there is something of our own narrative there; intimate yet shared, personal yet public.

Acknowledging that the myths of our lives are, in some fashion, commonly shared stories is not to imply that they are a static constellation of events. Precisely because the myth is a story its beginnings are born in the imagination's capacity to conceive of and describe on-going, lived experience in intimately meaningful ways. Myth-making is that practice where we invent, through language, those stories that depict our unique encounters with the world. That there is an element of familiarity for us in the imaginings of others should come as no surprise, given that narration (language) is a critical dimension of our existence. In this regard, we recognize that the wording of life is intrinsic to its being lived and that institutional expressions of our culture (in this case jurisprudence) originate through the instrumentality of language promulgated by the selected mythology that we create through it.

Experiential feminism as myth-making is the process whereby one authors their life. This chronicling is a personal recounting of the journey of one's lived experience. The work of experiential feminism through myth is to render the telling of narratives that more authentically depict the experience of women and the situations in which they find themselves. Starting from the phallocratic power structure that subtends the feminine frame of reference, MacKinnon (1987 pp. 38-9) argues that whatever women claim as their own (including the claim to their own stories or myths) is based on "... what male supremacy has attributed to [this sex] for its own use." For MacKinnon (1987; 1989) to speak of a woman's mythology is to describe what the misogynous language system says the feminine narrative is. Moreover, she contends that this misogynous assigning reflects the real social relationship between the sexes as organized male dominance over and subordination of women. MacKinnon's (1987; 1989) solution to the absence of a non-bastardized feminine point of view is to construct an action-oriented praxis. She maintains that this praxis should be built around consciousness-raising in which, through discourse (myth-making), women can better understand their sexuality and the implications this language holds for others, systematically forging an altered situational politics for feminine consciousness.

In summary, the application of experiential feminism to the rendering of a feminist jurisprudence requires one to identify and resist those metaphors, symbols and myths that represent our phallocentric system of law and justice. The limitations of this article neither permit me to canvass fully the theoretical or the methodological elements of this undertaking. On a more general level, though, experiential feminism seeks to displace the metaphors of "rules", "facts", "proofs", "burdens", "evidences", etc., as constituents of juridical (patriarchal) truth. In addition, experiential feminism rejects the misogynous implications of such symbols as the courtroom; the legal method; the reasonable man standard; case precedent; judge-dominated decision making and so forth. As the ingredients of a linguistic register, these metaphors and symbols are founded on a unitary morality, representing the myth-making of the masculine imperative. The work of experiential feminism in its rendering of a feminist jurisprudence is to de-center law and reconceptualize justice. Following Irigaray's (1985) psycholinguistics, this deconstruction of jurisprudence must occur in such a way that masculine categories of thought and reason are not codified. This language working must be grounded in reflexive, concernful, imaginative discourse so that the feminine in consciousness can announce the unadulterated experiences of women.

EXPERIENTIAL FEMINISM AND THE QUESTION OF ESSENTIALISM

Experiential feminism as a juridical code both accepts and resists the essentialist position. In brief, the essentialist question identifies the rigorous search for an uncultivated discourse for and about women as the intellectual pursuit and linguistic work (trap) of the masculine. The systematic reconstitution of the feminine experience is a phallocentric endeavor. It implies an elemental inventory of characteristics, a checklist, that forms a unitary set of guiding principles. The work of Grosz (1990), Sellers (1991), Kristeva (1980; 1984), Ragland-Sullivan (1986) to name just a few, has examined the concept of an *écriture féminine*. In addition, each in their own way has crossed this Rubicon. Like Irigaray (1985), I advocate the necessity for a grammar, a sign system, that seeks to establish a woman's *jouissance*. Also like Irigaray (1985) and Foucault (1970; 1972) before her, I recognize that any linguistic code as a system assumes the form of the expression of power. In other words, language legitimizes, indeed privileges, *only* that communication that conveys meaning through its defined coordinates (Milovanovic 1986; Habermas 1984; 1975). The discourse of experiential feminism is therefore essentialistic on two fronts. First, it is an attempt to discover, to identify, a particular language. Second, the argot of this grammar is specialized. Effective communication requires that transmitters and receivers of its messages (whether they be verbal or otherwise) understand the coded signs of this uncultivated feminine discourse.

What is not of the essentialist mystique, however, is *how* experiential feminism unfolds. This unfolding in the domain of jurisprudence is polymorphous and subject to the insights of literary scholarship. As previously described, my postmodern perspective on law and justice attempts to resist the masculine seduction to reduce experience to uniaccentuality. I submit that this approach to jurisprudence is quite novel among the academic community. Thus, this paper endeavors to extend the analysis in the area of feminist sociolegal studies.

EXPERIENTIAL FEMINISM, RAPE AND PRAXIS

To frame the phenomenon of rape in the language of experiential feminism, I describe an event constituted by four images: sexuality, the body, violence and power. The task of de-centering rape, then, requires an investigation of two issues: 1) the apparent universality of patriarchal domination (power) over women's bodies, and 2) the specific forms (sexual and violent) this domination takes in our present society. Within the context of experiential feminism, these questions are raised from the rape victim's point of view and then examined within the context of jurisprudence.

In view of Foucault's (1979) desexualization of the body phenomenon, rape is linked to power and the linguistic coordinates that define it as such. In other words, the crime of rape signifies an activity that affirms the law's claim to power (i.e., rape is a *sexual* crime rather than a physical assault because our misogynous system of jurisprudence has selectively codified the nonconsenting appropriation of a women's body as such). Sexuality for Foucault (1979) is understood to be a discursive formation. In other words, sexuality is *not* a property of the body (i.e., the genitalia), but, rather, a productive (inventive) knowledge-truth. (E.g., our "modern episteme" tells us that the illicit act (pleasure) of sodomy has been replaced by the licit category (orientation) of the homosexual). The point is that "truths about sexuality do not exist outside the operations of these power/knowledge networks" (Bell 1991:87; Butler 1990). Moreover, Foucault (1979) argues that particular forms of socially constructed sexuality encode our understanding of the "proper" relationship between the sexes as well as what types of sexual pleasures are socially accepted. In other words, these knowledge-truths function as the form of the expression of power. Foucault (1979) seeks to resist the deployment of sexuality understood as a domain saturated with power. For Foucault (1979), an effective resistance to the contemporary understanding of sexuality, with all of its gender constructed, power-differential relationships, is the strategy of desexualizing sexuality. In other words, the genitalia, regarded as "the sex" and more important than other parts of the body, need to be neutralized. This neutralization of sexuality entails a proliferation and diffusion of various forms of sexual pleasure so that the prevailing paradigm of sexuality is disrupted.

For Foucault (1979) the body too is organized by power. That is to say, power, as power/knowledge-truth, determines our understanding of the body. This organization of the body, this physiognomic interrogation, promulgated by the productive mechanism of power, is diffuse throughout the social order. Foucault's historical archeology of sexuality is a deliberate attempt to resist the traditional conception of body which privileges the genitalia (Bouchard 1977). In other words, the historical deployment of sexuality linguistically depicts the body's genitalia as something other, something more, than what is conveyed when one speaks of the body's arm, limb, face or fist. Indeed, the discourses on the genitalia conceive of this organ as marked off from the rest of the body, deserving special consideration (Bell 1991).

Missing from Foucault's (1979) analysis, however, is the recognition that underscoring the mechanisms of power and its rendering of sexuality and the body is a phallocratic linguistic system that subtends the experiences of women (MacKinnon 1987; 1989). As Irigaray (1985), the phallic economy of sameness (the masculine reductionistic imperative) underpins and privileges the *masculine* genitalia so that the coordinates of the dominant linguistic code are defined by this imagery. Foucault does not present his power/knowledge concept with this understanding of the genitalia in mind. For Foucault (1979), the body, through the discourses on the deployment of sexuality, renders the genitalia as set apart from and beyond the physiognomic structure. Thus, *contra* Irigaray (1985), the power that Foucault (1979) intends is unstable and productive, not certain and oppressive.

Investigating the question of rape requires that one take into account Foucault's understanding of sexuality and the body viz., power, but also Irigaray's injunction on how such notions are phallocratically constituted. For Foucault (1977) the analysis of rape is problematic. Notwithstanding his dilemma, the discursive label of sex in which the genitalia are understood to be outside the body (privileged) is reconciled by him in the act of rape. In addition to recommending that the body (the genitalia) be desexualized, Foucault (1979) insists on how the activity of rape should be coded. In short, he calls for a desexualizing of this experience in which the act of rape is likened to any other form of aggression. As Foucault explains:

> And when one punishes rape one should be punishing *physical* violence and nothing but that. And to say that it is nothing more than an act of aggression: that there is no difference, in principle, between sticking one's fist into someone's face or one's penis in their sex. (As cited in Kritzman 1988, p. 200) (emphasis added)

Thus, we see that for Foucault (1979), rape is understood not as an act of sexuality but, rather, as an act of violence. This assault to the body is likened to any other violent crime against a person. It is in response to this characterization of rape that Foucault's archeology of sexuality finds its staunchest criticism (e.g., Plaza 1980; MacKinnon 1987; 1989; Barry 1985; Dumaresq 1981).

Commenting on Foucault's (1979) critique of rape, MacKinnon (1989) rejects the idea that this activity be regarded as comparable to any other violent experience.

> [Foucault's] analysis would suggest that assault by a man's fist is not so different from assault by a penis, not because both are violent but because both are sexual....[Force *is*] the desire dynamic, not just a response to the desired object when desire's expression is frustrated. (MacKinnon 1989, pp. 178-186)

Elsewhere, however, MacKinnon (1982; 1987; 1989) does state that rape is about sex *and* power. In other words, the two metaphors are not opposed. Her argument is that male sexuality is constructed and experienced as patriarchal domination over women. Therefore, as others have concluded, rape "express[es] that power through violent intrusion...experienced [by men] as sexually arousing" (Bell 1991, p. 94).

A somewhat different analysis is provided by Dumaresq (1981). Her argument is that the rape victim is transformed into a "sexual" being. The victim's own intent/desire, dress, verbalizations, previous sexual history, interactive behavior, etc., create, as discursively articulated through event generating apparatuses (e.g., the media, the judiciary, the police), a semiotic field constituting the raped person as sexual. Depending on the particular discourse construction, the person may be identified as a "true" rape victim (non-sexual) or a "false" rape victim (sexual). In either case, the language of sexuality informs the outcome.

Interestingly, we see a diversity of interpretation on the meaning of rape. The phenomenon is about violent sexual power (MacKinnon 1989), discourse on sexuality (Dumaresq 1981), an act of aggression comparable to any other assault (Foucault 1979). However, none of these interpretations adequately address how the rape phenomenon, as constructed, legitimizes the juridico-linguistic communicative market. Thus, the argument that rape is power-sex, or sexuality, or violence to the body, ignores the implication these meanings convey regarding the power vested in our phallogocentric system of law and justice. It is upon these matters that an experientially-informed feminist jurisprudence is most instructive.

The act of rape is understood to be a grand transgression inexorably linked and fundamentally opposed to the law (Woodhull 1988, pp. 169-170). The law, too, is a Foucauldian discursive formation wielded through the complex disciplinary mechanisms of power (Smart 1989; Foucault 1980). The law possesses its own language, method, testing ground and system of results that distinguish it from other disciplines. Moreover, law's claims to truth are indivisible from the exercise of its power. Through the essentialism of its legal method (i.e., boundary definition, defining relevance and case analysis), law sets itself outside the social order rendering sound, rational judgements concerning complex and contradictory life circumstances occurring within this arena. In this way, this system of jurisprudence functions as a force, believing that it has the power to right wrongs.

Notwithstanding this analysis, law's claim to truth as a form of the expression of power also disqualifies other knowledges that cannot fit into legal theorems. Common sense, everyday experience, intuition, feelings, interpersonal truth, etc. (crucial ingredients for a feminist praxis), are routinely discounted because they cannot be adequately condensed into legal dictums (Smart 1989, Arrigo 1992). Thus, law's truth (phallogocentric) outweighs other (polymorphous) truths. The result is that the discourse of an *écriture féminine* is denied the possibility of articulation.

One of the wrongs our misogynous system of jurisprudence claims to right is the act of rape. In desexualizing rape, law's claim to power would be unalterably diminished, provided we acknowledge that juridical truth presupposes a unitary code of sexually acceptable (phallocentric) behavior. The greater the construction and acceptance of diverse sexual pleasures, the greater the reduction of law's normalizing grip on what constitutes sanctioned and proscribed sexual conduct, and, more importantly, law's claim to truth. By this analysis one is not to infer that rape be experienced as devoid of inflicting harm. It is a physical intrusion with a multitude of psycholinguistic implications, brought about by real or imagined power and having profound results.

The desexualization of rape, as a productive form of resistance to power, must be interpreted in such a way that our present system of jurisprudence is not affirmed. To do otherwise would be to acquiesce to the prevailing power differential in sexual relations (subversion of the feminine), articulated through legal statutes and codes. The work of experiential feminism in unveiling the meaning of rape for particular individuals so harmed is threefold. It must: 1) unpack how the vagina (in the case of a raped man, the anus) has come to be coded as a place of emptiness and vulnerability, the penis as a weapon of potential harm (intrusion) and the act of rape as violation (Woodhull 1988, p. 171), 2) disrupt these images by inventing, through imaginative discourse, interpretations that more authentically describe the many meanings our sexual bodies hold for us rather than accepting and announcing descriptions that our misogynous language and thought have permitted us, and 3) usher these re-situated interpretations into our culture, so that language, thought and reality can be transformed.

As we discover the unfolding significations sexuality and the body hold for individuals and de-sexualize and re-communalize them by granting that sexual pleasure abounds in multiplicity, the experience of rape is neutralized to the extent that it does not affirm the power of the law. Rape is no longer understood as a grave infraction undermining society. That rape is merely about discourse on sexuality is what our phallocratic culture has bequeathed to us. That rape is about violence relegates and reduces the violation to masculine sameness (i.e., rape is like a fist in the face). That rape is about sex *and* violence affirms the power of our present system of jurisprudence, a system that misogynously characterizes the feminine. Again, this is not to argue that the meaning of rape for persons so violated is not injurious. The jurisprudential questions that are posed here for further review are as follows: what metaphors, symbols and myths have come to constitute the rape situation in the preceding way; do these language constructs speak for a rape victim's experience of this phenomenon; and what impact would an experientially-based feminine discourse have in redefining (shattering) the rape experience in particular and our system of jurisprudence in general?

CRITIQUE OF EXPERIENTIAL FEMINISM

1. Throughout this paper I maintain that language is phallocratically constructed but employ it in its own deconstruction. Is not experiential feminism as presented nothing more than a masculine articulation of the

feminine in consciousness dilemma?

Through our languaged imagination we can semiotically disrupt what has been given to us (language and thought) and seek ways to ameliorate it. This is because the feminine in consciousness modality is not outside our experience of it. Like its counterpart (the masculine register), we always and already engender this code. The historical problem in the law (and society in general) has been a deliberate and, at times, unconscious effort to limit its value and quash its existence.

2. No systematic articulation of experiential feminism's methodology has been presented. What form does it take?

The systematization of experiential feminism is rejected because, like all methodologies, it involves the oppression of those who do not subscribe to its postulates. Experiential feminism is not a what or a unitary code. Experiential feminism is a how. It is polymorphous. How experiential feminism is lived out will depend on the imaginings of individuals to unpack the multitude of meaning experience holds for them. This will inevitably vary from persons to person as much as from community to community.

3. If we accept the principle that experiential feminism is an articulation of the feminine in consciousness encounter with lived experiences, why not construct a collaborative epistemology, one that includes the masculine in consciousness modality, so that others, who experience this description as foreign, might understand its importance?

As Irigaray has enumerated, the genealogy of the history of philosophical discourse gives ascendancy to the rational, sequential, logical paradigm. This is the prevailing seduction and, by taking on a collaborative effort, would ultimately invade the notion of experiential feminism, thereby destroying its meaning.

4. Even if we accept the premise that our existences are already of the feminine in consciousness, how can a man speak for and about the feminine in consciousness with any significant degree of authenticity?

The feminine in consciousness is not necessarily or even exclusively the domain of the female. The same can be said of the masculine in consciousness for the male. We are existentially multiplicity in our gender. Moreover, I have done my best to bracket my masculine consciousness in unpacking the meanings experiential feminism holds for us.

5. A central theme in this paper on experiential feminism is the deconstruction of our present system of jurisprudence. But if science is the pedagogic perpetrator of what language and thought constructs we esteem, why not disrupt its exalted status?

The work of existential phenomenological psychology, especially over the past twenty-five years, continues to demonstrate the need to take up the primacy of discourse (especially science) as a "human" project (Giorgi, 1970). The prestige afforded jurisprudence while conceded, has never been so critiqued.

6. Even if the description of experiential feminism in theory is accepted, there is very little hope of an identifiable integrated praxis. Therefore, it functions as a mere intellectual fantasm.

The search for praxis typically entails the application of identifiable form to everyday situations. This is the masculine way. Experiential feminism is polymorphous. In this regard, it is elusive; resisting singularity of expression, and illusive; grounded in enchanting images. The marriage of these allows for the possibility of praxis situated in the everyday imaginings of our lives.

7. When I speak of reality being socially constructed by the masculine register, how can this insight be reconciled with the experience of the male gender for minorities?

The understanding of socially constructed reality that is intended is that reality constituted by white males predominantly of Western European descent. This subjugates all other realities (including those of male minorities) to a lower prestige level. But even within minorities, we can discern what expression of reality is affirmed and what expression is not. The extent to which the masculine in consciousness code permeates the existences of minority races (in their gender relationships to one another) or even of other minority cultures (in the way they regard members of their own society), informs us of the power differential that colors their respective ethics or laws.

8. Is not the notion of disunity and a search for styles of existence that are as different from one another as possible, in fact the unitary principle of experiential feminism?

The activity of resistance to society's (particularly law's) claim to unitary truth and knowledge is a discursive process without boundaries. If this be unity, it is most definitely of the sort that allows for diversity in the absence of oppression. But here the question that is raised is decidedly of the masculine register. That phenomena possess form or unity is essential for masculine sense-making. Even in conceding the notion of experiential feminism as polymorphous, this criticism relies on a masculine in consciousness construct (unity) to deem appropriate the disunity of experiential feminism. This is precisely the problem of languaging experiential feminism in the masculine way. It intends the primacy of rationality and order which experiential feminism places in abeyance.

CONCLUSION

The rendering of an experientially-informed feminist jurisprudence situates the coordinates of its discourse in the realm of the imagination. These coordinates must resist the phallic economy of sameness in describing experience. Metaphor, symbol and myth are three constitutive elements of this *écriture féminine*. Resisting form, thesis, unity, identicality, sameness, all of which phallomorphically privilege oneness, resituates this uncultivated discourse for and about the feminine in multiplicity, ambiguity, plurisignification, inconsistency and, contradiction.

In applying these principles to rape, we discover that an experientially-based feminist interpretation of this phenomenon considers one's relationship to sexuality, violence, the body and power. If the power of the law, as phallocratically constructed, is to be neutralized, the body must not only be desexualized but so too must the act of rape. This does not mean, however, that rape necessarily be construed as an act of violence. To do so reduces the rape phenomenon to the normalizing, unitary paradigm that feminism must resist. The meaning of rape is polymorphous. The work of experiential feminism is to encode its own mythology, codify its own grammar, through metaphorical and symbolic modalities. To fall back upon the phallic economy of sameness (rape as power-sex, as discourse on sexual, as a physical attack), is to fall prey to the coordinates of the masculine seduction, thereby obliterating the possibility for an *écriture féminine*. The point is not that rape is not injurious but that articulations of this phenomenon have been assigned (selected out) to women as the "proper" code.

* *This is a revision of a previously published work that appeared in Humanity and Society 17(1): 27-48 (1993).*

** *Bruce A. Arrigo is Assistant Professor of Law and Justice Studies at Rowan College of New Jersey.*

NOTE

1. This paper provides a more theoretical reconceptualization of a feminist jurisprudence in its relationship to an *écriture féminine*,

precisely because "first wave" feminism, through its action-oriented legal reforms, did not *existentially* advance women's claims against the justice system. Simply changing the content of law still privileges the law which is, after all, a phallocratic construction. (For a good review explaining this process and the legal system's failure thus far see: Smart 1989; Los 1990).

REFERENCES

Adler, Z. 1987. *Rape on Trial*. London: Routledge & Keagan Paul.

Arrigo, B. 1992. "Deconstructing Jurisprudence: An Experiential Feminist Critique." *The Journal of Human Justice* 4(1):13-30.

Barry, K. 1985. "Social Etiology of Crimes Against Women." *Victimology* 10: 1-4.

Bell, V. 1991. "'Beyond the "Thorny Question" ': Feminism, Foucault and the Desexualization of Rape." *International Journal of the Sociology of Law* 19: 83-100.

Bottomley, A. 1987. "Feminism in Law Schools." In *Women and the Law*, edited by S. McLaughlin London: University College of London Press.

Bulter, J. 1990. *Gender Trouble: Feminism and the Subversion of Identity*. Routledge: London.

Cain, M. 1979. "The Gender Practice Lawyer and the Client: Towards a Radical Conception." *International Journal of the Sociology of Law* 7: 331-354.

Dews, P. 1987. *Logics of Disintegration: Post-structuralist Thought and the Claims of Critical Theory*. London; NY: Verso.

Diamond, I. and Quinby, L. 1988. *Feminism and Foucault*. Boston: Northeastern University Press.

Duchen, C. 1986. *Feminism in France*. London: Routledge & Keagan Paul.

Dumaresq, D. 1981. "Rape--Sexuality in the Law." *M/f: A Feminist Journal* 1: 1-5.

Foucault, M. 1970. *The Order of Things: An Archeology of the Human Sciences*. New York: Pantheon.

_____. 1972. *The Archeology of Knowledge*. New York: Pantheon.

_____. 1977. Debate and Change collective. *La folie Encerlee*. Seghers/Laffont: Paris.

_____. 1977. *Language, Counter-memory, Practice: Michel Foucault, Selected Essays and Interview*, Edited by D. Bouchard, Cornell University Press: Ithica, NY.

_____. 1979. *The History of Sexuality: An Introduction*. Penguin: Harmondsworth.

_____. 1980. *Power/Knowledge: Selected Interviews and Other Writings 1972-1977*. London: Harvester.

Freud, S. 1949. Three essays on the theory of sexuality. In *The Standard Edition*, Edited by J. Strachey. London: The Hogarth Press.

Gilligan, C. 1982. *In A Different Voice*. London: Harvard University Press.

____, Lyons, N.P. and Hanmer, T.J. 1990. *Making Connections*. Cambridge: Harvard University Press.

Giorgi, A. (1970). *Psychology as a Human Science; A Phenomenologically Based Approach*. New York: Harper & Row Publishers.

Goodrich, P. 1984. "Law and Language: An Historical and Critical Introduction." *Journal of Law and Society* 2: 173-206.

_____. 1987. *Legal Discourse*. New York: St. Martin's Press.

Grosz, E.A. 1990. *Jacque Lacan: A feminist Introduction*. London; New York: Routledge.

Habermas, J. 1984. *The Theory of Communicative Action. Vol. One. Reason and the Rationalization of Society*. Translated by T. McCarthy. Boston: Beacon Press.

_____. 1975. *Legitimation Crisis*. Boston: Beacon Press.

Heidegger, M. 1962. *Being and Time*. New York: Harper & Row.

Husserl, E. 1983. *Ideas Pertaining to a Pure Phenomenology and to a Phenomenological Philosophy*. Translated by F. Kersten. The Hague: Martinus Nijhoff Publishers.

Irigaray, L. 1985. *This Sex Which Is Not One*. Translated by C. Porter. Ithica: Cornell University Press.

Kristeva, J. 1984. *Revolution in Poetic Language*. New York: Columbia University Press.

_____. 1980. *Desire in Language*. New York: Columbia University Press.

Kritzman, L. 1988. (Ed.). *Michel Foucault: Politics, Philosophy, Culture. Interviews and Other Writings*. London: Routledge

Lacan, J. 1977. *Ecrits: A Selection*. Translated by A. Sheridan. New York: W.W. Norton.

_____. 1978. *The Four Fundamental Concepts of Psycho-analysis*. Translated by A. Sheridan. New York: W.W. Norton.

_____. 1982. *Feminine sexuality*.Edited by J. Mitchell and J. Rose. Translated by J. Rose. New York: W.W. Norton.

Lahey, K. 1985. "...Until Women Themselves have Told All that They have to Tell...". *Osgoode Hall Law Journal* 23: 519-541.

Langer, S. 1951. *Philosophy in a New Key*. New York: New American Library.

Lemert, C.C. and Gillan, G. 1985. *Michel Foucault: Social theory in Transgression*. New York: Columbia University Press.

Littleton, C. 1987. "In Search of a Feminist Jurisprudence." *Harvard Women's Law Journal* 10: 1-8.

Lyotard, J. F. 1984. *The Postmodern Condition: A Report on Knowledge*. Minneapolis: University of Minnesota Press.

MacKinnon, C. 1983. "Feminism, Marxism, Method and the State: Toward Feminist Jurisprudence." *Signs* 8: 635-658.

_____. 1987. *Feminism Unmodified: Discourses on Life and Law*. London: Harvard University Press.

_____. 1989. *Towards a Feminist Theory of the State*. Cambridge, Mass: Harvard University.

Merquior, J. G. 1982. *Foucault*. London: Fontana Press/Collins.

Milovanovic, D. 1986. "Juridico-linguistic Communicative Markets: Towards a Semiotic Analysis." *Contemporary Crises* 10: 281-304.

_____. 1988. *A Primer in the Sociology of Law*. Albany, NY: Harrow and Heston.

_____. 1992. *Postmodern Law and Disorder: Psychoanalytic Semiotics, Chaos and Juridic Exegeses*. Liverpool: Deborah Charles Publications.

Murray, E. 1975. "The Phenomenon of Metaphor." Pp. 270-293 in *Phenomenological Psychology*, edited by A. Giorgi, C. Fischer, and E. Murray. Pittsburgh, Pa: Duquesne University Press.

_____. 1986. *Imaginative Thinking and Human Existence*. Pittsburgh, Pa: Duquesne University Press.

O'Farrell, C. 1989. *Foucault: Historian or Philosopher?*. London: MacMillan Press Ltd.

Peirce, C. S. 1958. *Collected Papers: 1931-1935*. 8 vols. P. Edited by Weiss, C. Hartshorne and A. Burks. Cambridge: Harvard University Press.

Plaza, M. 1980. "Our Costs and Their Benefits." *M/f: A Feminist Journal* 4: 1-10.

Ragland-Sullivan, E. 1986. *Jacque Lacan and the Philosophy of Psychoanalysis*. Urbana: University of Illinois Press.

Ricoeur, P. 1973. "Creativity of Language." *Philosophy Today* 17: 97-112.

_____. 1975. *The Rule of Metaphor*. Toronto: University of Toronto Press.

Robertshaw, P. 1980. "Structuralism and Law." *Liverpool Law Review* 31: 46-62.

____. 1984. "Semantic and Linguistic Aspects of Sex Discrimination Decisions." In D. Carzo and B. Jackson (Eds.). Semiotics, Law and Social Science. *Liverpool Law Review* 203: 310-319.

Rowland, J. 1986. *Rape: The Ultimate Violation*. London: Pluto Press.

Sartre, J. P. 1979. *Imagination: A Psychological Critique*. Ann Arbor: University of Michigan Press.

Scully, D. and Marolla, J. 1984. "Convicted Rapists' Vocabulary of Motive: Excuses and Justifications. *Social Problems* 31: 530-544.

Sellers, S. 1991. *Feminist Criticism, Theory and Practice*. Edited by S. Sellers. New York: Wheatsheaf.

Smart, C. 1984. *The Ties that Bind*. London: Routledge & Keagan Paul.

____. 1989. *Feminism and the Power of the Law*. London and New York: Routledge.

Taylor, C. 1986. "Foucault on Freedom and Truth." In D. Couzens Hoy (ed.), *Foucault: A Critical Reader*. Oxford: Blackwell,

Temkin, J. 1987. *Rape and the Legal Process*. London: Sweet & Maxwell.

Thorton, M. 1986. "Feminist Jurisprudence: Illusion or Reality?" *Australian Journal of Law and Society* 3: 5-29.

Tiefenbrun, S. W. 1986. "Legal Semiotics." *Cardozo Arts and Entertainment Law Journal* 5: 89-156.

Volosinov, V. 1986. *Marxism and the Philosophy of Language*. Cambridge, Mass: Harvard University Press.

Wheelright, P. 1968. *Metaphor and Reality*. Bloomington: Indiana University Press.

Woodhull, W. 1988. "Sexuality, Power and the Question of Rape." Pp. 161-181 in *Feminism and Foucault: Reflections on Resistance*, edited by I. Diamond and L. Quinby. Boston: Northeastern University Press.

Chapter IV

INSCRIBING THE BODY WITH A SIGN: SEMIOTICS AND PUNISHMENT*

Dragan Milovanovic**

How to conceptualize and measure movement in space, in four or more dimensional space-time, chaotic multiplicities? This is the pivotal question of postmodern science. Postmodernism made its abrupt appearance in the social and the physical sciences in the 1980s. Key figures of the former include Deleuze, Guattari, Foucault, Kristeva, Derrida, and Baudrillard, who, to various degrees, advocate a Nietzschean conception of time, space, [decentered] subjectivity, and the centrality of a materialistically grounded psychoanalytic semiotics. For the latter, Penrose, a physicist/cosmologist, with his novel notions of "twisters," "twister space," "null lines," and the significance of imaginary numbers (1989; see also, Peat, 1988; Hawkins, 1988), nuclear physicists Green and Schwarz (1984) with their notions of "strings" (open, closed, heterotic), "world-lines," multidimensional space, and "compactification," and, finally, those associated with chaos theory (Mandelbrot, 1983; Pierre and Pomeau, 1984; Gleick, 1987; Hayles, 1990; Stewart, 1989) and their notions of fractal geometry, orderly disorder, and non-linearity have ushered in a new conception of space and time. A new language is emerging to capture the discoveries of the new science.

In this essay we want to explore the Deleuzian/Guattarian notion of the territorialized body as an alternative conceptualization of body surfaces and its connection with space-time. We want then to extend these developing notions into a more contemporary statement of the territorialized body by incorporating some emerging discoveries in the physical sciences. Of particular application will be the penological. Foucault has already begun the discussion in his *Discipline and Punish*. Elsewhere, Deleuze has critiqued and extended this penological model (1988). We would like to explore alternative ways of conceptualizing how the body is coded, or inscribed with signs; how, that, is desire through discursive practices is brought within the control and service of the state. We would also like to apply our analysis to the metaphorical construction of the empirical, legal, deviant, and normal subject particularly as this construction is related to historically and politically economically sensitive discursive formations.

We feel justified in crossing boundaries since, more often than not, ideas float between disciplines and are often incorporated, be it in idiosyncratic styles, into predominating mainstream paradigms. Fritjof Capra's book, *The Tao of Physics* (1983) has demonstrated some connections of ideas between quantum physics and Eastern religion. In both quantum physics and the religions of Hinduism, Buddhism, and Taoism a world view often runs along similar lines. To capture this new science a new language reflective of the new discoveries is necessitated. Physicists at the turn of the century found that ordinary language is totally incapable of adequately describing atomic and sub-atomic processes (Ibid.: 32-39; Pagels, 1983: 72-74, 133-35, 155). This search for a new physics has been carried over into the social sciences. Deleuze, in his book on Nietzsche (1983), Deleuze and Guattari in their discussion of space (1987), and Foucault in his work on the evolution of prisons (1977) all focus on an analysis of the physics of phenomena. (See also, in criminology, Hal Pepinsky's book (1990) on the "geometry of violence.") The Cartesian semiotics that has reigned since the Renaissance is archaic and needs to be replaced with one rooted in postmodern science (see, also, Best, 1990, 1991; Pagels, 1983).

In this essay we make no pretenses of describing the nexus between conceptions of space with its flows and the nature of the decentered subject. The two are related indeed; we merely wish to examine the conceptualizations of space that inform our writings. Remaining for another day is a precise analysis of the interdependencies of the two.[1] Absent this of course, ours is too formalistic a picture devoid of a subject that desires.

BERGSONIAN CONCEPTION OF SPACE-TIME

Bergson, in his now classic *Time and Free Will* (1960; originally in 1889), focused on explaining how to conceive of consciousness, primordial sense data, will, and how it was that duration takes on homogeneous form in language. Fundamental to his enterprise is the idea that all conceptualizations begin within some idealized conception of space: "When we speak of material objects, we refer to the possibility of seeing and touching them; we localize them in space" (1960: 85, 94-94). In other words, the intuition of space is the metaphysical starting point of constructing and explaining phenomena.

Two spaces can be distinguishable: pure duration and homogeneous space. The latter is associated with making clear cut distinctions and representing them as things, it's a world of symbolizations, the Symbolic Order of Lacan; it's an imposition of some ideal space on pure duration. The former, pure duration, is composed of heterogeneous space, "succession without distinction...an interconnexion and organization of elements, each one of which represents the whole and cannot be distinguished or isolated from it except by abstract thought" (Ibid.: 101). In homogeneous space we project duration as extensity as a continuous line distinguishable as the past, present and future and capture it in words; we produce quantitative changes where in fact only qualitative changes exist (i.e., pure heterogeneity).

In coming to a decision, we often reflect and project a line in imaginary space that encounters a junction at which point we convince ourselves a decision was consciously arrived at, where in fact, the decision was already arrived at in the activity itself. As Bergson would argue: "this figure does not show me the deed in the doing but the deed already done" (Ibid.: 180). In fact there was no segmented line of conscious states, no point in time where a clear juncture was reached, no two subsequent lines projecting outward from the juncture as pure abstract possibilities. The question of whether one chooses one direction or another at the assumed juncture is meaningless. "To ask such a question," Bergson tells us, "is to admit the possibility of adequately representing time by space and a succession by a simultaneity" (Ibid.: 176, 179-80). In short, "we project time into space, and we base our reasoning, consciously or unconsciously, on this geometrical figure. But this figure represented a thing and not a progress..." (Ibid.: 181). We constantly create, in other words, fictional spaces, segmented time, and within their coordinates we attribute conscious acts. Rather than heterogeneous duration with interpenetrating moments we have a segmented, spatial line along which moments are affixed (Ibid.: 237). As Bergson tells us, "we forget that states of consciousness are processes and not things; that if we denote them each by a single word, it is for the convenience of language..." (Ibid.: 196).

Nietzsche, of course, has warned us of these "semiotic fictions." We in fact have only doings, becomings. In language we create the fiction that the subject is separate from the doing, that it is the subject that activates action, and that free will informs the process (Nietzsche, 1968: 481).

We will like now to move to a more modern, or more accurately, a postmodern conception of space from a Deleuzian/Guattarian perspective.

DELEUZE AND GUATTARI'S CONCEPTUALIZATION OF SPACE-TIME

Underlying any conception of the subject, cause, and explanation of phenomena is a conception of space and time, as Bergson so convincingly argues. It seems that much of Lacan's rather obtuse, highly esoteric, but yet very precise and self-coherent "ouvre" (1977) was a struggle with an alternative conceptualization of space -- his embracing of Klein bottles, Mobius strips, topology and knot theory, etc. -- and with developing an adequate discourse that would be its expression. Deleuze and Guattari's work, owing much to Lacanian insights, especially in *A Thousand Plateaus* (1987; hereafter referred to a TP), can be seen as a struggle with this very same theme.

Much of Deleuze and Guattari's formulations, too, are based on Nietzsche and, much earlier, Spinoza. Deleuze's book on Nietzsche (1983) can be seen as an exercise in the clarification of Nietzschean physics. Thus for Nietzsche, the body can be conceptualized as the totality of quanta of energy in dynamic relation to other quanta of energy, and it is the "will to power" that coordinates forces of the body (will to power is not to be confused with a conscious agency separatable from the action, a semiotic fiction, but rather an affirmative desire manifesting itself in its coordination of forces of the body, see, especially Bogue, 1989: 22); and for Spinoza, it is seen as "a complex relation between differential speeds, between a slowing and an acceleration of particles" (reported in Bogue, 1989: 133). A Spinozist conception then has it that a body is made up of differential speeds, intensities, rhythms (Deleuze, 1981; Bogue, 1989: 133-34). At its primordiality, the Spinoza model would have it that we need to discern elements without function or form that are merely distinguishable by "movement and rest, slowness and speed" (TP: 254, Bogue, 1989: 134). These amorphous forms, termed "haeccities" reside within "planes of consistency" (Ibid.). It is this notion that Deleuze and Guattari develop in their opus, *A Thousand Plateaus*. As to haeccities:

> They are not atoms, in other words, finite elements still endowed with form. Nor are they indefinitely divisible. They are infinitely small, ultimate parts of an actual infinity, laid out on the same plane of consistency of composition. They are not defined by their number since they always come in infinities. However, depending on their degree of speed or the relation of movement and rest into which they enter, they belong to a given Individual, which may itself be part of

> another Individual governed by another, more complex, relation, and so on to infinity (TP: 254).

Thus haeccities are heterogenous, reflecting degrees and intensities, relations of rest and movement, and having a power of being affected and a power of affecting (Bogue, 1989: 134; TP: 256; 261). (In anticipation of what is to follow, haeccities have much similarity to a conception of "strings" being currently developed by cosmologists and nuclear physicists and, with some reservations, to "floating signifiers" of Lacan, and generally many postmodernist theorists who have followed him.) They are singularities defying strict expression. They populate "planes of consistency," defined by the Spinozean dimensions of "longitude" and "latitude" (TP: 260). Longitude defined as "the sum total of the material elements belonging to it under given relations of movement and rest, speed and slowness." Latitude as "the sum total of the intensive affects it is capable of at a given power or degree of potential." It is along this plane of intersecting lines that "becomings" take place. Haeccities are amorphous, individuations, having no discernible end nor beginning, composed of lines not points (TP: 263), caught in constant territorializations and deterritorializations and reterritorializations. Corresponding to this plane of consistency is a semiotic grid that serves as its expression.

To pause for a moment. This essay is an excursion into alternative conceptualizations of the body and the constitution of desire. Necessarily we need to alter our sociological imagination in order to prepare for the possibility of transcending conventional thought. In order to do this, as physicists have already done, an alternative discourse is needed to capture an alternative form of conceptualization. Some who would argue that this ultimately ends in jargonistic analysis miss the point that novel conceptualizations conjure up an alternative space-time dimensionality. Ultimately, too, the question becomes one of whether this bears fruitful lines of inquiry. Let us continue.

The plane of consistency is caught in tension with a "plane of organization" that attempts to superimpose a diagram that imparts structure, form, a univocality, and a historicity. The plane of organization attempts to "plug the lines of flight, stop or interrupt the movements of deterritorialization, weigh them down, restratify them, reconstitute forms and subjects in a dimension of depth" (TP: 270). It is much like desire originating from the plane of the unconscious attempting to take form on the plane of the perceptual-conscious system of Freud (TP: 284).

For Deleuze and Guattari, the plane of consistency may give way to the plane of organization, or the "arborescent," a striated space composed of points, linear coordinates that capture flow (TP: 293-98, 478-500). A plane of consistency, however, may behave as a "smooth" space, much like the Bergsonian notion of duration, an amorphous space with haeccities, singularities, that reflect "continuous variation, continuous development of form; it is the fusion of harmony and melody in favor of the production of properly rhythmic values, the pure act of the drawing of a diagonal across the vertical and the horizontal" (TP: 478). It is essentially Hamiltonian (Penrose, 1989: 174-84) in character with haeccities specified by position and momentum coordinates (momentum=velocity x mass). Smooth spaces are composed of lines, or vectors with directionality without dimensionality, haeccities in states of being and becoming. "Smooth space is occupied by intensities, wind and noise, forces, and sonorous and tactile qualities..." (TP: 479). Striated space produces the conventional sciences; smooth space the becomings, transcendence, the quantum leap beyond, a necessary condition as Einstein once said, in establishing an Absolute Postulate from which further research will progress. Smooth space is much in line with Kristeva's notion of a "semiotic chora," a pre-symbolic (prior to language structuration) amorphous space with uncoordinated desire; striated space connected more with the effects of the child entering the sphere of language (the Symbolic sphere) and its structuring qualities.

Finally, planes of consistency can be characterized by the "lines of flight" that traverse it. These are defined as converging lines, imaginary lines that converge on the vanishing point such as we find in painting (Bogue, 1989: 110). Imagine, if you will, desire awakened, energized, seeking catharsis. The lines of flight connect multiplicities -- "a multiplicity has neither subject nor object, only determinations, magnitudes, and dimensions that cannot increase in number without the multiplicity changing in nature" (TP: 8); they can be characterized as "rhizomes." Here there are only lines, no points. A multiplicity is composed of a finite number of dimensions, or better, "directions in motion" (TP: 21), which is further composed of lines of flight (TP: 9). Rhizomes tend to deterritorialization; they tend to rupture, and the releasing of the lines of flight by which they are composed (Ibid.).

> the rhizome is made only of lines: lines of segmentarity and stratification as its dimensions, and the lines of flight or deterritorialization as the maximum dimension after which the multiplicity undergoes metamorphosis, changes in nature... [it]

> operates by variation, expansion, conquest, capture, offshoots...[it] has multiple entryways and exits and its own lines of flight....(TP: 21).

Lines of flight can be conceptualized as lines along which desire flows. In other words, the body can be conceptualized as a crisscrossing of flows following lines of flight (See also Lecercle, 1985: 177; Deleuze and Guattari, 1986: 59). So, in opposition to Lacan, not letters, but "unordered, unstructured lines, without beginning or end" (Lecercle, 1985: 177) are inscribed on the body, are territorialized on the body in the form of distinct distributions, producing the "diagram" (Deleuze, 1988: 34-37, 44, 72-73, 84).

Both Foucault (1977) and Deleuze and Guattari (1987, 1988) indicate that every society has its diagrams; they are abstract machines that give static form to the flow of desire; they map desire; they inscribe desire on the body; they produce space-time multiplicities; they superimpose (overlay) the plane of organization on the plane of consistency or immanence. Desire itself can be conceptualized (a) in the more passive sense as a response to lack, a filling of a void, as in Lacan (analogous to what Nietzsche criticizes as the negation of a negation of Hegel, the slave mentality), or (b) in a more active, joyous sense as in Deleuze and Guattari, best expressed by Lecercle as "a flight towards an object which always eludes our grasp, the attempt, never successful but never frustrating, to reach the unattainable by exploring the paths of the possible" (Lecercle, 1985: 196: Bogue, 1989: 88-90). The second form of desire is consistent with Nietzsche's alternative conception of value creation: where the will to power actively and affirmatively produces values, an affirmative transpraxis (desire is not defined as a lack of lack), and with Freud's notion of the libido (see, also, Milovanovic, 1991).

Historically, Deleuze and Guattari tell us, distinct abstract machines, diagrams, become predominant forms of territorializing desire. They identify: (1) the "territorial machine" corresponding to primitive organizations where desire is inscribed along the lines of hierarchy, kinship relations, taboos, gift-exchanges (particularly of women) (Lecercle, 1985: 184; Bogue, 1989: 96-98; Deleuze and Guattari, 1972); (2) the "despotic machine" corresponding to the development of the early state where flows are inscribed, increasingly abstractly, according to bureaucratic imperatives and imageries (Lecercle, 1985: 184; Bogue, 1989: 98-100); and (3) modern capitalism, corresponding to the alienation and commodification of the worker where the equivalence-form increasingly predominates (whether in the form of the juridic subject, in principles of formal equality in law, or in the form of the empirical subject assumed in positivistic oriented sciences -- recall Quetelet's conception of the "average man" in his early and ground-breaking development of statistical analysis) -- desire becomes commodified; lack is fabricated, is deliberately created, is the creation of the hegemonic group (Ibid.; see also Bogue, 1989: 88-95; 100-104).

In *A Thousand Plateaus* Deleuze and Guattari extend this conceptualization to two additional abstract machines (nomadic, passionate-subjective) and to the corresponding "regimes of signs," or, put in another way, to particular discursive regions that become sedimented. Each regime of signs is composed of "mots d'ordre," order-words that lay down the law.

To focus on the contemporary form, "post-signifying regimes," Deleuze and Guattari specify lines commencing from a "point of subjectification," the origination point that does not necessarily imply a conscious, conspiratorial agent at the controls, but rather lines emanating from capital logic, technological imperatives, bureaucratic rationalism, phallocentric logic, to name a few, that traverses the speaking subject (in the Lacanian sense as the "sujet d'énonciation") and makes its appearance in discourse via the subject of speech (Lacan's "sujet d'énoncé") as a signifier, the personal pronoun, the "I" of speech production (utterance) (Deleuze and Guattari, 1987: 127, Lecercle, 1985: 186-190; Bogue, 1989: 141-145). More generally, the point of subjectification "can be anything" (Deleuze and Guattari, 1987: 129): for the anorexic, food; for the fetishist, a shoe; for the lover, the beloved; for the patient, the psychoanalyst, etc. We are always already in language, in an abstract machine that produces lines of flight emanating from these points of subjectification. Metaphysical you ask? No, our own biases concerning the subject as being the center of the universe, conscious, determining, and self-transparent militates against our awareness of forces that have their own originations with effects. Indeed a "point" can develop from nothing; just as highly concentrated energy can change qualitatively and quantitatively into mass.

This line of flight is completed, ultimately, in the "doubling" of the subject, by which Deleuze and Guattari mean that the separate subjects (Lacan's subject of speech and subject of the statement) are now reduced to One, the one constituted, or as Althusser would say, interpellated. At each point that the doubling is completed the line is terminated, but new ones once again appear. Self-subjectification is the end point; the subject finds him/herself situated in discursive regions within a flow of signifiers that are appropriated in constructing speech and ultimately an illusory unified conception of self, well-suited for the abstract machine in terms of functionality and control.

In sum, languages can be envisioned as coordinating mechanisms for action, hence my appropriation, linguistic coordinate systems (Milovanovic, 1986, 1988; Henry and Milovanovic, 1991). Space that is heterogeneous, and conceptions of duration that are derivatives, are overlaid by particular, historically specific discourses. We want to now move onto recent developments, particularly in the 1980s that have revolutionized our conception of space. Chaos and string theory have ushered in a new paradigm with a multitude of novel conceptions which have not yet made inroads into the social sciences. It is our contention that this evolving paradigm offers us alternative insights into conceptualizations of how the body is inscribed with the sign.

CHAOS: IRREGULAR BEHAVIOR GOVERNED BY DETERMINISTIC SYSTEMS

> "You believe in a God who plays dice, and I in complete law and order." Albert Einstein

In 1687 Isaac Newton published his *Principia Mathematica* that established the main paradigm for mathematical thought until the twentieth century. His ideal: that all phenomena could be brought within formal mathematical understanding. Chance and indeterminacy played no role, space was absolute, at rest, and definitively non-changeable: the universe was orderly and logically constructed. This mechanistic (deterministic) view prevailed for almost three centuries. On a grand scale and in most everyday activity he formalized the physical laws well enough for orderly planning and execution from riding bicycles to sending a spacecraft to fly by the planets and out of the solar systems with great precision. First Albert Einstein with his relativity theory, then Niels Bohr and Werner Heisenberg with their notion of quantum mechanics with its uncertainty principle (to which Einstein heavily contributed but yet later was to resist), together undermined this orderly conception. Space and time were interrelated and the relationship varied as a function of, on the one hand, the grand cosmological and on the other, the very small -- nuclear particle interactions. (In some contemporary explorations in cosmology, by the use of imaginary numbers, the distinction between space and time disappears altogether.) Relativity and quantum theory remains unreconciled to this day. But in the 1980s, in particular, chaos theory has become the new person on the block.

Chaos is a misnomer. The dictionary meaning is not what its scientific enterprise is about: "complete disorder, utter confusion." At a recent meeting of the Royal Society in London a more precise definition was offered and accepted: "stochastic behaviour occurring in a deterministic system" (Stewart, 1989: 17). By "stochastic" it is meant "random"; thus chaology is the study of random behaviour occurring in a deterministic system. Hence, chaologists study deterministic chaos. Some have even referred to chaos as "orderly disorder" (Hayles, 1990). As contradictory as this sounds this novel view is offering us a new way of viewing multidimensional space, of constructing more meaningful representations of phenomena, and has produced a novel way of conceptualizing dynamic systems. We would like here to give its essential elements and indicate how it can broaden the Deleuzian/Guattarian conception of lines, points, and planes of consistency.

First, chaos theory stresses the importance of initial conditions. Much in accord with the findings of quantum mechanics, in particular the uncertainty principle of Heisenberg, defining accurately initial conditions is always plagued by uncertainty and hence subsequent projected outcomes are inherently inaccurate. Any initial condition is assumed to have some minimal level of fluctuations which defies exact measurement. Hence, initial conditions can not totally predict subsequent observable phenomena. In fact, a corollary of this idea is the discovery by chaologists that initial conditions can have disproportional macro scale effects. A butterfly flapping its wings in Asia, it is said, may produce a hurricane in the Florida Keys (chaologists have referred to this parable as the "butterfly effect"). Social theorists such as Derrida have developed a similar idea where it is posited that no foundation for any posited truth-claim can be found from which absolute Truth can be determined, since any "foundational" position in turn can be undermined by another "foundational" position and that, in turn by another, and so forth. This anti-foundationalism has been carried over into the critique of the Critical Legal Studies movement by such contemporary theorists as Stanley Fish.

Second, scale dependent measurements is the idea that in measuring some phenomena, a coastline for example, the researcher is dependent on the instrument that is being employed. Make use of a yardstick and one result is reached; an "inch stick" would give another, and so forth. Social scientists have already seen this in the form of experimental effects where the very intrusion of the researcher and his/her frame often contaminates accurate understanding of the phenomena under investigation.

Third, non-linearity, a critical point for chaologists, is the idea that the mathematics of dynamic systems do not proceed according to linear logic as in traditional differential equations. In linear geometry some added input produces an incremental or proportional increase in some output. In non-linear geometry some small incremental increase at a micro level may have large, disproportional effects at the macro level (i.e., the butterfly flapping its wings in Asia).

Fourth, chaologists explore the effects of iteration, a mathematical concept meaning doing the same calculation over and over again with a particular starting formula (algorithm). The output of one calculation is the input for the next calculation, and that result in turn for the next and so forth; each calculation is dependent on the function specified. For example, by using a calculator and the x-square function key one can plug in a number between zero and one, hit the key and get a result. Now if we continue to hit the x-square function key the end result is smaller and smaller until by the ninth hit, many calculators would have zero as a result. Each time the function key was depressed iteration has occurred. Next step. If following Stewart's (1989: 18-20) example, we invent a "x^2 minus one" key, we choose a number such as .54321 and iterate we get a diagram that indicates regular oscillations such as in the following where x is plotted on the vertical scale, and the iterations on the horizontal scale (example taken from Stewart, 1989: 19):

Figure 1
Iteration of x^2-1

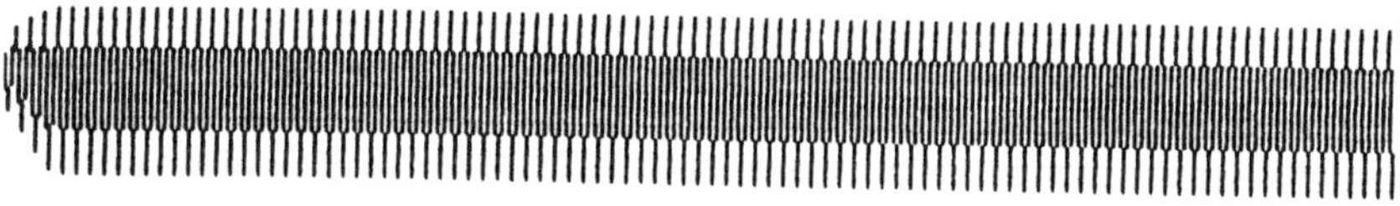

Now if we were to take a "$2x^2$-1" key and iterate by starting with an x value between 0 and 1 we get a chaotic looking diagram. If we then change a fifth decimal value very slightly (say by in .54321 and iterate and produce a graph; then change the last value, in other words start with .54322, after about fifty iterations the two graphs start looking completely different (example taken from Stewart, 1989: 18-20).

Figure 2
Iteration With Slight Change of Fifth Place Value

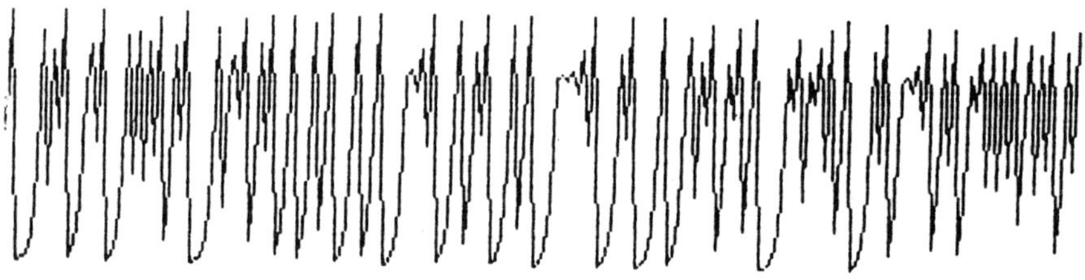

It is just this logic that led Lorenz, in 1961, to a startling conclusion. In trying to predict weather he ran (iterated) a program on his computer that had an initial value of .506127. Then, because of wanting to save printout space, and making the assumption of the inconsequentiality of slight rounding, he rounded to .506 but found that the resulting weather patterns diverged dramatically until the two patterns had no similarity at all. A car polluting the air in New York City might have dramatic effects on the weather in Warren, Ohio.

Similarly, cosmologists have explained the nature of the universe within a split second of the occurrence of the Big Bang and then assumed a logical unfolding of processes, where in fact the fluctuations within this split second after the Big Bang, following the logic of chaologists, might have vastly disproportionate effects on the evolution of the universe.

In the social sciences, a similar assumption is made in research. It is assumed that some initial values plugged into some formulation of say the causes of crime, will have uniform effects at each stage of the unfolding of a phenomena. The ideas behind non-linearity, iteration, uncertainty in initial conditions, and scale dependent measurement undermine any accurate prediction of social phenomena. Linear progression for example would produce self-similarity at all scales, an idea referred to as scale invariance. Non-linearity is not so kind.

It should be added, in anticipation of the next section of this article, that cosmologists have developed string and superstring theory that mathematically predicts the necessary existence of 26-dimensional, or in later forms, 10-dimensional space/time (Peat, 1988; Hawkins, 1988). Thus, for example, if we assume 10 dimensions, three would be of space as we know it and one of time. These are manifest. The other six dimensions are "compactified" (curled up), and held together by enormous energies. Could it be, following the logic of chaologists, that these hidden dimensions exert some measurable effects (proportional and disproportional) that are currently not accounted for in research? "Unexplained variance" of methodologists may provide the sphere within which otherwise "minor" variables may have significant long range effects.

Fifth, fractal geometry is the language of chaos. "Fractals," coined by Mandelbrot in his now classic *The Fractal Geometry of Nature* (1983), is an added fraction of a dimension. In Euclidean space we are familiar with the concept of a dimension. A line has a dimension of one; a plane a dimension of two; a sphere three. A point is dimensionless. A fractal line, however, "spills over" into a two-dimensional space. For example a coastline. Thus we have a dimension between one and two. A fractal plane, a mountain for example, is something between a plane and a sphere; hence possessing a fractal dimension between two and three (Goldberger, Rigney and West, 1990: 44-45). Fractallike structures abound in the human body -- network of blood vessels, ducts, nerves (ibid.), as well as elsewhere -- villi of intestinal walls, trees, coastlines, clouds, rivers. A fractal dimension of 2.7, for example, has been computed for human arteries (Jurgens, Peitgen and Saupe, 1990: 67). A coastline has a fractal dimension of between 1.15 and 1.25; a snowflake around 1.26 (Stewart, 1989: 219). Fractals are more often expressed in algorithms (a precise mathematical procedure) rather than in primary shapes (Jurgens, Peitgen and Saupe, 1990: 61). A snowflake, for example, can be expressed as log4/log3 = 1.2619 (Stewart, 1989: 220).

Two types of fractals exist: linear and nonlinear. Linear fractals possess a self-similarity quality; in other words, as iteration proceeds, the initial image is duplicated infinitely. It always approaches a "limit image," an approximation of the initial image (Ibid.: 62). The algorithm states the precise rules in reductions or displacements of the initial image.

Nonlinear fractals are more consistently chaotic. The diagrams generated by rather simple algorithms and the iteration of nonlinear fractals -- Mandelbrot and Julia sets -- produce incredibly complex patterns.

Sixth, chaologists have constructed a novel way of imaging dynamic systems, diagrams which they call phase spaces. Phase spaces are designed to map multi-dimensional systems in movement. The result of these imagings have uncovered profound phenomena referred to as "attractors" -- regions of phase space that attract trajectories (attractors "live" only in phase spaces). A point in phase space specifies the coordinates of, for example, position and velocity. As a dynamic systems changes, the point moves to a new position in phase space. The changing system produces a trajectory in phase space (Gleick, 1987: 49-50, 134-137; Hayles, 1989: 147-150). The point represents the dynamic system, no matter how complicated, as it exists at that precise time and at that precise location. A two-dimensional phase space plots two factors, say for a pendulum swinging -- the velocity and the precise location of the pendulum (thus this phase space also has two degrees of freedom). Given zero frictional forces the phase space will look like a loop or an orbit. A pendulum swinging faster and farther out will form a similar loop but much larger than the first. With frictional forces taken into account the orbit will spiral inward. Here the phase space would look like a spiral toward a center, a zero point (x=0, y=0) (here, also referred to as the "fixed point" attractor).

Figure 3
Phase Space of a Swinging Pendulum

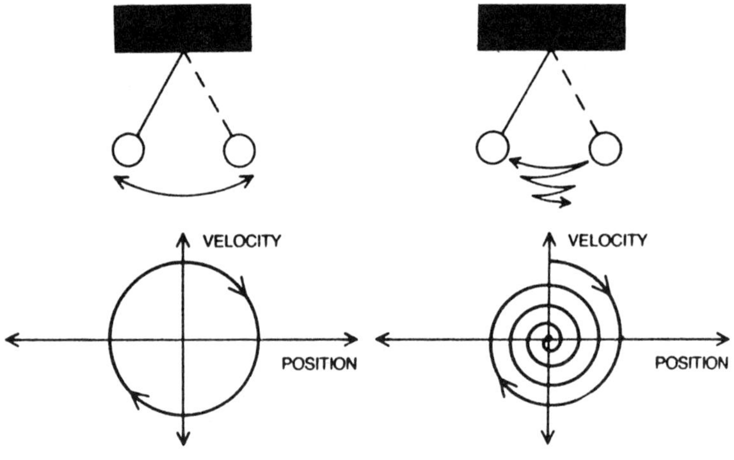

The beauty of phase spaces is that it gives a picture of movement in a dynamic system, one in which variables change continuously. Phase spaces expose patterns in movements that may have been invisible before. Phase spaces should not be confused with our everyday understanding of real movement through space, nor should they be confused with what we previously described as haeccities existing in Hamiltonian space-momentum coordinates, but rather, they represent (diagram) changes in a dynamic system's behavior over repeated cycles. Imaginatively, the investigator can look at the phase space and reconstruct the system itself (Gleick, 1987: 135). However, with added variables, say with three degrees of freedom the phase space must include an additional dimension to accurately reflect in a point the complex movement that is taking place. For example, one number, say temperature, might accurately reflect all the researcher's needs (here we have a one-dimensional line). Two numbers, one reflecting velocity the other location in space accurately reflects a pendulum in movement (here we have a two-dimensional space). But Lorenz's equations had three dimensions, and hence three degrees of freedom account for weather predictions. In other words, it took three variables to predict weather fluctuations. His three-dimensional phase space looked very much like two butterfly wings (also called a Lorenz Attractor).

With systems with more than three dimensions a visual apprehension of what's going on becomes increasingly difficult. However, it is not to say we cannot work, intuitively, with everyday practical results, within multidimensional spaces. Take for example, riding a bicycle. It is said that it has five degrees of freedom: left and right pedal, handlebar, front wheel, rear wheel and crank assembly. But it takes ten-dimensions to represent bicycling: five for velocity and five for position (Stewart, 1989: 91-92). It is Stewart's view that our socialization experiences limit us to experiencing and understanding three spatial dimensions, and what is needed is the development of "a new kind of geometrical intuition" (Ibid.: 90; see also, Weeks, 1985: 195-99). It also seems that this is behind Lacan's, Deleuze's, and Guattari's often esoteric expository styles. Stay within our conventional paradigms and all their work will be judged as jargonistic, obtuse, babble; venture forth in the spirit of openness and profound insights develop.

This leads us to specifying the seventh main element of chaos theory, the notion of attractors. An attractor which only has existence in phase spaces can be defined as "a region of phase space that attracts trajectories" (Goldberger, Rigney and West, 1990: 48; Hayles, 1990: 147; Stewart, 1989: 95-125). Stewart even provides a simpler definition: "an attractor is defined to be... whatever it settles down to!"(1989: 109). Three basic attractors exist: (1) fixed point attractors are those where the system settles down to a particular point, a pendulum swinging for example in a frictional space; (2) the limit attractors are those that indicate periodicity, a regular path, one that is circular or elliptical for example, such as in the frictionless pendulum swinging; and (3) the strange attractors are those that are neither periodic or static (Goldberger, Rigney and West, 1990: 48). In the latter we have chaotic behavior where trajectories on the phase space may diverge then change dramatically over the long run (Ibid.). For example, it has been demonstrated that the normal heartbeat can be represented by a phase space that contains a strange attractor, not, as expected by conventional wisdom, by a periodic attractor; the normally functioning heartbeat is chaotic! (Ibid.: 48).

These seven core elements of chaos theory are suggestive for undoing the rationalistic bias of post-enlightenment thought, and provide potential lines of inquiry that promise to constitute a new basis of a humanistic orientation in the social sciences. Whether we talk about the empirical subject of positivistic methodology, the legal subject of law-practices, or the deviant subject of criminology, chaos theory undermines the orderly, stable, and formalistic conceptualizations employed.

Before we continue, we want to briefly tour some new directions within cosmology and nuclear physics and then once again return to show how all this contributes to alternative ways of conceptualizing the body.

POSTMODERN SCIENCE

> "There remains a possibility that some new version of quantum mechanics might replace the probabilistic nature of the wave-function by something deterministic but chaotic." Ian Stewart

Yoichiro Nambu, the original creator of "string theory" has called the new era "postmodern physics." The mid 1980s to present has ushered in a new era in ways of conceptualizing the very nature of the universe. String and twister theory, in particular, have forced us to reconceptualize the very way we perceive space-time (Peat, 1988; Hawkins, 1988; Penrose, 1989). We want to explore, in brief, some of the main conceptions of the "new science" and see if in fact these new visions offer the social sciences alternative ways of conceptualizing space, time, and dimensionality.

Cosmologists have grown accustomed to explaining events in four-dimensional space on what is called space-time diagrams. Let the horizontal line represent space, and the vertical line time and we can trace the "world-line," the history of any object through time. Here we have a two-dimensional diagram (See Capra, 1983: 147-73). We could increase dimensionality to four by adding depth to the two-dimensional diagram. Hence we would have the following:

Figure 4
Visualizing 4-Dimensional World Lines

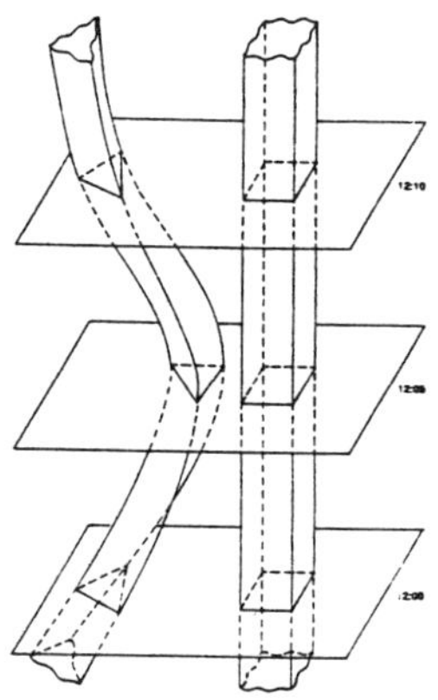

Faced with the problem of integrating a quantum physics with relativity theory in explaining the beginnings of the universe (and in explaining subatomic particle interactions), cosmologists were, especially in the 1980s, to develop more complex models. One of these models that exploded on the scene in 1984 concerned string theory (see especially, Hawkins, 1988: 158-169; Peat, 1988).

In essence superstring theory has mathematically predicted a 10-dimensional space/time (initially it was 26-dimensional). Four we know (3 of space, one of time); but the other six are said to be "compactified," curled up tightly, and held together by enormous forces. We need not go into all the details here, but the essence of string theory is that the very basic objects of the universe are not particles but "things that have a length but no other dimension, like an infinitely thin piece of string" (Hawkins, 1988: 159). Strings, if you could try and stretch your imagination, are extremely small (10 to the minus 33cm!), spinning, rotating, vibrating, massless, rays of light, held together by enormous tensions (Peat, 1988: 57). It thus has a series of energy levels (Ibid.: 108). With Einstein's formula $E=mc^2$, these enormous energies can change into mass and vice versa. In fact, what accounts for particles with masses, is the compactification of 10-dimensions into four, leaving strings looking very much like particles in a 4-dimensional space-time (Ibid.: 293).

Unlike space-time mapping, conceptualized by quantum physicists as objects occupying one point of space at each instant of time producing a historical "world-line," string theorists see strings as one-dimensional lines occupying a space at each specific moment of time. Here, the string's history can be conceptualized as a 2-dimensional plane called a "world-sheet" (Hawkins, 1988: 159; Peat, 1988: 107-109, 123-131). Hence, a particular point on this world-sheet indicates two numbers, one reflecting position of the point along the string, the other, time. Strings can be either "open" or "closed"; the world-sheet of the former looks like a strip; the latter, like a cylinder (figure 5). If we take a slice through the closed string that is moving through time, much as chaologists would take a slice called a "poincaré section" through a doughnut shaped object in phase space, we arrive at the specific position of the string at any particular time; a point, then, can be located somewhere on this slice (Ibid.). The best we can do is to say that the point has a high probability of being somewhere in this circumscribed plane.

Figure 5
Strings (Closed, Open) and World Lines

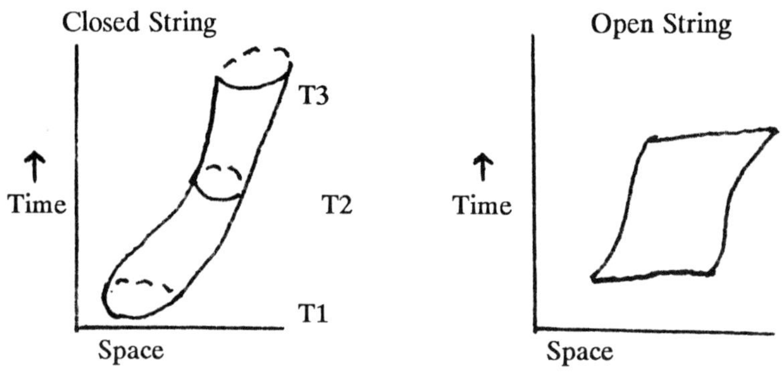

Strings can join together; closed strings joining together can be pictured as two legs of trousers (Ibid.). Previously pictured particles can now be pictured as waves moving down the strings (Ibid.: 160). One of the difficulties of current string theories, however, is in depicting strings of 2-dimensions in a 10-dimensional space/time (Peat, 1988: 319).

This imagery is very useful for alternative conceptualizations of movement of desire through space. Let's turn to this mapping of desire.

POSTMODERNITY: INSCRIBING THE BODY WITH A SIGN

How does all this help us in our project? Deleuze and Guattari have envisioned a space, the plane of consistency (unfortunately conceptualized narrowly in 2-dimensional space), with crisscrossing lines, lines of flight having beginnings and converging on some distant point (as in a vanishing point in paintings), expending themselves of energy, and being territorialized by abstract machines associated with a particular political economy. Points of subjectification, you will recall, originate not necessarily in some conscious design, but rather may be due to capital logic, bureaucratic rationalism, phallocentric logic, technological imperatives, etc. Bourgeois conceptualists could indeed give idealized expression to these phenomenal forms, without necessary understanding the deeper significance (recall the principle of commodity fetishism homologous to legal fetishism and how the equivalence-form becomes ubiquitous and omnipresent). String theories provide us some provocative stimuli for conceptualizing these lines of flight and what Deleuze and Guatteri refer to as "lines of continuous variation." It would seem fruitful to conceptualize not lines, as a series of linear connected points, but lines on a world-sheet of the closed variety. Thus we posit the unpredictability of accurately delineating points in space, but yet these points are limited in their possible variation. Let me explore this point in a moment.

It seems to me that what we would like to describe in the social sciences is dynamic systems but are incapable of finding an accurate representation of movement in space-time. Part of the problem is that we are imprisoned within the paradigms of our age. How is it that we can better conceptualize space-time and phenomena within dynamic systems? To this end we have briefly explored some recent innovations in theorizing in the mathematical sciences, specifically chaos and string theory. We would like now to apply some of these provocative ideas, first to Deleuze and Guattari, then to Foucault in his analysis of the panopticon, and finally to penal policy and outcome in general.

Whether we turn to Bergson with his notion of the subject as a becoming, or to Lacan with his notion of "speakings" we note that a conceptualization of space becomes critical. In his polemic on Spinoza, Deleuze has said that a body can be conceptualized as "a complex relation between differential speeds, between a slowing and an acceleration of particles" (reported in Bogue, 1989: 133). We have seen that for Deleuze and Guattari, haeccities exhibit this

movement -- the power of being affected and of affecting; haeccities then have a similar functional role to strings in string theory. (Too, we see a similar idea expressed by Nietzsche as to the body being a repository of quanta in dynamic relation to other quanta; left for another day, too, is an extended analysis of to what extent there are similarities and dissimilarities between Lacan's notion of floating signifiers, conceptualized as perhaps the inseparatness of thing-presentations and word-presentations, and haeccities.) Abstract machines, a particular diagram of power, arranges these haeccities along lines of flight that normally crisscross the body. Lines of continuous variation have variability within a limited space; hence we posit the existence of both determinism and indeterminism. Particular regimes of signs, sedimented discourses, or my appropriation, linguisitc coordinate systems, impose structure on these otherwise amorphous forms of duration. In post-signifying regimes, and I would extend these to all hierarchically arranged political economies, continuous exposure to these various points of signification can be diagramatically depicted, appearing much like closed strings moving through time, producing world-sheets. Thus if we were to take a slice from this tube-like structure, we would have defined accurately a line of flight.
Thus:

Figure 6
World-Sheet of Haeccities, Line of Continuous Variation, and Hypercathected Space

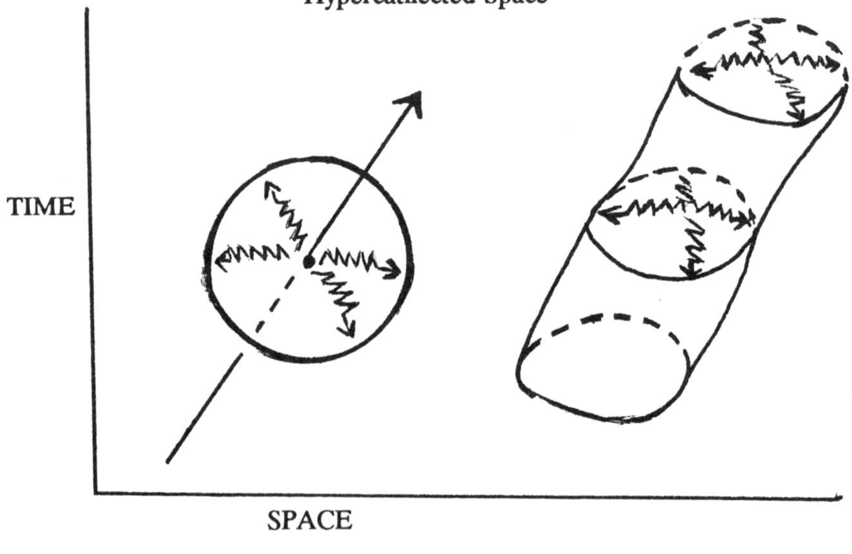

Figure 7
Poincaré Section of a Continuous Line
of Variation And Haeccities

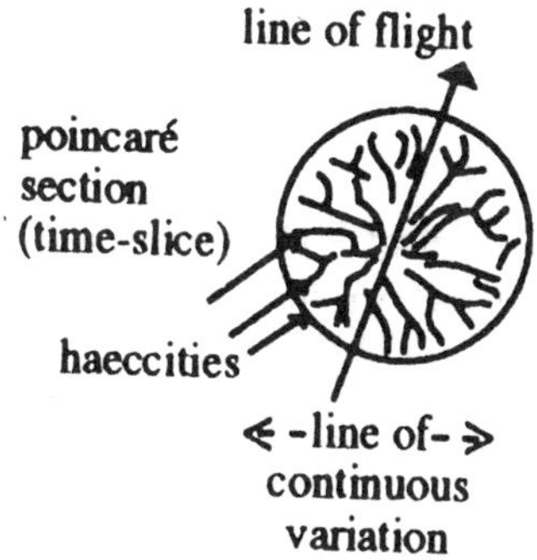

--Range of variation--

Language, for Deleuze and Guattari, must not be defined "by its constants and homogeneity but on the contrary by a variability whose characteristics are immanent, continuous, and regulated in a very specific mode" (1987: 93-94). In other words, signifiers (words) are better conceptualized as being in "continuous variation" (Ibid.). Signifiers are in perpetual states of change or variation. Just as Lacan has told us that signifiers' natural state is that they float, or slide over signifieds (1977) and it is at particular politically economically determined anchoring points that signifiers are attached to specific signifieds producing momentary stabilized meanings (see also Laclau and Mouffe, 1985), for Deleuze and Guattari another dimensionality exists one by which particular signifiers proliferate in variability producing in turn particular nuanced meanings.

For semioticians of the Lacanian psychoanalytical persuasion a sign is dualistically constituted. The signifier stands for the acoustic-image (psychologically, the sound-image); the signified, the referent of the signifier, or the concept referred to. The signifier represents an absence; say the word tree and a tree appears in its absence. Or as Hegel tells us, saying the thing is the killing of the thing. A subject finds its place in discourse by the use of a personal pronoun (signifier), but at the same time distances itself from the Real; it is a presence of an absence. For the construction of an utterance a semiotic grid must be evoked: a signifier must first be selected from the paradigmatic axis (within this vertical axis signifiers develop value in their differences with other signifiers), and then placed in some linear order along the syntagmatic axis (the horizontal axis, governed by syntactical and grammatical rules). Thus speech production entails: (1) selection from a repository of available signifiers circumscribed by a particular speech genre (linguistic coordinate system) -- here the periodic arousal of desire animates the process; (b) placement of these signifiers in a distinct order; and, (c) in the final step, as Lacan tells us, after the punctuation that ends the process of selection and placement, a retroactive glance to the beginning of these strings of signifiers takes place whereby the whole utterance is grasped and given precise meaning. Normally, signifiers "float" within the realm of the unconscious. They only refer to other signifiers; meaning is thus self-referential; look up a word in the dictionary and the words used in the definition must be further looked up and these in turn looked up, and so forth.

Introducing a critical, materialistically-based psychoanalytical semiotics we can say that discursive regions exist (alternatively, regimes of signs, or linguistic coordinate systems), each of which can be pictured as a depository of value-laden signifiers, and each of which is characterized by a distinct patterned interaction between the paradigmatic and syntagmatic axes. Political economies fix otherwise floating signifiers to particular signifieds, giving particular meaning to phenomena (see also Laclau and Mouffe, 1985; Milovanovic, 1986).

Extending on what we have done so far, the vertical axis, the paradigmatic axis, can be envisioned as a line of continuous variation and can be depicted, diagramatically as a closed string moving through space-time producing a world-line. At each poincaré section a range of resonating haeccities, signifiers, are perturbed, are activated from their quiescent states, or as Freud has told us are hypercathected. Which signifier is actually chosen as the representative of desire to be placed in a syntagmatic structure, the utterance, is never definite, but is conditioned somewhat by the pragmatics of place and by the force of restrictive "major literatures" that tend toward dominance over resonating "minor literatures" that know no closure (see figure 6 and 7); hence, we have the dominance or hegemony of male discourse rather than female, white rather than black, older rather than younger generation, upper class rather than lower, etc., prevailing at times of signification, or speech production. It is the hidden, repressed voice that critical feminist analysis, for example, seeks to recover (Irigaray, 1985; see also Grosz, 1990; Giroux, 1988).

As an example of lines of continuous variation, take, for example the word "dog." Alternatively it could be pronounced "dawg" or "dag" (Lecercle, 1985: 145-46). Or take the sworn testimony introduced in a recent trial I attended concerning police brutality where the question focused on the meaning of the instruction (utterance) by the police supervisor to officers who had just arrested a suspect for killing two police officers, "take him to the station." Did it mean "take him to the police station and book him" as the police contended? Or did it mean "take him to the station and work him over there" as the defense contended? In other words, we have variability within a semantic space, with one pronunciation or one implied meaning being more statistically common, although none are permanently fixed or stable. Thus we have continuous lines of variation rather than linear constants (Deleuze and Guattari, 198: 94-96; Bogue, 1989: 146). Each signifier in a linguistic coordinate system has this characteristic of being in a constant state of variation. Say the word "dog" or make the utterance "take him to the station" and all other variations resonate. "It is the sum of such lines of variation" Bogue paraphrasing Deleuze and Guattari tells us, "that comprises the 'abstract machine' of a given language, and it is the collection of 'concrete machines' of a regime of signs that determines which variables will be standard and which will not" (1989: 146). These lines of continuous variation also reflect contextual colorations. The statement "I swear" has different meaning according to whether it is pronounced by a child to her father, by a witness in court, or by a lover to his/her beloved (Deleuze and Guattari, 1987: 94). Thus "I swear" is a continuous line of variation producing three specific meanings. Which specific variation is stabilized ultimately is a function of context, specific discourse employed, and unique (person-specific) desire generated.

In a given time interval the subject passes continuously and indescernibly from one particular discourse to another; utterances reach a level of stability due to the circumvention of lines of continuous variation that traverses a particular linguistic coordinate system (Ibid.).

Deleuze and Guattari posit the existence of "major" and "minor" language/literatures (1987: 104-110; 1986: 16-42; Bogue, 1989: 147); in the former, they restrict variation producing rigidity in meaning, in the latter producing continuous variation (see figure 7). Writers such as Kafka and Beckett, Deleuze and Guattari tell us, have embraced minor readings (see Deleuze's and Guattari's analysis of Kafka, 1988); said more specifically, these writers embrace lines of continuous variation, allowing them to manifest their resonations (compare the very rich poetic to the very dry scientific writings). Bogue has a clear example: "when e.e. cummings writes 'they went their came,' he does not simply combine the standard phrases 'they went as they came, they went their way, they came and went," etc., but rather sets the standard phrases in disequilibrium by availing himself, through the atypical phrase, of a line of variation" (1989: 147). Consider also the feat of a skydiving colleague of mine who parachuted from the Statue of Liberty in 1986 and the subsequent newspaper headlines which read:

STA-CHUTE OF
LEAP-ERTY!

A regime of signs (linguistic coordinate systems) thus is composed of these lines of continuous variation, which can be depicted as existing as potentialities: "they dictate no single, determinate course of development, but many possible directions of metamorphosis" (Bogue, 1989: 148). It is the plane of consistency and its haeccities that lines of continuous variation traverse, resonating the field, but always driven by the abstract machine with its diagram of power inscribing the body with lines of flight, representing a mapping of desire. Diagramatically this can be depicted in our world-sheet. If we take a slice, place it upright we can pinpoint a 2-dimensional circular plane that is but one slice passing through the line of continuous variation (see figure 7); the precise utterance is always indeterminable; a range exists from which one variation of a signifier is chosen. This slice also can be seen as composed of haeccities that are hypercathected and arranged by the effects of the traversing line of continuous variation.

A better understanding of these phenomena can be had by bringing Foucault into the picture. Foucault has acknowledged the work of Deleuze and his physics as being influential. He has said that "perhaps one day this century will be known as Deleuzian" (cited in Deleuze, 1988: xli). It is particularly apparent in Foucault's *Discipline and Punish*. Here he presents concepts such as "micro-physics of power," the "political anatomy of the body" and many more that offer a new way of conceptualizing the body and its powers. Deleuze's treatise on Foucault's work, particularly the sections commenting on *Discipline and Punish* (1988) extends this analysis. Deleuze following Foucault sees power as operational, as defined in its exercise, rather than in its possession (1988: 25-27). A diagram or the abstract machine, the panopticon according to Foucault, posits relations between forces (Ibid.: 36). Or to put it in our vocabulary, it is a way of structuring haeccities, of inscribing the body with the sign. As Foucault has told us,

> discipline organizes an analytical space...[it] is a political anatomy of detail...[it] produces subjected and practised bodies, 'docile' bodies. Discipline increases the forces of the body (in economic terms of utility) and diminishes these same forces (in political terms of obedience) (1977a: 138-19, 143).

It can be equally used in the workshop, school, hospital, army, or prison. Its sole function is to produce bodies of docility and utility; docility in terms of subservience, utility in terms of usefulness for some organizational end. In the U.S. at the present moment there are about 750,000 imprisoned, almost 500,000 on parole, and about 2.5 million on probation; an outstanding figure approaching almost four million people under supervision, under the eyes of the panopticon and its disciplining force. Elsewhere, Gary Marx (1988) makes a convincing case that police surveillance practices have become increasingly proactive and hence all in society are subject to the gaze of the panopticon: we are in the throws of a "maximum-security society."

The penal policy at any given time can be seen, in its manifest form as the point of subjectification, a point from which lines of continuous variation run their course in the social formation. But others exist. Bureaucratic rationalism and the culture of informal secondary adjustments by the kept will have their say. But so, too, resistance to the absurdities created by contradictory lines of continuous variation intersecting produce moments of liberated space within which a minor literature can be recovered or constructed (Milovanovic and Thomas, 1989). Put in another way, whereas major (hegemonic) literatures/discourses produce particular lines of variation, in their effects producing the tendency for the inscription of desire on the body along the form of the diagram that is historically specific, minor literatures deterritorialize (Deleuze, 1988: 16), they set in resonance thc line of continuous variation expressing maximal potentials. In addition, minor literature is political; it expresses collective rather than individual utterances; it produces ruptures; it liberates repressed voices; it is revolutionary (Ibid.: 16-18; Bogue, 1989: 119). A minor literature deconstructs and reconstructs; deterritorializes and reterritorializes. It's the initial step in producing a more stable oppositional linguistic coordinate system within which repressed subjects may take a political stance by being effected by politically stimulated lines of continuous variation.

Deleuze, Guattari, and Foucault have offered us novel ways of conceptualizing body-space. How does the body get inscribed by the sign? The mechanism is a regime of signs, structured according to a diagram, a map, that, by the points of subjectification and lines of continuous variation that emanate from it, structures haeccities along lines of flight, along which desire flows. The terrain: dynamic quanta in relation, varying between speed and rest, haeccities with potential for affecting and being affected, lying on a plane of consistency, a striated space that is always in tension with minor revolutionary literature that undermines it.

Deleuze and Guattari's direction is refreshing. It can be greatly augmented by the ideas from chaos theory. First, they already acknowledge the usefulness of fractals (1987: 486-88) in describing the nature of smooth space. They argue: (1) striated space is representable by non-fractional dimensions, (2) that smooth space is constituted by lines with fractional dimensions, hence a fractal line greater than one and less than two dimensions, or by a surface with dimensionality between two and three, (3) that these fractals represent directionality with continuous variation, (4) that "it does not have a dimension higher than that which moves through it or is inscribed in it," (5) that space and that which occupies it become one, (6) that, finally, a smooth space is occupied by "proximities" -- more than the dimensionality of a line but less than a plane, more than the dimensionality of a plane but less than a volume (Ibid.: 488; for literary theorists who reflect chaos in their writings see Serres, 1982a, 1982b; Hayles, 1990: 196-208).

Second, postulating the indeterminacy of the lines of continuous variation presence a clearer picture of movement. In other words, within any slice from our world-sheet, we have variability without stability or absolute determination; we cannot define in all situations at what point along the lines of continuous variation a particular configuration will stabilize; at best, we, as in the uncertainty principle, will witness probabilities of occurrence. It would seem that critical feminism, particularly being done by the French postmodernists, Kristeva (1984), Irigaray (1985), and Cixous (1976) indicates a way of recovering the feminist voice. We may conceptualize the lines of continuous variation following a major literature where the feminist voice has been relegated to the minor. What postmodernist feminists might argue is that the strategy is to place in resonance the lines of continuous variation and allow variability to play itself out, in the process uncovering all the repressed voices without, at the same time, falling trap to an essentialist position concerning the question of agency.

Third, and closely connected to the second, non-linearity dynamics assure imprecision in predicting social phenomena. An incremental increase in some value does not necessarily translate into a proportional increase in an effect; rather, the initial value may combine with others in such a way that disproportional effects may occur. Someone exposed to a particular situation may thereafter dramatically alter his/her life course, way out of proportion to the prima facie message of the situation itself. Or, to approach it differently, an initially stipulated measurement error cannot be assumed to be constant over time; hence, outcomes are never totally predictable by initial states alone.

Fourth, Deleuze and Guattari's enterprise can be augmented by chaos theory by stipulating non-scale invariance; in other words, phenomena that take place at one level, say the micro do not necessarily work themselves out in a linear, self-same form at some other level. Compare, for example, the Hegelian/Marxian linear dynamics of dialectical materialism (i.e., the logical working out of the Absolute Spirit) with the notion of genealogy advocated by Nietzsche which questions linear causality (Love, 1986: 67-111; Foucault, 1977b: 139-64; Sarup, 1989: 63-64).

Fifth, the notion of attractors offers much speculation. Could we envision the following direction of inquiry: since haeccities are defined as dynamic quanta with differentials in speeds, having the capacity of being affected and having affects (could they also be Lacan's signifier + X ?), then couldn't we benefit more in quantifying and predicting phenomena by picturing phenomena on a phase space, pinpointing speed and place of haeccities, and watching for attractors appearing, rather than embracing the static graphs and regression analyses of contemporary positivistic empirical analysis? In other words, couldn't we observe some repeating situations or contexts to see if some attractors develop on the phase space diagrams, and couldn't this then be the definition of the subject; a tendency toward certain points and no more? Could we then define Nietzsche's "eternal return" as a passage through a specified space, a "poincaré section," never duplicating precisely previous points but, nevertheless, falling within a predictable range of occurrences, an inner sense of unity that reflects both an indeterminacy and a deterministic structure? -- an entity that cannot be precisely defined in space but has certain tendencies with multiple degrees of freedom along lines of continuous variation? Could this, perhaps, be the basis of a new humanistic orientation in the social sciences: the subject seen as being both determining and determined? Would this allow us, then, to escape from the fetishistic categories created of the empirical, legal, and the deviant subject and prepare us for the return of a science appreciative of the uniqueness of being human? A new focus, the inscribing of the body with the sign, may offer illuminating lines of inquiry. Foucault has well-stated the direction:

> The body is the inscribed surface of events (traced by language and

> dissolved by ideas), the locus of a dissociated Self (adopting the illusion of a substantial unity), and a volume in perpetual disintegration. Genealogy, as an analysis of descent, is thus situated within the articulation of the body and history. Its task is to expose a body totally imprinted by history and the process of history's destruction of the body (1977b: 148).

CONCLUSION

This has been a highly speculative study. But at a time where theory finds itself locked within the paradigm of the age, what is necessary is a leap forward. Postmodern science in the 1980s has already witnessed a profound break in theorizing, from the nature of the universe to the nature of particles. String theory on the one hand, and chaos theory on the other provide new visions for a more complex understanding of dynamic systems in space-time. We, in the social sciences, need new visions in conceptualizing space, time, subjectivity, and social action. It is toward this end that this essay strives.

* *An earlier version of this paper was presented at the Annual Meeting of the American Society of Criminology, November, 1990.*

** *Dragan Milovanovic is Professor of Criminal Justice at Northeastern Illinois University.*

NOTE

1. We have focused on one component of post-modernism, the nature of the conceptualization of space. A necessary next step is to indicate the nexus with agency (the nature of subjectivity) and political economic structures. Elsewhere we have developed the idea of the decentered subject (Milovanovic, 1989, 1991), of the dialectics of resistance to oppressive structures (Milovanovic, 1988; Milovanovic and Thomas, 1989; Bannister and Milovanovic, 1990), of how in fact conceptions of crime and the criminal are constructed in discourse by way of a constitutive criminology (Henry and Milovanovic, 1991), and the beginnings of a replacement discourse (Lynch, Lynch, and

Milovanovic, this volume). The demands for integrating a conception of space with a convincing conception of agency as these relate to a political economy remains the challenge of the postmodernist enterprise.

REFERENCES

Bannister, Shelley and Dragan Milovanovic. 191. "The Necessity Defense, Substantive Justice and Oppositional Linguistic Praxis," *International Journal of the Sociology of Law* 18: 179-198.

Berge, Pierre, Yves Pomeau, and Christian Vidal. 1984. *Order Within Chaos*. New York: John Wiley.

Bergson, Henri. 1960. *Time and Free Will: An Essay on the Immediate Data of Consciousness*. New York: Harper and Row

Best, Steven. 1990. "Chaos and Entropy in Postmodern Science and Social Theory" (unpublished manuscript)

Best, Steven. 1991. *Postmodern Theory*. London: Macmillan.

Bogue, Ronald. 1989. *Deleuze and Guattari*. New York: Routledge.

Cixous, H. 1976. The Laugh of the Medusa," *Signs*, 7 (1).

Deleuze, Gilles. 1983. *Nietzsche and Philosophy*. New York: Columbia University Press.

_____. 1988. *Foucault*. Minneapolis: University of Minnesota Press.

_____. 1981. *Spinoza*. Paris: Minuit.

____ and Felix Guattari. 1987. *A Thousand Plateaus*. Minneapolis: University of Minnesota Press.

____ and Felix Guattari. 1988. *Kafka*. Minneapolis: University of Minnesota Press.

Foucault, Michel. 1977b. *Language, Counter-Memory, Practice*. New

York: Cornell University Press.

_____. 1977a. *Discipline and Punish*. New York: Pantheon Books.

Gleick, James. 1987. *Chaos: Making a New Science*. New York: Viking

Goldberger, Ary, David Rigney and Bruce West. 1990. "Chaos and Fractals in Human Physiology," *Scientific America* (February): 42-49.

Grosz, Elizabeth. 1990. *Jacques Lacan: A Feminist Introduction*. New York: Routledge.

Hayles, Katherine. 1990. *Chaos Bound: Orderly Disorder in Contemporary Literature and Science*. Ithaca: Cornell University Press.

Hawkins, Stephen. 1988. *A Brief History of Time From the Big Bang to Black Holes*. New York: Bantam Books.

Heisenberg, Werner. 1958. *Physics and Philosophy*. New York: Harper and Row.

Henry, Stuart and Dragan Milovanovic. 1991. "Constitutive Criminology," *Journal of Criminology*. 29: 293-315.

Irigary, L. 1985. *Speculum of the Other Woman*. Itrhaca: Cornell University Press.

Jurgens, Hartmut, Heinz-Otto Peitgen and Dietmar Saupe. 1990. "The Language of Fractals," *Scientific American* (August): 60-67.

Kristeva, Julia. 1984. *The Revolution in Poetic Language*. New York: Columbia University Press.

Lacan, Jacque. 1977. *Ecrits*. New York: Norton

Laclau, Mouffe. 1985. *Hegemony and Socialist Strategy*. New York: Verso.

Lecercle, Jean-Jacque. 1985. *Philosophy Through the Looking Glass*. London: Hutchinson.

Love, Nancy. 1986. *Marx, Nietzsche, and Modernity*. New York: Columbia University Press.

Lynch, Michael, Lynch, and Dragan Milovanovic (see This volume) "Deconstruction and Radical Criminology, Contradictions and the Problem of 'The Text.'"

Marx, Gary. 1988. *Undercover: Police Surveillance in America*. Berkeley, California: University of California Press.

Milovanovic, Dragan. 1986. "Juridic-Linguistic Communicative Markets: Towards a Semiotic Analysis," *Contemporary Crises* 10: 281-304.

____. 1988. "Jailhouse Lawyers and Jailhouse Lawyering," *International Journal of Sociology of Law* 16: 455-475.

____. 1989. "Critical Criminology and the Challenge of Postmodernism," *The Critical Criminologist* 1(4): 9-10, 17.

____. 1991. "Images of Unity and Disunity in the Juridic Subject and the Movement Toward the Peacemaking Community," in Harold Pepinsky and Richard Quinney (eds.) *Criminology as Peacemaking*. Bloomington Indiana: Indiana University Press.

____ and Jim Thomas. 1989. "Overcoming the Absurd: Prisoner Litigation as Primitive Rebellion," *Social Problems* 36 (1): 48-60.

Nietzsche, Friedrich. 1968. *Basic Writings of Nietzsche*. Ed. W. Kaufman. New York: The Modern Library.

Pagels, Heinz. 1983. *The Cosmic Code: Quantum Physics as the Language of Nature*. New York: Bantam Books.

Peat, E. David. 1988. *Superstrings and the Search for The Theory of Everything*. Chicago: Contemporary Books.

Penrose, Roger. 1989. *The Emperor's New Mind*. New York: Oxford University Press.

Pepinsky, Harold. 1990. *The Geometry of Violence and Democracy*. Bloomington, Indiana: Indiana University Press.

Prigogine, Ilya and Stengers, Isabell. 1984. *Order Out of Chaos*. New York: Bantam Books.

Rifkin, Rifkin. 1989. *Entropy: Into the Greenhouse World*. New York: Bantam

Books.

Sarup, Madan. 1989. *Post-Structuralism and Postmodernism*. Athens, Georgia. University of Georgia Press.

Serres, Michel. 1982a. *Hermes: Literature, Science, Philosophy*. Ed. Josue Harari and David Bell. Baltimore: Johns Hopkins University Press.

____. 1982b. *The Parasite*. Trans. Lawrence Schehr. Baltimore: Johns Hopkins University Press.

Stewart, Ian. 1989. *Does God Play With Dice?* New York: Basil Blackwell.

Weeks, Jeffrey. 1985. *The Shape of Space*. New York: Marcel Dekker, Inc.

CHAPTER V

TWO IDEOLOGICAL MONSTERS: THE SUBJECT OF THE BAR AND THE OBJECT OF DESIRE IN BLEAK HOUSE

David S. Caudill*

> "... It won't do to have truth and justice on his side, he must have law and lawyers," exclaims the old girl, apparently persuaded that the latter form a separate establishment,and have dissolved partnership with truth and justice for ever and a day.[1]

The famous image of sluggish legal processes and decayed legal institutions in Dickens' *Bleak House* strikes many as capturing some truths about Western law generally, even in its current forms. Of course *Bleak House* is a fictional construct --a detective story or mystery full of exaggerated characters and situations -- and not an historical account, but that distinction fades in light of the narrativity of (and devices of emplotment that appear in) historiography. Moreover, cases like *Jarndyce v. Jarndyce* did[2] and do[3] arise; and while such cases are rare, some of their features are not. Lawyers recognize in *Bleak House* certain characteristics of contemporary law practice, client relationships, judicial processes, and so forth. To the extent that Dickens predicted a cataclysmic collapse of the English legal system (and even society), he was (so far) wrong,[4] but his literary descriptions of people and society are generally viewed as compelling and insightful.[5]

The use of literature as a source of understanding about law, as well as the use of law to understand literature, are growing enterprises in legal scholarship.[6] This essay falls in the former category insofar as my concern is not with interpreting the intended meaning of, or identifying Dickens' well-placed themes in *Bleak House*. Just as Jacques Lacan used Poe's *Purloined Letter*,[7] or Slavoj Zizek uses popular culture (i.e., jokes, films, science fiction),[8] to illustrate some of the unfamiliar, counter-intuitive, and controversial features of contemporary psychoanalytic theory, I treat certain representations in *Bleak House* as allegories. If that practice seems reductionistic, I make no claim to have captured the essence of the novel.[9] On the other hand, in terms of postmodern consciousness, the meaning of *Bleak House* is not severely limited by the text or by Dickens,[10] thus I may accidentally "use law to understand literature."

The purpose of this essay is to explore two forms of the critique of legal ideology, the first being relatively well understood and the second -- based on Zizek's reading of Lacan --quite complicated and unfamiliar. In Section I, I focus on certain passages in *Bleak House* about law, including lawyers, clients, lawsuits, and Chancery. Section II acknowledges the psychological themes in those passages and summarizes some of the psychoanalytic criticism that *Bleak House* invites. In Section III, I consider Zizek's contrast between a critique which presumes ideology to be an illusion about reality, and a critique which views ideology as structuring reality itself. Finally, in Section IV, I use Dickens' materials to elucidate some of Lacan's complex notions of desire and fantasy, and I conclude that the critique of legal ideology can be enriched by psychoanalytic theory.

I
LAW'S SUBJECTS AND OBJECTS OF DESIRE

> "Kenge," said my guardian, ..."do you ask *me* to believe that any good is to come of Jarndyce and Jarndyce?"
>
> "Oh, really, Mr. Jarndyce! Prejudice, Prejudice. My dear sir, this is a very great system, a very great system. Really, really!" (576)

John Jarndyce, firmly within the network of law, maintains (in his "animosity") a psychical distance from its promises. When attorney Kenge says of a will that it is a perfect document, that it could not "have been stated more plainly and to the purpose if it had been a case at law", Jarndyce asks, "Did you ever know English Law, or equity either, plain and to the purpose?" (576)

Even those characters less experienced in legal matters -- especially those characters -- have little faith in the possibilities of justice in law. Law is an impossibility, thus any "honorable" Chancery Court lawyer would give the warning: "Suffer any wrong that can be done to you rather than come here."

(2) Mr. George, for example, as a subject of law generally and specifically (in his business debts), will trust no lawyer even when he is wrongly accused of murdering attorney Tulkinghorn. Trooper George proposes to tell the truth as his defense:

> "But the mere truth won't do," rejoined [John Jarndyce].
> "Won't it indeed, sir? Rather a bad look- out for me.!" Mr. George good-humoredly observed.
> "You must have a lawyer,"....
> "I ask your pardon, sir", said Mr. George...."But I must decidedly beg to be excused from anything of the sort.... No lawyer! I don't take kindly to the breed...." (482)

In fact, Mr. George opines, if he had kept clearer of law and lawyers, he wouldn't be in "this place"; moreover, even if he was guilty, and a lawyer could "get him off" by keeping him quiet, by chopping "the evidence small," and by quibbling, he

> would rather be hanged in [his] own way.... What I say is I must come off clear and full or not at all.... If they can't make me innocent out of whole truth, they
> are not likely to do it out of anything less.... And if they are, it's worth nothing to me. (484)

However, Mr. George's mother "impresses upon" him that he needs the best advice obtainable by money and influence". Only for her, to alleviate her suffering, is he willing to "yield up his case to the greatest lawyers that can be got; [he] must not be self-willed, however right...." (515)[11] Nevertheless, as with John Jarndyce, the belief in law's possibilities are absent -- Mr. George remains self-willed and suspicious, in contrast to the subjects of the bar and those who desire law's objects.

Lawyers

> "I [Lady Dedlock] dread one person very much....He is Sir Leicester Dedlock's lawyer, mechanically faithful with attachment.... I may keep him at a standstill, but I can never shake him off.... He is indifferent to everything but his calling." (347-48)

Tulkinghorn, one of Dickens' major lawyer-figures, is known by John

Jarndyce "both by sight and by reputation, and it was certain that he was a dangerous man." (406) Dedlock's lawyer is impenetrable -- he "melts" in and out of rooms; he dwells "among mankind," but without consortion, nesting in the "holes and corners of human nature", not in "its broader and better range." (396) One knows Tulkinghorn to one's sorrow:

> He is a confoundedly bad kind of man. He is a slow-torturing kind of man. He is no more like flesh and blood than a rusty old carbine is. (434)

Trooper George's "rusty carbine" comparison is confirmed as a metaphor in Dickens' description of the late-night assassination of Tulkinghorn:

> What's that? Who fired a gun or pistol?... Has Mr. Tulkinghorn been disturbed?... It must be something unusual indeed to bring him out of his shell.... What power of cannon might it take to shake that rusty old man out of his immovable composure? (450-51)

While Tulkinghorn is exceptional, a "high priest of [his] noble [clients'] mysteries" (396), his death does not even wound the law generally, as plenty of lesser priests with lesser clients populate the world of the novel, each of whom share to some degree the ideals embodied in Tulkinghorn. I consider only Vholes, since I will in the next section consider his client Richard Carstone as one who does not keep his psychical distance from the law -- Richard in his delusion believes in law's possibilities, in law as the place of truth and justice.

Vholes, with his less-glamorous practice, is not unlike Tulkinghorn in reputation among the lower classes of litigants in Chancery: "You don't like Vholes, I hope? *Don't* like Vholes. Dan-gerous man!" (560) But in society at large,

> Mr. Vholes is a very respectable man. He has not a large business, but...is allowed by the greater attorneys...to be a most respectable man. He never misses a chance in his practice, ...never takes any pleasure,...is reserved and serious, [and his] digestion is impaired, [all of] which is highly respectable. (371)

Vholes follows the "one great principle of English law" -- "to make business for itself" at the expense of others[12] -- thus his fidelity to his client Richard is always limited by respectability, by business interests:

> I wish to say no more of any third party than is necessary. I wish to leave my good name unsullied. I also desire to live in amity with my professional brethren.... [Your] interests are now paramount in his office. I shall not rest... and when I ultimately congratulate you... on your accession to fortune,... all between us is ended. (374-75)

Such wordiness and proprieties make Richard angry and impatient, but Vholes always offers some immediate relief to the dejected litigant, some rekindling of hope in the suit. Thereafter, Richard neither blames himself nor his lawyer, neither the suit nor Chancery, as he is slowly consumed; but this

> fighting with shadows and being defeated by them necessitates the setting up of substances to combat; from the impalpable suit which no man alive can understand, the time for that being long gone by, it has become a gloomy relief to turn to the palpable figure of [John Jarndyce] and make *him* his enemy. (375-76)

Richard, fully aware that John Jarndyce now embodies for him the abstractions of the lawsuit, nevertheless believes in the accuracy, the truth, of that symbolism -- Jarndyce really is, for Richard, his antagonist and oppressor.[13] This inability to see the gaping flaws in legal processes and institutions -- including law practice -- is a carefully analyzed form of delusion in Dickens' account of law.

Lawsuits

Richard's delusion is on the surface identical to that of the mad Miss Flite, but due to her years of experience there is a difference. Miss Flite keeps her place in Chancery long after she recognizes the futility of her (and Richard's) cause:

> "...I expect a judgment. Shortly. My father expected a judgment", said Miss Flite. "My brother. My sister. They all expected a judgment...."
>
> "Would it not be wiser", said I, "to expect this judgment no more?"
>
> "Why...of course it would.... But...there's a dreadful attraction in

> that place.... You *can't* leave it. And you *must* expect." (337-38)

Chancery *draws* people, and draws out of them their sense, good looks, good qualities, nightly rest -- "I went to look at the Monster...and I was drawn to stay there." (338) She knows all the signs, and she sees them "beginning" in Richard -- "Let someone hold him back. Or, he'll be drawn to ruin." (339)

Richard, "young and handsome, and in all respects so perfectly" Miss Flite's opposite, is "so dreadfully like her" in his "clouded, eager, seeking look." (335) And he knows that he, like Miss Flite, appears deluded; but if his critics only knew the accumulated papers in the case, if they would apply themselves, they would see what he sees.

> "But do you think that among those many papers there is much truth and justice, Richard?"
>
> "There is truth and justice somewhere in the case, Esther."
>
> "Or was once, long ago," said I.
>
> "Is -- is -- must be somewhere," pursued Richard impetuously, "and must be brought out." (358)

Yes, the suit has changed him, yes, others have failed to bring it to an end, but "I devote myself to it. I make it the object of my life." (358) Much later, when he looks "worn and haggard", he explains: "Call it madness.... But it is no such thing; it is the one object I have to pursue." (415, 417) Even later, Richard's pursuit in Chancery is almost seen as a mistake, but then as destiny:

> To make short of a long story, I am afraid I have wanted an object; but I have an object now -- or it has me -- and it is too late to discuss it. Take me as I am, and make the best of me. (472)

Miss Flite will discuss "it"; Richard will not (and he dies on the eve of his worthless victory in Chancery).

II
DICKENS AS PSYCHOLOGIST

> [N]othing can obscure the illusions and the greeds and disputes that drive people to place their reliance on Chancery and help to sustain

> it. Richard is the classical case in point.... A goodnatured, improvident man places his faith in riches and in the Court's capacity to satisfy this desire.[14]

Joseph Gold argues that "one of Dickens' principal concerns and talents was the exploration of the psychology of behavior," and notes the fascination of psychiatrists in Dickens' novels.[15] In the opening chapter of *Bleak House*, to be "In Chancery" is a state of mind, a condition of perception, "as though one were to speak of being...'in a trance.'"[16] Gordon Hirsch's explicitly psychoanalytic approach to *Bleak House* (which novel is "concerned primarily with mystery, curiosity, and investigation -- with making connections and finding links") uses Freudian categories to explore the effects of Chancery:

> The mysteries of *Bleak House* are connected at root with the child's curiosity about parental sexuality and his struggle to manage his own complex and ambivalent feelings about that sexuality.[17]

Hence Richard is a self-destructive obsessional neurotic, his major symptom being his inability to choose a profession; his uncertainty and procrastination mirror Chancery, into which he was born and where his Oedipal conflicts are re-constituted -- "Chancery becomes the institutional symbol for the parents."[18]

More recent studies of *Bleak House* also include recourse to psychoanalytic and even Lacanian theory. For example, Pam Morris' *Dickens's Class Consciousness: A Marginal View* (1991) utilizes Lacan and Althusser to "reposition" Dickens' novels outside his authorial intentions; the representation of law in *Bleak House* as an ultimate structure of mystification is justified, since

> law is the...guarantor of the existing "providential" dispensations of property, privilege, and power. Moreover, law is the formal institution for defining...what is legitimate.... [Law] is unveiled as the mechanism of submission constructing subjects who "willingly" subject themselves to subjections.[19]

In this reading, the social orders of discourse, including law's "mystifying systems of meaning which sustain" power structures, become examples of Lacan's Symbolic order and Althusser's ideological structures of interpellation.[20]

Audrey Jaffe's *Vanishing Points: Dickens, Narrative, and the Subject of*

Omniscience (1991) focuses on Ester's narrative in *Bleak House*:

> Esther comes into existence for herself already structured by what Lacan calls the symbolic: by language, morality, and the law. Feeling herself both guilty and innocent, she fashions her narrative to confirm her as the latter but not the former [-- she denies her "unpleasurable self"].[21]

In the end, she constructs the imaginary "world which reflects only the self she wishes to see."[22]

> Esther's narrative thus reflects the conflict necessitated by the taking of a place within the social world, for empowered as narrator to construct an identity for herself, she can only do so by choosing one identity and rejecting another.[23]

This "almost allegorical enactment of [Lacan's] mirror stage" recurs, Morris demonstrates, at various moments in Dickens' novels.[24]

Without challenging the careful readings of *Bleak House* by Morris and Jaffe, their work betrays the tendency to appropriate Lacan's seemingly quite accessible notions of the symbolic and imaginary "registers" in cultural studies, at the expense of Lacan's conception of desire. In the case of Morris and Jaffe, whose psycho-analyses focus on Esther and not on those lawyers and litigants caught up in Chancery, the cost is negligible. For critics of legal ideology, however, the terms "symbolic" and "imaginary" can function to reduce Lacanian theory to the commonplace. As Slavoj Zizek has demonstrated, the failure to take desire and its object into account in ideology-critiques can render such critiques ineffective. It is not so much that the terms "symbolic" and "imaginary" are not useful markers in social theory, but rather that such terms alone tend to support an ideology of subjects as being *determined*, as if the desire and enjoyment of the subject are beside the point.

III
ZIZEK'S FANTASY

> [B]elief, far from being an "intimate", purely mental state, is always *materialized* in our effective social activity: belief supports the fantasy

which regulates social reality.[25]

The place of Lacan in the critique of ideology, including legal ideology, is not clear. Conceiving ideology as "false consciousness" is now out of fashion, giving way to a conception of ideology as a human condition. Lacan's notion of the subject constituted in imaginary and symbolic relations seems to fill that bill, as Althusser's appropriation of Lacan for neo-Marxism demonstrated,[26] but aficionados of Lacan are less than comfortable with such syntheses -- either because the hope for liberation (through an active, historical subject) seems unjustified or, almost conversely, because psychoanalytic categories are somehow reduced to the terms of socio-historical determinism.[27] However, the suggestion of postmodernism that we live in a post-ideological era -- because the beliefs that support ideologies have been called into question -- is also not compelling to Lacanians, because, in Marxian and Lacanian terms, people's

> beliefs, superstitions and metaphysical mystifications, supposedly surmounted by the rational, utilitarian personality, are embodied in the "social relations between things." They no longer believe, *but the things themselves believe for them.*[28]

That is, rather than people having interior beliefs and exterior knowledge, "it is belief which is radically exterior, embodied in the practical, effective procedure of people."[29] A place for Lacan in ideology theory therefore remains, but only in a reconsideration of Lacan and in a new definition of ideology.

Zizek -- in a series of contrasts involving Freud and Marx, Lacan and Althusser -- identifies two types of ideology-critique. With respect to Freud's dream theory, for example, one can characterize the latent text as containing the hidden meaning of the manifest test (which appears meaningless); interpretation of a dream is then a translation of the latent text into everyday language. Such an approach, however, identifies unconscious desire as the latent thought, the dream's signification, rather than recognizing the latent text as an articulation of something else. Zizek therefore argues that the

> structure [of the dream] is always triple; there are always three elements at work: the *manifest dream-text*, the latent *dream-content* or thought and the *unconscious desire* articulated in a dream. This desire attaches itself to the dream, it intercalates itself in the

> interspace between the latent thought and the manifest text; it is therefore not "...deeper" in relation
> to the latent thought, it is decidedly more "on the surface"...its only place is in the *form* of the "dream".[30]

Just as we must get rid of our fascination with the "hidden meaning" of the dream -- "the content concealed behind the form" -- and focus on the form itself, so in ideology critique we must examine the process by which an ideology installs itself as effective.[31]

To clarify this distinction between form- and content-based analyses, Zizek contrasts two views of the ideological "dream". If one conceives "of ideology as a dreamlike construction hindering us from seeing the real state of things", then the critique of ideology consists of "throwing away the ideological spectacles", just as we awaken from a dream into reality and realize we were confused. In psychoanalytic theory, however, one is mush closer during the dream to the "fantasy framework which determines our activity" in reality; the ideological dream is not

> an illusion masking the real state of things, but... an (unconscious) fantasy structuring our social reality itself.... The only way to break the power of our ideological dream is to confront the real of our desire which announces itself in this dream.[32]

We might say, paraphrasing Zizek on Freud on dreams,[33] that the structure of ideology is always triple: (1) *unconscious desire* attaches itself to the form of ideology, intercalating itself in the interspace between (2) *ideological "thought" content* and (3) *manifest reality*. The

> illusion is not on the side of knowledge, it is already on the side of reality itself, of what people are doing.... What they overlook, what they misrecognize, is not the reality but the illusion which is structuring their reality, their real social activity.[34]

The significance of ideology is not that it hides reality from us, but rather that it announces our reality. Fantasy, in Lacan's sense of an answer to unconscious desire, is on the side of reality, not the dream.[35]

Anti-Semitism, for Zizek, exemplifies the operation of fantasy in ideology.

> It is not enough to say that we must liberate ourselves of so-called

> "anti-Semitic prejudices".... We must confront... how the ideological figure of the "Jew" is invested with our unconscious desire, with how we have constructed this figure to escape a certain deadlock of our desire.[36]

That is, the remedy for ideological anti-Semitism is not simply production of evidence that "Jews are really not like that", as if ideology is opposed to reality, because ideological anti-Semitism has nothing to do with Jews -- it "is a way to stitch up the inconsistency of our own ideological system."[37] Thus in Germany in the 1930's, the experience of having a Jewish neighbor who was *not* unclean, scheming, or exploitative could actually be turned into an argument for anti-Semitism:

> "You see how dangerous they really are? It is difficult to recognize their real nature. They hide behind the mask of everyday appearance...." An ideology really succeeds when even the facts which at first sight contradict it start to function as arguments in its favour.[38]

The paranoid construction of anti-Semitism is not a matter of misapprehended facts -- each new experience of reality can be re-determined or structured by ideology. Thus in *Bleak House*, the evidence that Chancery is *not* bringing relief to its litigants tends to demonstrate, for Richard, how much more he needs it and how much harder he must work within its processes; John Jarndyce's apparent kindness to Richard demonstrates as well how bad Jarndyce really is.

Some critics of ideology emphasize the discursive field, a symbolic order, that operates to determine subjects in their language. Thus a discourse analysis of anti-Semitism might identify the association of Jews with financial dealings, and show how social antagonism is (linguistically) displaced into antagonism between a sound society and the Jew, or how various features (profiteer, schemer, corruptor) are (linguistically) condensed into a coded message. But this logic, Zizek notes,

> is not sufficient to explain how the figure of the Jew captures our desire; to penetrate its fascinating force, we must take into account the way "Jew" enters the framework of fantasy structuring our enjoyment.[39]

Fantasy, in Zizek's account, is a "scenario filling out the empty space of a fundamental impossibility, a screen masking a void".[40] The fantasy at work in fascist anti-Semitism is that of a social Whole, without antagonism, and the "Jew" -- an external element that has caused antagonism -- is a "fetish which simultaneously denies and embodies the structural impossibility of 'Society.'"[41] Society without antagonism does not exist, yet a social fantasy operates to mask this "nothing" and give its "internal negativity" a "positive existence".[42] In working through the fantasy, we can recognize that the excesses attributed to the Jew reveals the ideological subject's -- society's -- character.

IV
TWO IDEOLOGIES IN *BLEAK HOUSE*

> Custom is the whole of equity for the sole reason that it is accepted. That is the mystic basis of its authority. Anyone who tries to bring it back to its first principle destroys it.[43]

The ideological system in which Dickens' lawyers operate in *Bleak House* can be viewed as primarily discursive, as a symbolic order. To be named a lawyer is to hold a position of power: legal documents determine the existence of property and wealth, and judges create order with their words. Lawyers know how, and are the only people allowed, to make the system "work". Dickens' lawyers avoid feelings, including any notions of truth and justice that do not serve the symbolic conventions. If one is accused of breaking the law, one needs a lawyer to present a workable defense -- otherwise, the innocent can be prosecuted, and the guilty will never get off. The system is ideological in the most obvious sense: the pronouncement of guilt or innocence does not necessarily match reality. In Chancery as well, a victorious litigant may lose everything to legal fees, or die before victory is won, which reveals an ideological, not real, benefit of law.

Such a critique, however, does not explain Richard's unique attachment to the law. Indeed, the ideological features of law are transparent for many characters in *Bleak House*, from the wealthiest like John Jarndyce to the poorest like Miss Flite. Both will have recourse to the law, but not with any confidence in its truth or justice. For Richard, however, the impossibility (or lack) of truth and justice is covered over by a fantasy of victory -- the justice due him -- in the lawsuit.

One might simply view Richard as lazy or greedy, as someone who is willing to set aside a normal life to gamble on a lottery, but Dickens clearly constructs a deluded subject in Richard. Richard believes he is going after justice, *and* that law is in that business. His subjection to the symbolic order of law is surely complete, but there is more to his delusion than confidence in law -- his foolhardy belief in legal processes is not the fantasy but its "support". Recall the triple structure of Zizek's dream-based ideology theory; in Richard's case, there is the promise of law (ideological content), the miserable actualities of Chancery (manifest reality), and his more than active pursuit of his case which announces his (unconscious) desire to patch up the cracks in law so visible to those around him. Obviously, in the world of Dickens' *Bleak House*, the ideological promise of law is not by itself effective -- as each year passes, the "coded message" of the symbolic order is fooling less and less Londoners.

Richard's fantasy, the justice due him in Chancery, is like the fantasy of the "social Whole" in fascist anti-Semitism -- there is nothing *behind* the fantasy except the impossibility or lack, which must be filled to support the fantasy. Richard's lawsuit, together with his lawyer's representation of his interests therein, provides an object of his unconscious desire -- unconscious not because Richard is not aware of his anxiety for justice, but unconscious insofar as he desires to fill a void with a fantasy. Richard is decidedly *not* aware of the impossibility of justice in Chancery, an impossibility constructed by Dickens and disclosed to omniscient narrators and readers of *Bleak House*. While the spell of legal ideology can explain Richard's delusion, the fantasy of justice in Chancery supported by an object of desire -- his lawsuit -- can explain why the ideology affects Richard and not all others.[44]

CONCLUSION

> Like the author, the fictive character has [in recent literary theory] been deconstructed into an effect of textual codes, a kind of thematic mirage, and the psychoanalytic study of the putative unconscious of characters has also fallen into disrepute.[45]

It would not be enough to say that Richard should have worked through his fantasy, and seen in the excesses of his projection of evil upon John Jarndyce a truth about himself. Richard's delusion is, among other things,[46] an illustration of how ideology can work. Traditional critiques of ideology that focus on the blinders created by social and linguistic conventions tend to be either deterministic, which calls into question critics' presumed position outside ideology, or rationalistic, insofar as ideology is viewed as a temporary condition affecting an otherwise free-thinking subject. The recourse to the psychoanalytic, exemplified in Zizek's analysis, offers an explanation of the effectiveness of ideology without lapsing into symbolic-order determinism or post-ideological optimism. In *Bleak House*, it is true that most of the lawyers, in their lifelessness, have become dupes of the symbolic order; moreover, Ester and John Jarndyce, in their wisdom, seem to have avoided the traps of Chancery; but Richard is trapped in the extreme, not merely because the law structures his experience, but because his fantasy materializes the law that structures his experience.

* *David Caudill is Associate Professor of Law at Washington and Lee University.*

NOTES

1. CHARLES DICKENS, *BLEAK HOUSE* (Garden City, N.Y.: Literary Guild 1953), 512. Page references to this novel will appear in parentheses in the text of this chapter.

2. *See* Johnson (1952: 145):

   > Nor are these sharp and bitter strictures unjustified by the actualities. The Day case, nowhere near settled at the time Dickens wrote, dated from 1834, had always involved seventeen lawyers and sometimes thirty or forty, and had already incurred costs of [70,000 pounds].... Jarndyce and Jarndyce was suggested by the notorious Jennings case, involving the disputed property of an old miser of Acton who had died intestate in 1798, leaving [1,500 pounds]. When one of the claimants died *in 1915* the case was still unsettled and the costs amounted to [250,000 pounds].

   See also Evans & Jack (1984: 383-85) (a common suit takes over five years due to procedural delays; during those delays, some parties become insolvent or die, new cross-actions arise, the pleadings increase in bulk, and a large part of any estate is swallowed up in fees).

3. *See* Gow (1990 : 518-19):

> The real *Jennens* case became the fictitious *Jarndyce v. Jarndyce*.... A more modern case in the *Jarndyce* mould is *Diplock's* case in 1945 [lasting nine years].... In re *Theobald Mathew's Estate*...is still running after six years.... [Mr. Mathew's eldest brother] has spent a total of six months in court and chambers in 249 appeals as applicant, respondent, plaintiff, defendant and appellant in proceedings over his brother's estate. As a litigant in person he claims...that he has appeared variously before thirty-three High Court judges, fourteen registrars, twenty-six masters, four stipendiary magistrates and four JPs.... [S]ome [286,000 pounds] has already been incurred in legal costs.

4. *See* Barnard (1978: 74-75):

> *Bleak House* is not so much a warning to society to reform itself as a picture of a society long past the stage at which reform is still possible.... [S]uggestions of rot and approaching collapse ... permeate the novel....Mines, or trails of gunpowder, are under Chancery.... The explosion, soon to come, will indeed be a "good one", destroying not partially but totally.... Nevertheless, it is certainly true that, in those parts of the novel that were intended
> to be prophetic, the prophecies have been proved false.

5. *See e.g.*, William (1984: 32-33):

> [Dickens] is uniquely capable of expressing the experience of living in cities.... [His characters act out] the real and inevitable relationships and connections, the necessary recognitions and avowals of any human society.

See also Brown (1985: xix) ("However engaging [Dickens'] novels are as independent verbal structures...their relation to real life cannot be dismissed so easily").

6. *See* Allen (1992: 178-182) (describing the law and literature movement, including efforts to explicate law in, as, and through literature).

7. *See* Lacan (1972).

8. *See* Zizek (1989).

9. This chapter includes, for purposes of clarifying Zizek's notion of ideology, character analyses.

> Character analysis, however, has a bad reputation.... [By treating] characters like people, ... analysts ... are perhaps enriching psychoanalysis but only at the price of misreading literature.
>
> [Some critics treat] a literary text... all too much like the raw materials of an actual analysis -- .... when they ignore the literal story or manifest argument in a text and try instead to see into it or through it and to relate its structure and conflicts to a drama within some human mind....

Skura (1981: 29,32). My intention, like Joyce Wexler's in her recent reading of Conrad, is not to "use psychoanalytic theory to illuminate [a literary text, but to use] literature to clarify theory." *See* Wexler (1991: 599):

> Lacan's use of fiction to articulate his theories offers a precedent for examining the connections between theory and text in either direction....[While] it would be absurd to argue that Lacan is the key to understanding [Conrad's short story,] I would claim instead that the story helps us understand Lacan's theory of the subject's entry into the Symbolic order.

10. *See* Clayten (1991).

> [Postmodernism] has no single, stable meaning. It refers to so many different things... that the multiplicity of references has itself been theorized as a major "lesson" of postmodernism: "that terms are by no means guaranteed their meanings, and that these meanings can be appropriated and redefined for different purposes, different contexts, and, more important, different causes."

Id. at 184, quoting Ross (1988: xi).

11. My "dear Mother, I'll be as tractable and obedient as you

can wish.... So now I am ready even for the lawyers." *BLEAK HOUSE, supra* note 1, at 516.

12. "Viewed by this light it becomes a coherent scheme and not the monstrous maze the laity are apt to think it." *Id* at 371.

13. *See id.* at 375, 376.

 "When will he awake from his delusion!"...
 "The more he suffers, the more averse he will be to me -- having made me the principal representative of his suffering." ...
 "So unreasonably!"
 "Ah ... what shall we find reasonable in Jarndyce and Jarndyce! Unreason and injustice at the top ... at the heart and at the bottom....

 Id. at 557.

14. Gold (1972: 189-90).

15. *Id.* at 1, citing (at n.2) medical and psychiatric authorities on Dickens.

16. *Id.* at 188.

17. Hirsch (1975: 132-133). Richard, for example, is indecisive about his future occupation, which frequently stems from inhibition of aggressiveness, which is a defense against rage, which is occasioned by frustration of infantile sexual desires. *Id.* at 144, citing Fenichel (1945: 178-83).

18. *Id.* at 143-46.

19. *Id.* at 2, 89.

20. *Id.* at 89; Morris acknowledges that Lacan's notions of desire and lack "provides a point of fracture within the total determinism Althusser seems at times to imply." *Id.* at 5. The Symbolic order, roughly the structure of language into which we are born (and in which we live), is one of Lacan's three cognitive registers, alongside the Imaginary realm of identificatory images and the unknowable Real, that orient (or are the dimensions of) subjectivity. *See* Lacan (1988: 161-71).

21. *Id.* at 137.

22. *Id.*

23. *Id.*

24. *Id.* at 19; regarding the mirror stage, which refers to an infant's identification with his image in an alienating moment by which a "self" is constructed, *see* Lacan (1977: 1-7).

25. Zizek, *supra* note 8, at 30.

26. *See* Althusser (1971).

27. *See* Ragland-Sullivan (1987: 272) (In "Althusser's famous misreading of Lacan,...the conscious subject is both master of Desire and of language!"); Smith (1988: 14-23).

> It is easy to see what is attractive to Althusser in Lacan's... symbolic order [which] seems to be offered as an overarching, even inescapable monolith having everything in common with the discursive formations which work ideologically....
>
> Such a view, however, misappropriates Lacan's concept of the symbolic which ...does not take on the characteristics of the historical real as Althusser wants it to....

Id. at 20.

28. Zizek, *supra* note 8, at 34.

29. *Id.*

30. *Id.* at 13.

31. *Id.* at 14-15.

32. *Id.* at 47, 33, 48.

33. Refer to text accompanying note 30 *supra*.

34. *Id.* at 32. One of Zizek's major theses, not discussed in this essay but implied in the above passage, is that traditional critiques of ideology

presume that the "spell" of ideology is broken upon disclosure or enlightenment; such critiques are ineffective, however, in light of today's cynical subjects who are quite willing to acknowledge the falsity or illusivity of ideology even as they fail to renounce it -- even while they act as if it is not an illusion. *See id.* at 28-33. Thus when Zizek suggests that ideology depends upon non-knowledge of "*its essence*", *id.* at 21, he is not saying that the cynical subject is outside the social effect of ideology, because just as the traditional subject of ideology does not know about his illusion, the cynical subject does not know *what he is doing*. Thus an ideological distortion is

> already at work in the social reality itself, at the level of what individuals are *doing*, and not only what they *think* or *know* they are doing. When [for example] individuals use money, they know very well that there is nothing magical about it -- that money, in its materiality, is simply an expression of social relations.... The problem is that in their social activity itself, in what they are *doing*, they are *acting* as if money... is the immediate embodiment of wealth as such.

Id. at 31.

35. *Id.* at 44 (fantasy in Lacan as "the support that gives consistency to what we call 'reality'").

36. *Id.* at 48.

37. *Id.*

38. *Id.* at 49.

39. *Id.* at 126.

40. *Id.*

41. *Id.*

42. *Id.*

43. Pascal (1966: 46). Zizek comments:

> [F]or the law to function "normally",...the dependence of the law on its own process of enunciation...must be repressed

> into the unconscious, through the ideological, imaginary experience of the "meaning" of the law, of its foundation in Justice, Truth (or, in a more modern way, functionality).

Zizek, *supra* note 8, at 37-38.

44. Less complicated reasons for Richard's seduction by Chancery can be offered: he is rebelling against his guardian (father-figure) and makes the conflict a legal one (Richard asserts that he is not accountable "to Mr. Jarndyce, or Mr. Anybody"); he is careless, impulsive and lacks commitment; and his fantasy is to avoid work and recuperate his class status, the pursuit of which leads to increasing desperation as he loses power and control over his life -- this latter explanation is consistent with the analysis -- above -- of Richard's "object" of desire in Chancery. *See generally* Bottfried (1990).

45. Brooks (1987: 335).

46. Refer to note 44 *supra*.

REFERENCES

Allen, A.L. (1992). "The Jurisprudence of Jane Eyre." *Harvard Women's Law Journal*. 15: 173- 238.

Althusser, L. 1971. *Lenin and Philosophy*. New York: Monthly Review Press.

Barnard, R. 1978. *Imagery and Theme in the Novels of Dickens*. New York: Humanities Press.

Bottfried, B. 1990. "Fathers and Suitors: Narratives of Desire in Bleak House," in M. Tinko, F. Koplan and E. Guiliano (eds.) *17 Dickens Studies Annual*. New York: AMS Press.

Brooks, P. 1987. "The Idea of a Psychoanalytic Literary Criticism." *Critical Inquiry*. 13: 334- 348.

Brown, J.P. 1985. *A Reader's Guide to the Nineteenth-Century English Novel*. New York: Macmillan.

Clayten, J. 1991. "Dickens and the Geneology of Postmodernism." *Nineteenth-*

Century Literature. 46: 181-95.

Evans, M. and R. Jack (eds.) 1984. "Some Account of the Proceedings in a Common Chancery Suit, and the Probable Time of its Duration, c. 1828." *Sources of English Legal and Constitutional History*. Sydney: Butterworths.

Fenichel, O. 1945. *The Psychoanalytic Theory of Neurosis*. New York: Norton.

Gold, J. 1972. *Charles Dickens: Radical Moralist*. Minneapolis: University of Minnesota Press.

Gow, N. 1990. "No Chance in Chancery". *Journal of the Law Society of Scotland*. 15: 518-19.

Hirsch, G. 1975. "The Mysteries in Bleak House: A Psychoanalytic Study," in R. Partlow (ed.). *4 Dickens Studies Annual*. Carbondale, IL: Southern Illinois University Press.

Jaffe, A. 1991. *Vanishing Points: Dickens, Narrative, and the Subject of Omniscience*. Berkeley: University of California Press.

Johnson, E. 1952. "The Anatomy of Society," in A.E. Dyson (ed.). 1969. *Charles Dickens, Bleak House: A Selection of Critical Essays*. Nashville: Aurora.

Lacan, J. 1972. "Seminar on 'The Purloined Letter' (trans. J. Mehlman)." *Yale French Studies*. 48: 39-72.

___. 1977. *Ecrits: A Selection*. (trans. A. Sheridan). New York: W.W. Norton.

___. 1988. *The Seminar of Jacques Lacan, Book II: The Ego in Freud's Theory and in the Technique of Psychoanalysis 1954-1955*. (trans. S. Tomaselli.) New York: W.W. Norton.

Morris, P. 1991. *Dicken's Class Conciousness: A Marginal View*. New York: St. Martin's Press.

Pascal, B. 1966. *Pensees*. Harmondsworth: Penguin Books.

Ragland-Sullivan, E. 1987. *Jacques Lacan and the Philosophy of Psychoanalysis*. Urbana: University of Illinois Press.

Ross, A. 1988. "Introduction." in A. Ross (ed.) *Universal Abandon? The*

Politics of Postmodernism. Minneapolis: University of Minnesota Press.

Skura, M.A. 1981. *The Literary Uses of The Psychoanalytic Process*. New Haven: Yale University Press.

Smith, P. 1988. *Discerning the Subject*. Minneapolis: University of Minnesota Press.

Wexler, J. 1991. "Conrad's Dream of a Common Language: Lacan and 'The Secret Sharer'." *Psychoanalytic Review*. 78: 599- 606.

William, R. 1984. *The English Novel from Dickens to Lawrence*. London: Hogarth.

Zizek, S. 1989. *The Sublime Object of Ideology*. London: Verso.

Chapter VI

WITNESS UNDER COVER

Maarten Henket*

The witness is an important source of evidence in any system of criminal adjudication. Modern insights as to the unreliability of human sense perception and memory cannot change this. We simply have no substitute.

The use of testimonial evidence is always subject to certain limits and precautions. These may vary between systems, and tend to change over time together with the political climate. In this paper I shall attempt to draw a comparison with regard to witness testimony between the situation in the United States - a common law country - and the Netherlands - a civil law country.

By way of introduction I shall first give a global comparison of criminal procedure and, then, the rules of evidence in the two systems. Then I shall describe in general the use of witness testimony in the Netherlands and compare it to that in the United States. Next I will examine a development in criminal procedure that is, I think, discernable both in the Netherlands and in the United States: the inquisitorial trend. Finally I shall speak about recent developments in the Netherlands under the influence of European law.

TYPES OF CRIMINAL PROCEDURE

In characterizing types of criminal procedure, it is customary to use the terms "accusatorial" and "inquisitorial". Roughly speaking, an accusatorial procedure is a public contest between the accuser and the accused, with the judge as referee. Equality of arms, directness and orality are important principles here. An inquisitorial procedure is indeed an inquiry, with an imbalance of power between the state (the inquisitor) and the accused. Important parts of the procedure may be secret and written.

It has often been said that in the civil law tradition criminal procedure is inquisitorial, while in the common law tradition it is accusatorial. As Merryman rightly observes, this generalization is inaccurate and misleading as applied to contemporary systems of criminal procedure, though it has some validity when put into historical context (1985, p.126). Nevertheless, I think there are certain important differences between the two systems that warrant the use of the characterizations just mentioned as points of orientation. To clarify this, I shall give a few of the most striking examples.[1]

First, there is the role of the judge. In Anglo-Saxon criminal procedure, the judge is an observer and an impartial referee. In principle he does not take an active part in the fact-finding process. In a civil law system, the criminal judge has a double role. He too is an impartial referee, but besides that he is the leader, director and principal agent who is actively engaged in seeking and checking evidence.

Secondly, the two systems differ as to the nature and importance of the last phase of the procedure- the trial. In the Anglo-Saxon world, the trial is "the heart of [the] criminal justice system" (Gora 1978, p. 146). In a civil law system, the pre-trial phase is in some ways more important. Most of the evidence is collected in the pre-trial or examining phase, which is not public. The trial serves mainly to present the case to the trial judge and to allow the prosecutor and the defendant('s counsel) to argue their case.

Thirdly, there is the practice of plea bargaining, which is common in the United States but unknown in the Netherlands and other civil law countries. There a guilty plea is acceptable as evidence, but does not prevent a trial; it is up to the court, not the parties to determine guilt.

It is sometimes suggested that in an accusatorial model the fairness of the procedure is more important than the quality of the result: just like in other oral contests, the best orator wins- and he is not necessarily the one who is right.[2]

As far as I know, this is not how most Anglo-Saxons see it. I have the impression that they do not feel a tension between fairness and truth seeking. On the contrary, a fair procedure is seen as the best way to find out the truth. To mention only one example pertinent to the subject of this paper, the right to cross-examine witnesses is not only a matter of fair trial, it is also "the principal means by which the believability of a witness and the truth of his testimony are tested" (*Davis v. Alaska 1974*).[3] Accordingly, the right to confrontation is not just defined as one of the defendant's basic trial rights; its "very mission" is to "advance 'the accuracy of the truth-determining process in criminal trials'" (*United States v. Inadi*).[4]

In other words, truth determination is the end, fair trial the means. As far as there are differences with the inquisitorial model, they are to be found in the means. According to the inquisitorial model, the best way to truth determination is to have competent and impartial investigators with ample discretion.

These observations may serve as a prelude to the next section, in which I shall say something about the differences between the models with respect to the rules of evidence.

RULES OF CRIMINAL EVIDENCE

A Dutch expert on criminal evidence gives the following global characterization of the difference between the rules of criminal evidence in Anglo-Saxon law and civil law. In Anglo-Saxon law, the rules of criminal evidence are production rules. They determine what kinds of evidence the parties may present to the jury. In civil law, the rules of evidence are justification rules. They determine what kinds of evidence the judge may use in his verdict to justify his decision, and what this justification should look like (Nijboer 1991).

For the subject of my paper this picture is very helpful. In the United States, evidence in criminal procedure is presented to the jury. The jury is, of course, regarded as impartial, but not as versed in the law nor as trained in weighing evidence. The jury decides in secret deliberations on the basis of the evidence presented. It's conclusion is either "guilty" or "not guilty". No justification is offered. No appeal from this decision regarding the facts is possible. In such a system, rules of evidence will naturally get the character of production rules.

In Dutch criminal procedure, the evidence is presented to the court. The court is not only regarded as impartial, but also as well versed in the law and trained in weighing evidence. Like the jury, the court reaches its decision in secret deliberations; however, its decision does not come without justification. A full appeal from the decision is possible. Even appeal to the Supreme Court is possible on the grounds of defective reasoning. One can see how in such a system rules of evidence may turn out to be largely rules of justification. The judge is impartial, competent and well versed in the law. And if he makes a mistake, it can be corrected on appeal. So, why not leave most things to him?

WITNESS TESTIMONY IN DUTCH CRIMINAL PROCEDURE

The Phase of Investigation

In the Netherlands, like in most other civil law countries, a criminal proceeding consists of three phases: the preliminary inquiries, the investigation, and the trial. The investigation, which is not public, is in practice often the most important phase. It is run by a member of the judiciary, the investigating judge. Under her supervision the evidence is collected. She hears the accused and the witnesses and expert-witnesses. She can invite the prosecutor to be present at the hearings. The accused's counsel is not invited, but has the right to be present unless the investigating judge objects "in the interest of the investigation." Prosecutor and counsel can only suggest questions; it is the investigating judge who actually asks them.

The investigating judge prepares a written record that serves as the basis for the trial- if the prosecutor decides there will be a trial. The dossier is open to inspection by the defense. If indeed a trial follows, the complete record is made available to the court, the prosecutor and the defense.

The Trial Phase

The trial is public. Contrary to what is sometimes thought in the Anglo-Saxon world, the accused is presumed to be innocent. The case is presented to the court by the prosecutor. Prosecutor and counsel for the defense argue their respective cases. Witnesses may be heard. A written statement of a witness made before the investigating judge can be used as evidence in the trial.

The judge is not an impartial referee. She is free to seek evidence and she controls the nature and objectives of the inquiry.

In the courtroom, the prosecutor's table is situated on the same level as that of the court, a few steps higher than the defendant and her counsel. There is no jury.

All witnesses, including those for the defense, are summoned by the prosecutor. In order to have a defense witness summoned, the accused's counsel has to enter a request to that effect. The prosecutor can refuse to call a witness if "it must be reasonably assumed that the defendant can not be hampered in his defense when [this witness] is not heard in court" (*Dutch Code of Criminal Procedure*, Article 263).[5]

As previously discussed, during the investigation phase witnesses are "heard" by the investigating judge. In court, the situation is as follows: witnesses are first interrogated by the judge or judges; thereafter, prosecutor and defense counsel may ask additional questions. (Article 284, 285).

Due to the fact that a statement of a witness made before the investigating judge may serve as evidence in the trial, the actual physical presence of witnesses at a Dutch trial is relatively rare.

THE WITNESS IN ANGLO-SAXON AND IN DUTCH CRIMINAL PROCEDURE

Jackson (1988) has proposed a model for the analysis of the common law trial. According to Jackson's model, the witness is a subject for whom a goal has been set, namely "to perform the task of persuading the court of the truth of certain propositions." The witness has a helper and an opponent. The helper is (the counsel for) the party who called the witness. This party commences the examination in a "friendly" manner. The opponent is (the counsel for) the opposing party, who conducts the "cross-examination," which is "a form of hostile questioning designed to plant doubts in the mind of the judge or jury as to the credibility, truthfulness or accuracy of the witness." The witness undergoes a test as it were; later, "there is a recognition of it, in the judge's summing up, and ultimately, but less explicitly, in the decision of the court."

Examination of a Dutch criminal trial from this perspective reveals some important differences. There is no cross-examination. The prime examiner is the judge. The main task of the witness is not "to persuade the court of the truth of certain propositions" (formulated by the party who called her), but to answer truthfully to the questions the judge sees fit to ask. Only in the second instance may the prosecutor and the counsel for the accused comment on the statements made by the witness and ask their own questions. This never takes the form of a procedure of examination-in-chief and cross-examination. Due to the fact that all witnesses are summoned by the prosecutor, there is little emphasis on whose side a witness is on. Finally, the recognition "test" undergone by the witness is only to be found (inexplicitly) in the decision of the court. There is no jury and consequently no summation. The judge is supposed to be impartial, but is not, as in common law criminal procedure, merely an "observer" of the pragmatics of the trial (Jackson 1988, p. 34). She plays an active part in the trial. Her part is a crucial one, since it includes refereeing and if necessary correcting the other players, while she herself is above correction.

Perhaps the most crucial element in the Dutch fact finding process is the importance of the pre-trial phase of investigation. Formally, Dutch criminal procedure is subject to the principle of directness. The *Code of Criminal Procedure* prescribes that the court shall base it's ruling upon evidence that is presented in court. In practice, most if not all evidence is produced in the non-public pre-trial phase. The court bases its ruling largely upon the written record prepared by the investigating judge. A model of the process of fact construction in Dutch criminal law would have to reflect this reality.[6]

However, I am not suggesting that the model is totally unsuited for Dutch criminal procedure; on the contrary, I only think that the roles of the participants are different. I agree with Jackson's (1988) theoretical claim that "we cannot separate the semantic and pragmatic dimensions of a [spoken or written] text" (p.35). Moreover, I suspect that the role of pragmatics in Dutch criminal procedure is as important as, albeit more hidden than, it is in common law criminal procedure. More hidden as a result of the aspiration of truth seeking and law application that is at the core of the inquisitorial system.

THE INQUISITORIAL TREND

Merryman (1985) describes the development of criminal procedure as follows:

> In a sense it can be said that the evolution of criminal procedure in the last two centuries in the civil law world has been away from the extremes and abuses of the inquisitorial system, and that the evolution in the common law world during the same period has been away from the abuses and excesses of the accusatorial system. The two systems, in other words, are converging from different directions towards roughly equivalent mixed systems of criminal procedure. (p. 126).

In my opinion, Merryman is only partly right. It is, of course, true that both Anglo-American and Continental European systems "contain hybrid mixtures of adversarial and inquisitorial features" (twining 1978, p. 78). It is probably true that the two systems are converging, but I do not think this happens by skipping extremes, abuses, and excesses. I believe that, especially in the last ten or twenty years, the convergence is caused by an increasing emphasis, both in common law and in civil law countries, upon "crime control," at the cost of "due process."[7] Furthermore, this development goes hand in hand with movement towards a more inquisitorial system, both in the Netherlands and in the United States.

The Inquisitorial Trend in the Netherlands

In the Netherlands, some "extremes and abuses of the inquisitorial system" have been brought back to life by the Dutch Supreme Court's construction of certain provisions of the *Code of Criminal Procedure*. It actually began right after the enactment of the *Code* in 1926. In that same year the Dutch Supreme Court sanctioned the use of hearsay evidence, as long as it was handled "with due care." (HR 20-12-1926, NJ 1927 p. 85). As a result, not only an ordinary witness can tell the court what someone else told him, but also a written report by, e.g., a police officer, containing a statement by a witness can serve as evidence.

The Dutch *Code of Criminal Procedure* makes this possible under certain restrictions only.[8] The Supreme Court, however, has expanded this possibility further and further. The culmination of this development so far has been an almost unlimited freedom for the courts to use statements by anonymous witnesses, given during the pre-trial stage, as evidence. The Supreme Court has sanctioned this practice in the beginning of the eighties.[9]

As a result of the lenient attitude of the Dutch Supreme Court, the criminal judge has been almost totally free in the choice and weighing of the evidence. Even a conviction based exclusively on statements by anonymous witnesses has been upheld by the Supreme Court (HR 12 November 1985, DD 86.147). The only restrictions were the following: the judge had to weigh and use the evidence "with due care," and- since 1984[10]- if he used an anonymous statement after the defense had cast doubt on its reliability or on the grounds for the declarant's fear, the judge had to justify the use. These two restrictions illustrate a point made earlier, namely, that the rules of evidence in Dutch law are mostly rules of justification directed at the judge.

The reader may have noticed that the last paragraph is written in the past tense. This is not because the Dutch Supreme Court has changed its course or because the Dutch legislature corrected the judges. It is because the European Court in Strasbourg has recently raised a warning finger in the direction of the Dutch judiciary. In *Kostovski v. The Netherlands* (1989), the

Court condemned the use of anonymous statements as evidence.

The Inquisitorial Trend in the United States

In the Netherlands, the use of pre-trial testimony from anonymous witnesses is closely linked to the rise of organized crime. The wish to stay anonymous is usually inspired by fear of revenge. Fear of revenge has become an important source of hearsay evidence.

I have the impression that this particular form of hearsay evidence is not officially admitted in the United States. In *Ohio v. Roberts* (1980), the United States Supreme Court held that "when a hearsay declarant is not present for cross-examination at trial, the Confrontation Clause normally requires a showing that he is unavailable."[12] According to Ramella (1992), "unavailable" has the same meaning here as in Rule 804(a) of the *Federal Rules of Evidence*. The final sentence of 804(a) states:

> A declarant is not unavailable as a witness if exemption, refusal, claim of lack of memory, inability or absence is due to the procurement or wrongdoing of the proponent of a statement for the purpose of preventing the witness from attending or testifying.

If I am right, the implication is that granting anonymity is officially not available as a means to procure admissible evidence from fearful witnesses. There is, of course, an alternative: witness relocation and protection. This alternative would probably never work in the Netherlands, a country twice the size of Vermont. An interesting example of how geography can shape the law.[13]

Given the alternative, the absence of testimony from anonymous witnesses in the United States is no argument against the existence of an inquisitorial trend. There are indications that crime control is coming to be regarded as more important than due process, which is another way of signalling an inquisitorial trend. Let me mention two areas that are directly relevant to our subject: the exclusionary rule and the confrontation clause.

For the development of the exclusionary rule, I refer to Janikowski (1991). Janikowski's analysis of the the relevant case law shows "a marked departure from the constitutional understanding of the [Supreme] Court(...) regarding the Fourth Amendment." He expresses the fear that the Court "may well be on the verge of doing further damage to the constitutional tradition in future decisions."

In regards to the confrontation clause, I refer to Haddad (1990) and

Ramella (1992). Paraphrasing Ramella, hearsay testimony is basically only allowed upon two conditions. First, the prosecution must either produce the declarant or prove that he is unavailable. Second, when the declarant is shown to be unavailable, the out-of-court declaration is only allowed if it contains "indicia of reliability."

The United States Supreme Court has given rather lenient treatment to these two conditions. In *United States v. Inadi* (1986), the Court held that the unavailability condition does not apply if the out-of-court statement was made by a co-conspirator (while the conspiracy was in progress). According to Haddad, the implication of *Inadi* is that ordinarily no demonstration of unavailability is necessary (p. 80). As to the showing of indicia of reliability, since *Bourjaily v. United States* (1987), this requirement does not hold for hearsay that falls within the criteria of a "well-rooted" hearsay exception.[15]

There are cases that point in a different direction, e.g., when the Supreme Court invalidates cross-examination without direct confrontation.[16] This causes Haddad to observe that "the differences in the results as they might be charted on a liberal-conservative graph are amazing"(p.78). He is waiting for the Court to "synthesize its precedents" (p. 97), and expects it to do so in an inquisitorial direction:

> If the Court does not take a sharp turn in favor of the rights of the accused, the philosophy of the hearsay-confrontation line of cases should prevail. (p. 78)

It is time to return to the Netherlands. Is the horizon equally dark there? Perhaps not. In the next section I shall present at some length a recent (1989) decision by the European Court of Human Rights at Strasbourg that may have considerable influence on the development of criminal procedure in the Netherlands. Thereafter I shall first discuss the status of European decisions for Dutch domestic law in general and then the impact of this decision in particular.

KOSTOVSKI V. THE NETHERLANDS

In order to give the reader an impression of the style of European Court decisions, this section is composed entirely of quotations from the *Kostovski* decision[17] (the decisions of the European Court are published in English).

The Facts

(...)

9. Mr. Slobodan Kostovski is a Yugoslav citizen born in 1953. He has a very long criminal record ..[including armed robbery and attempted manslaughter].

On 8 August 1981 the applicant escaped from Scheveningen prison together with one Stanley Hillis and others (...).

10. On 20 January 1982 three masked men conducted an armed raid on a bank in Baarn and made off with a substantial amount of currency and cheques.

Police suspicions centered on Stanely Hillis and his associates (...). These suspicions were strengthened on 25 January, when Amsterdam police received an anonymous telephone call from a man who said [that Stanley Hillis, Paul Molhoek and a Yugoslav were responsible for the hold-up in Baarn].

11. On 26 January 1982 a man visited the police in The Hague. For fear of reprisals he desired to remain anonymous. The reporting officer knew his identity. He stated as follows:

> A few months ago four men escaped from the remand centre (*huis van bewaring*) in The Hague, among them a Yugoslav and an Amsterdamer. (...) The Yugoslav, the Amsterdamer and Paul Molhoek carried out a hold-up a few days ago on a bank in Baarn.(...)

The man was shown some photographs included in the police file and picked out photos of Kostovski and Hillis.

(...)

13. On 23 February 1982 a person visited the police in The Hague. The two reporting officers drew up, on 22 March, the following account of the interview:

> On Tuesday 23 February 1982 there appeared before us a person who for security reasons wishes to remain anonymous but whose identity is known to us. He/she stated that he/she knew that [Kostovski and three others] who were known to him/her, were guilty of armed raid on a branch of the ... Bank at Nieuwstraat 1 in Baarn on or about 19 January 1982. (...) The said person also stated that Kostovski and the others knew each other from when they were detained in Scheveningen prison. Hillis and Kosotovski escaped from

the said prison on 8 August 1981 (...).

According to the person in question, [they] were in possession of powerful weapons. (...).

14. On 1 April 1982 Stanley Hillis and Slobodan Kostovski were arrested in Amsterdam. (...).

15. A preliminary judicial investigation (*gerechtelijk vooronderzoek*) was instituted (...). On 8 April 1982 Mr. Nuboer, the examining magistrate (*rechter-commissaris*), interviewed, in the presence of the police, but in the absence of the public prosecutor and of Kostovski and his counsel, the witness who had made a statement to the police in The Hague on 23 February (see paragraph 13 above). The magistrate, who did not know the person's identity, considered his/her fear of reprisals to be well-founded and therefore respected his/her wish to remain anonymous. His report on the hearing recorded that the witness made the following sworn statement:

> On 23 February 1982 I made a statement to the police in The Hague which was included in a report drawn up on 22 March 1982. You read out that statement to me. I declared that it is the truth and that I stand by it (...).

16. On 22 June 1982 the examining magistrate wrote to the lawyers acting for those concerned, enclosing copies of the officials reports, including the statements of the anonymous person he had seen. He indicated that they could submit written questions (...). Mr. Kostovski's lawyer, Mrs. Spronken (...) submitted fourteen questions (...).

On 22 June, as a result of those questions, the anonymous witness (...) was interviewed again, this time by Mr. Weijsenfeld (...). The police were present but neither the public prosecutor nor the applicant or his counsel. (...)

In the event, only two of Mrs. Spronken's fourteen questions (...) were answered. In this connection Mr. Weijsenfeld added the following in his report:

> The questions sent in (...) which have not been answered were either not asked by me (...) in order to preserve the anonymity of the witness, or not answered by the witness for the same reason.

17. The cases (...) came on trial before the Utrecht District Court on 10 September 1982. (...)

> The witnesses heard in court included the examining (...) and one of the police officers who had conducted the interview on 23 February (...). They had been called at the applicant's request, but the court (...) did not allow the defence to put to them certain questions designed to clarify the anonymous witness's reliability and sources of information, where answers would have revealed the latter's identity.

Mr. Nuboer stated that he believed the witness he had heard on 8 April 1982, who had made a 'favorable impression' on him; that he did not know the witnesses' identity and considered the fear of reprisals (...) to be a real one (...).

Mr. Weijsenfeld stated that he considered to be 'not unreliable' the witness - whose identity he did not know - whom he had interviewed (...)

Mr. Weijman [the policeman] stated that, in his view, the person he had interviewed (...) was 'completely reliable' because he/she had also given information on other cases which had proved to be correct. (...).

18. The anonymous witnesses themselves were not heard at the trial. Contrary to a defense submission, the official reports drawn up by the police and the examining magistrates on the hearings of those witnesses were used in evidence. Also the sworn statements made by one of them to the magistrates were read out and designated as statements by a witness made at the trial (...)

In its judgements of 24 September 1982 the Utrecht District Court recognized, with regard to the use of the statements of the anonymous witnesses, that their sources of information could not be checked, that it could not form an independent view as to their reliability and that the accused were deprived of the possibility of being confronted with them. By way of justification for its decision nevertheless to use this material in evidence the court stated that it had been convinced of Mr. Kostovski's guilt, considering that the statement strengthened and partly complemented each other and having regard to the views it had heard as to the reliability of one of the anonymous witnesses (...)

[Both the Court of Appeal and the Supreme Court dismissed Kostovski's appeal, who then took his case to Strasbourg.]

The Opinion of the European Court

37. The essence of Mr. Kostovski's claim was that he had not received a fair trial. In this connection he relied mainly on the following provisions of Article 6 of the Convention:

> 1. In the determination of ... any criminal charge against him, everyone is entitled to a fair and public hearing ... by an independent and impartial tribunal...
> 3. Everyone charged with a criminal offence has the following minimum rights:...
>
>   (d) to examine or have examined witnesses against him and to obtain the attendance and examination of witnesses on his behalf under the same conditions as witnesses against him; (...)

41. In principle, all the evidence must be produced in the presence of the accused at a public hearing with a view to adversarial argument (...). This does not mean, however, that in order to be used as evidence statements of witnesses should always be made at a public hearing in court: to use as evidence such statements obtained at the pre-trial stage is not in itself inconsistent with paragraphs 3(d) and 1 of Article 6, provided the rights of the defence have been respected.

As a rule, these rights require that an accused should be given an adequate and proper opportunity to challenge and question a witness against him, either at the time the witness was making his statement or at some later stage of the proceeding (...).

42. Yet such an opportunity was not afforded to the applicant in the present case, although there could be no doubt that he desired to challenge and question the anonymous persons involved. Not only were the latter not heard at the trials but also their declarations were taken, whether by the police or the examining magistrate, in the absence of Mr. Kostovski and his counsel (...). Accordingly, at no stage could they be questioned directly by him or on his behalf.

It is true that the defence was able, before the Utrecht District Court and the Amsterdam Court of Appeal, to question one of the police officers and both of the examining magistrates who had taken the declarations (...). It was also able, but as regards only one of the anonymous persons, to submit written questions to him/her indirectly through the examining magistrate (...). However, the nature and scope of the questions it could put in either of these ways was considerably restricted by reason of the decision that the anonymity of the authors of the statements should be preserved (...).

The latter feature of the case compounded the difficulty facing the applicant. If the defence is unaware of the person it seeks to question, it may be deprived of the very particulars enabling it to demonstrate that he or she is prejudiced, hostile or unreliable. Testimony or other declarations inculpating an accused may well be designed untruthfully or simply erroneous and the defence will scarcely be able to bring this to light if it lacks the information permitting it to test the author's liability or cast doubt on his credibility. The dangers inherent in such a situation are obvious.

43. Furthermore, each of the trial courts was precluded by the absence of the said anonymous persons from observing their demeanor under questioning and thus forming its own impression of their reliability. The courts admittedly heard evidence on the latter point (...) and no doubt - as is required by Netherlands law (...) - they observed caution in evaluating the statements in question, but this can scarcely be regarded as a proper substitute for direct observation.

It is true that one of the anonymous persons was heard by examining magistrates. However, the Court is bound to observe that - in addition to the fact that neither the applicant nor his counsel was present at the interviews - the examining magistrates themselves were unaware of the person's identity (...), a situation which cannot have been without implications for the testing of his/her reliability. As for the other anonymous person, he was not heard by an examining magistrate at all, but only by the police (...).

In these circumstances it cannot be said that the handicaps under which the defence laboured were counterbalanced by the procedures followed by the judicial authorities.

44. The (Dutch) Government stressed the fact that case-law and practice in the Netherlands in the matter of anonymous evidence stemmed from an increase in the intimidation of witnesses and were based on a balancing of the interests of society, the accused and the witnesses. They pointed out that in the present case it had been established that the authors of the statements in question had good reason to fear reprisals (...).

As on previous occasions (...), the Court does not underestimate the importance of the struggle against organized crime. Yet the Government's line of argument, whilst no without force, is not decisive.

Although the growth is in organized measures, the Government's submissions appear to the Court to lay insufficient weight on what the applicant's counsel described as 'the interest of everybody in a civilized society in a controllable and fair judicial procedure'. The right to a fair administration of justice holds so prominent a place in a democratic society (...) that it cannot be sacrificed to expediency. The Convention does not preclude reliance, at the investigation stage of criminal proceedings, on sources such as anonymous informants. However, the subsequent use of anonymous statements as sufficient evidence to found a conviction, as in the present case, is a different matter. It involved limitations on the rights of the defence which were irreconcilable with the guarantees contained in Article 6. In fact, the Government accepted that the applicant's conviction was based 'to a decisive extent' on the anonymous statements.

45. The Court therefore concluded that in the circumstances of the case the constraints affecting the rights of the defence were such that Mr.Kostovski cannot be said to have received a fair trial. There was accordingly a violation of paragraph 3(d), taken together with paragraph 1, of Article 6.

[This concludes the decision of the European Court].

Prior to discussing the impact of the decision in the Netherlands, attention will be directed to a discussion of the relationship between European judicial decisions and Dutch domestic law in general.

EUROPEAN DECISIONS AND STATE LAW

There are various reasons why a decision by a European Court may only have limited consequences for the Dutch province of criminal procedure. All kinds of factors, both semantic and pragmatic, play their part. I shall briefly dwell on a few of the most relevant factors.

Background and Status of the European Convention

The European Convention on Human Rights is a European document. Of all the members of the Council of Europe that stood at its cradle, only one has a common law system: England. Still, in the wording of the treaty a strong Anglo-Saxon influence is visible. The explanation of this phenomenon is not difficult. When in September 1949 the Council of Europe asked the Committee of Ministers for a draft convention, the request was

> to cause a draft Convention to be drawn up as early as possible, providing a collective guarantee, and designed to ensure the effective enjoyment of al persons residing within their territories of the rights and fundamental freedoms referred to in the Universal declaration of Human Rights. (Van Dijk, 1983, p. 12).

The Convention is to a large extent a copy of the Universal Declaration, which has strong Anglo-Saxon traits because at the time England and the United States were practically the most influential members of the United Nations.

When the Netherlands signed the Convention in 1951, the official picture presented by the Dutch government to the public was, that Dutch law was entirely in compliance with the Convention and that accordingly there was nothing to hide and nothing to fear from the European Court.[18] And the public, including most jurists, believed it. How is that possible, in view of the Convention's so clearly Anglo-Saxon character?

The answer can be found in the following qualification of the Convention by Justice Martens of he European Court, made in his dissenting opinion in *Brogan v. Great Britain* (1989):

> (...) its wording is not seldom better suited to a manifesto than to an international treaty designed to provide, for a considerable time and for a great number of different legal orders, answers to fundamental but often delicate questions of law (quoted in Groenhuijsen, 1990, p. 89).

Indeed, a manifesto. fruit of the post war 'never again' atmosphere. Drafted and adopted in little over a year. Felt to be generally humanitarian, not particularly Anglo-Saxon. A collection of principles rather than detailed rules. No one could foresee how these principles would be developed into more concrete rules by the growing body of European case law.

Construction Upon Construction

When a Dutch court has to apply a provision from the European Convention, it will probably apply that provision *as constructed in the European case law*. Often, the relevant cases will not have resulted from a complaint against the Netherlands. In as far as the law of the country involved differs from Dutch law, the implications of the decision for the Netherlands will probably be unclear and its relevance arguable.

Even if the Netherlands is involved, as in the *Kostovski* case, the decision of the European court is a decision in an isolated case. The European Court is very reluctant in formulating general rules and always makes it very clear that its decision is dependent upon the facts of the particular case. The consequences of the *Kostovski* decision for Dutch criminal procedure in general are therefore not at all clear.

In any case, application of an application is a construction upon a construction and involves judicial discretion to the second degree.

Constitutionalism Versus Raison d'Etat

We are still discussing some of the factors that influence the impact of European cases upon Dutch domestic law. The title of this sub-section refers to two schools of thought, so christened by Van Hoof (1989), concerning the relation of the Strasbourg organs to the national authorities in questions of interpretation of the Convention. Simplifying the debate, we can say that the 'Constitutionalists' stress the 'individual rights and freedoms' character of the convention, whereas the adherents to the Raison d'Etat approach look upon the interpretations of the Convention as a weighing of interests of the individual and the state.

Van Hoof (1989) sees a trend in many states of declining acceptance of the decisions of the Commission and the judgements of the European Court, an increasing dissatisfaction with the judicial activism of the Court. He mentions, as an example, the reaction of the British Government to the *Brogan* case.[19]

Given the interpretive freedom indicated previously, it is clear that the attitude of the interpreter towards the Convention plays an important role in determining the outcome of her interpretation. Summing up this section we may say that the impact of a European decision upon state law is uncertain.

Groenhuijsen (1989) remarks: "Article 6 ECHR still has a few surprises in store. A the end of the century one will wonder with amusement why so many of the consequences of this key-provision were not foreseen today"(p. 93). He is right of course. But in as far as this passage suggests that the consequences have always been there, only undiscovered, his words are misleading. The meaning of Article 6 is not given but made. Accordingly, against this background we can examine and appreciate the actual impact of the *Kostovski* decision.

THE IMPACT OF THE *KOSTOVSKI* DECISION IN THE NETHERLANDS

The *Kostovski* decision set off a chain of reactions in the Dutch law journals. Some of the first commentators concluded that the decision meant the end of the anonymous witness, others felt that a few minor adjustments would be enough to make Holland respectable again. Since then, other decisions of the European Court have caused a growing awareness that the *Kostovski* case was not an isolated incident but part of a general development in the Court's interpretation of Article 6. This has resulted in an almost general feeling that the present practice of Dutch criminal procedure does not pass the test concocted in Strasbourg.[20]

As could be expected the Dutch judiciary has given narrow interpretation to the *Kostovski* decision. In three subsequent decisions (two of them unpublished) the Supreme Court states that Dutch law does not support the view that anonymous statements can not be used at all, or that they can not be used to establish and support reasonable conjecture with regards to committed crime.[21]

Finally the legislator. Taking into consideration the proverbial slowness of legislator's reactions- if they react at all - the Dutch legislator has moved with astounding speed. On 6 January 1992, little over two years after *Kostovski*, Minister of justice Hirsch Ballin sent a draft to the Dutch parliament which aims at reconciling the Dutch code with Strasbourg case law whiling limiting the use of anonymous statements as little as possible.[22] The main provisions are the following.

- The draft introduces the concept of the "threatened witness." The investigating judge can label a witness "threatened" ("bedreigd") if it can be reasonably expected that the statement he wants to make will lead to serious violence against himself or another person and if the witness refuses to testify because of this threat. The investigating judge then issues an order to conceal the identity of the witness from others.
- The investigating judge investigates the identity and the reliability of the threatened witness
- If for security reasons the defendant's counsel is excluded from being present at the pre-trial hearing of the threatened witness, the prosecution must be also excluded. In such cases both parties are given the opportunity to enter questions they wish the investigating judge to pose to the threatened witness.
- The investigating judge can decide to withhold an answer by a threatened witness from the parties, in which case he mentions in his report that the question has been answered.
- The trial judge can not base a conviction solely on anonymous statements.
- Threatening a witness to prevent him from testifying is a crime, punishable with a maximum of four years imprisonment.[23]

Thus far, it appears like a Dutch version of witness protection. Indeed, Holland is too small for witness protection American style (as long as it is not part of a united Europe).

As to the use of anonymous statements by other than threatened witnesses, (e.g., undercover agents) the draft contains some extra limitations.

-Anonymous statements by other than threatened witnesses can only contribute to a conviction if

a. the conviction is based to an important extent on other evidence,

b. the defendant does not wish to interrogate the witness.

The draft has not yet been discussed in Parliament. Commentators differ regarding the question of whether these proposals go far enough.

CONCLUSION

Merryman (1985), writing about the future of the civil law tradition, predicts three fundamental changes. On of them is constitutionalization.[24] The *Kostovski* case is an example of this development. The European Convention of Human Rights can be seen as a kind of European constitution or bill of rights, comparable to the American constitution, and the European Court acts as a sort of constitutional court, much like the American Supreme Court.

Given the nature of modern constitutions, a movement towards constitutionalism means a growing influence of individual rights like the right to due process in civil and criminal law. And this in turn seems to imply a movement away from inquisitorialism.

If the European Court continues to interpret the Convention the way it does at present, it seems clear that the legal unification of Europe - ironically consisting of countries that all but one have civil law traditions - brings along a recasting of criminal procedure in a more accusatorial, "Anglo-Saxon" mold. On the other hand, the American system appears to be acquiring a few "civil" traits.

An "eminent comparative scholar" once stated that if he were innocent, he would prefer to be tried by a civil law court, but that if he were guilty, he would prefer to be tried by a common law court.(Merryman, 1985, p. 132). Could it be that the eminent scholar will have to reverse his preferences in the future?

* *Maarten Henket is Assistant Professor of Law in the Department of Legal Theory at Utrecht University, The Netherlands.*

NOTES

1. For further details, see Merryman (1985), chapter XVII.

2. According to Twining (1989, p. 78) "it is generally recognized that inquisitorial systems are more directly and consistently concerned with the pursuit of Truth and the implementation of law than adversarial proceedings, the primary end of which is legitimated conflict-resolution."

3. Mr. Chief Justice Burger in *Davis v. Alaska* (1974).

4. Mr. Justice Powell for the majority in *United States v. Inadi* (1986), at 396, quoting two other Supreme Court decisions.

5. The defendant can ask the court to overrule such a refusal, and the court may do so, but may also uphold the refusal (Article 280).

6. According to Jackson (1988), his model is applicable, "with only relatively insignificant modifications", to the process of fact construction in the civil law tradition (p. 32, n. 55). This is perhaps true for civil cases, where the judge is "passive", but in my opinion not for criminal cases.

7. The origin of these labels can be found in Packer (1968). In the 'crime control' approach, the primary aim of the law of criminal procedure is to facilitate the solving of cases. In the 'due process' approach, the emphasis is upon the protection of the individual against excessive exercise of power by the authorities.

8. Article 187 states that if the investigating judge wants to hear a witness who probably will not be able to appear at the trial, he must invite the prosecutor, the accused and the counsel to attend at the hearing unless the interest of the investigation does not allow for any delay.

9. HR 5-2-1980, NJ 1980, 319 and HR 4-5-1981, NJ 1982, 268. For

critical discussions of this development, see, Swart (1986) and Prakken (1990).

10. HR 25-9-1984, NJ 1985, 426 and 427.

11. *Ohio v. Roberts* (1980) at p. 66.

12. Regulated in United States Code, title 18, sec. 3512.

13. Another instance may be found in the paucity of malpractice suits in Holland, caused perhaps in part by the fact that the members of the medical profession live too close together to be willing to testify against each other.

14. *United States v. Inadi* (1986).

15. *Bourjaily v. United States* (1987) at p. 171.

16. *Coy v. Iowa* (1988). The case involved testimony by young, alleged victims of a sexual assault against the alleged offender while they are behind a screen. For more details and other examples, see, Haddad (1990, p. 92-93).

17. *Kostovski v. The Netherlands*, (1989).

18. Internally, the government felt less at ease. See, Klerk and van Poelgeest (1991).

19. In the *Brogan* case, the Court held *inter alia* that the British Act of 1984 which authorized detention during a period of up to seven days without the accused being brought before a judicial authority, was incompatible with the requirement of "promptness" in Article 5(3). The British Government then claimed the right to derogate from its obligations pursuant to article 15, which allows a state to derogate in "time of war or other public emergency."

20. Even the Minister of Justice has openly stated that the Dutch Code of penal procedure does not pass the European test (E.M.H. Hirsch Ballin on 19 April 1991, quoted n Myer (1992, p. 563)).

21. On the unpublished decisions (9-1-1990 and 6-2-1990) see

Borst and Nijboer (1990, pp. 61-62). IN HR 2-7-1990, NJ 1990, 692, the High Court also gives a strict interpretation to the *Kostovski* decision, leaving room for using anonymous statements as evidence under certain not very restricting conditions.

22. Draft nr. 22 483 (protection of witnesses).

23. This is the same maximum punishment as for theft.

24. The other two are decodification and federalization.

REFERENCES

Borst, W.L. and J.F. Nibjoer. 1986. *Inleiding tot het strafrechtelijk bewijsrecht* (3d ed. by J.F. Nijboer), AAL Nijmegen.

van Dijk, P. 1983. *The Right of the Accused to a Fair Trial Under International Law*. Utrecht.

European Commission on Human Rights. 1990. *Report of the Commission 3 April 1990: Application No. 11069/84; Jean-Claude Cardot against France*. Strasbourg.

Gora, J.M.. 1978. *Due Process of Law*. New York: American Civil Liberties Union.

Groenhuijsen, M.S., 1990. "Artikel 6 EVRM en de dagelijkse rechtspraktijk. Inleiding en perspectief" Pp. 89-94 in *Artikel 6 EVRM en de dagelikse rechtpraktijk*, edited by R.R. M. de Moor. Zwolle.

Haddad, J.B. 1990. "The Futureof Confrontation Clause Developments: What Will Emerge When the Supreme Court Synthesizes the Diverse Lines of Confrontation Decisions." *The Journal of Criminal Law and Criminology*. 81(1): 77-98.

van Hoof, F. 1989. "The Future of the European Convention on Human Rights: Judge Martens' Position on Questions of Construction; A Dissenting Opinion." *Netherlands Quarterly of Human Rights*. 451-464.

Jackson, B.S. 1988. *Law, Fact and Narrative Coherence*. Deborah Charles

Janikowski, W.R. 1991. "'Good Faith', 'Bad Faith': Rhetoric, Ideology and the United States Supreme Court." Paper presented at the 7th colloquium of the International Association for the Semiotics of Law, Utrecht, The Netherlands.

Klerk, Y.S. and L. van Poelgeest. 1991. "Ratificatie a contre coeur: de reserves van de Netherlnds regering jegens het Europees Verdag voor de Rechten van de Mens en het individueel klachtrecht." *RM Themis* 1991, p. 220-246.

Merryman, J.H. 1985. *The Civil Law Tradition*. Stanford, CA: Stanford University Press.

Myer, E. 1992. "De Europese dimensie: meer dan vrijblijvende versiering." *Delikt en Delinkwent* 21, afl.6:563-580.

Nijboer, J.F. 1991. "Strafrechtelijk bewijs van een andere kant bekenen." *Delikt en Delinkwent* 21, afl. 4:332-344.

Packer, H. 1968. *The Limits of the Criminal Sanction*. Stanford, CA: Stanford University Press.

Prakken, T. 1990. "Verdeiging: hoezo equality of arms?" *Nederlands Juristenblad* 1990:887-893.

Ramella, R.K. 1992. "The Confrontation Clause and Hearsay in Child Abuse Cases: *United States v. Spotted War Bonnet*." *Creighton Law Review*. 25: 1043-1078.

Swart, A.H.J. 1986. "Anonieme getuige en eerlijk proces" *Recht als norm en als aspiratie*. Nijmegen.

Twining, W. 1989. "Rationality and Scepticism in Judicial Proof: Some Signposts." *International Journal for the Semiotics of Law*. 2(4): 69-83.

United States Code Annotated, Title 18, Section 3521.

TABLE OF CASES

United States Supreme Court

Bourjaily v. United States, 483 U.S. 171 (1987).

Davis v. Alaska, 415 U.S. 308 (9174).

Ohio v. Roberts, 448 U.S. 56 (1980).

White v. Illinois, 112 S. Ct. 736 (1992).

Dutch Supreme Court

HR 20-12-1926, N.J. 1927, p. 85 (*De auditu*).

HR 5-2-1980, N.J. 1980, nr. 319.

HR 4-5-1981, N.J. 1982, nr. 260.

HR 25-9-1984, N.J. 1985, 426 and 427.

HR 12-11-1985, DD 86.147.

HR 2-7-1990, N.J. 1990, 692.

European Court of Human Rights

Kostovski v. The Netherlands, 20 November 1989; publ ECHR, Series A 166.

Brogan v. Great Britain, publ. ECHR, Series A 145 (1989).

Chapter VII

LICENSE AND COMMODIFICATION: THE BIRTH OF AN INFORMATION OLIGARCHY[1]

Dion Dennis*

This essay has one general topic. That topic is an assessment of the possible and actual effects of an escalation of market logics across higher educational sites. In surveying these effects, I focus on two objects of analysis. The first is the construction and deployment of *hypertextual ensembles*. The second are those sets of administrative practices that circulate under the name of *Total Quality Management*. Let me tell you what I mean by each term.

There are multiple and contested definitions of hypertext. My characterization of hypertextual systems exceeds those definitions that equate hypertext with MacIntosh-based hypercards. (These make up one small subset of hypertexts). Within this essay, the term hypertext refers to a full-text informational search and retrieval ensemble. That is, a hypertext is a full-text computerized database or database structure that is reasonably user-friendly and has an accessible and extensive cross-referencing system. Within the system's storage capacity and access and design limits, users can move around the database in a non-linear manner and generate conceptual links with other parts of that database. In this essay, the hypertextual system is constituted through a micro-mainframe interaction mediated by a telecommunication shell. Hypertexts signify an emergent form of electronic literacy and textuality. They embody new and productive configurations of information access and exclusion. As a commodity form, they represent the digitalized manufacture and licensing of information, images and sounds. As pedagogical practice, they reshape the distribution of resources in classrooms and libraries. They are part of socioeconomic and cultural practices that are reconfiguring social fields. And, they are the both products and effects of sets of those market logics that are being mapped onto educational sites.

Total Quality Management also has many definitions. In its name, discourse and practice at thousands of bureaucratic sites have been reconfigured. Institutional modes of persuasion, promises, seduction, coercion and deception are enacted under its umbrella. To pledge visible and public support for TQM is often considered an act of political correctness. The acronym has developed local variants. TQM now has several names. It is also TQS (Total Quality Service) and TQE (Total Quality Education) and CQI (Continuous Quality Improvement) and QQ (Quantum Quality). Across all these designations, definitions and implementations, there are two definitive traits of current regimes of TQM. First, TQM is a common and flexible set of regulative practices that emphasize consistency, conformity and standardization. Secondly, TQM's objects of quality control have shifted from its historical roots. As information, images, sound and speech have become digitalized and commodified, the objects of TQM techniques are no longer the processes by which material goods are produced. Rather, they are now the communicative fields that shape the imaginative range of public identities. In the 1990's, regimes of TQM's deploy a melange of market ideologies and behaviorist techniques. The goal is to reinscribe and then police the realms of viable self-definitions. That is, TQM discourses constitute a globalizing and impoverished domain of identities. Within the TQM *marketverse* (the universe seen as organized by the "Invisible Hand" into producer/ consumer), there are only three possible identities. In its positivity, TQM constitutes two (and only two) viable subject-positions. We are, depending on the activity of the moment, either happy customers or perky and attentive producers/providers. Nothing else exists in the TQM marketverse except those who would utter sentiments of evil resistance. In the Manichean world of TQM, resistance is to be deftly coaxed from the shadows. Then it can be crushed! Among other things, TQM represents a regime of obedience constituted in the name of "the market."

Both these objects, hypertextuality and Total Quality Management, come into educational fields deeply etched with the promises and effects of market logics and practices. This essay is a narration and reflection of how these circulate at two local sites.

A SCENE FROM A HALL

K., a young graduate student, called out my name as she briskly walked over. "I've had some major problems in getting research materials for my thesis," she said. "Everything in the library," she continued, "is outdated. When I ask for a title through interlibrary loan, they want an exact article." She paused and took a quick breath. "They won't order an issue of anything. I've heard that you can help me." I listened as she told of the passage of a punitive anti-abortion law in Poland. Doctors that perform abortions now face stiff criminal penalties. Nearly overnight, post-Communist Poland had become a battleground for women's reproductive rights.

For her thesis, K. wanted to do some textual analyses on the Polish abortion debates just before the referendum. Finding our State University library ineffectual, she approached prominent feminist scholars. Several had relevant source materials. But they all refused to share these with K. It was only after these snubs that she remembered that some academic units had access to **OSTRICH** *(the Olympian System of Text Retrieval and Information Collection and Hoarding).*[2] *OSTRICH* is the world's largest commercial compiler and vendor of electronic texts. These include medical journals and references, law review articles, incorporation documents, tax records, legislative bills, court decisions, and liens. *OSTRICH* also digitally catalogs the texts of hundreds of national and international newspapers, TV news transcripts, wire service reports and consumer magazines. One distinctive feature of electronically-stored texts is that they are simultaneously available. Subjects and themes can be simultaneously explored across thousands of newspapers, journals and law reviews with powerful search commands. The results are available in seconds. A CITE format permits a fast eyeballing of the data. But that's not all! *OSTRICH* is not just a fancy reference-list. Full-texts of articles can be viewed on-line and then downloaded, via modem, to a standalone PC.

K. learned that *OSTRICH* had English-language translations of *The Warsaw Voice* and *The Polish Press Agency.* These were just what she needed. K. went to the State Law Library first. She'd seen the PC's lined-up in a glass room at one end of that library, fiber-optically wired to the mainframes in Mall City, *OSTRICH's* home, half-a-continent away (Fawcett 1992).

K. was again refused. She was denied access under the terms of a license-agreement between *OSTRICH* and the State Law Library. That is, since she wasn't a law student, she couldn't use *OSTRICH.* She then went to a member of her department, Dr. Holmes, who had "grey" use of *OSTRICH.* Holmes couldn't legitimately use *OSTRICH,* but he was on the committee that had approved funds for the *Legitimacy Program's OSTRICH* license. (And the rest, as they say, is history). In talking with K., he first denied any knowledge of *OSTRICH* access. By the end of their chat, he told her "to see those graduate students in the *Legitimacy Program* who have on-line access." K. knew that (then) I was the chief training and development liaison for *OSTRICH* in the *Legitimacy Program (LP)*. I had some discretion within the access guidelines. That is, I understood that neither the software nor the passwords could be circulated without his prior knowledge and approval. He wanted a tight lid put on wide-scale abuses. But, there was nothing in those walking orders that prevented me from logging on to *OSTRICH* and then turning that session over to her. She did her research. She downloaded her texts. I worked the ambiguity within the guidelines, wanting to empower a talented friend. But I began reflecting on this scene. Her experience of exclusion, as a near-loser within an information hierarchy, was a local event that resonated within larger relations (of information as commodity) and emerging social fields that are strewn with power and knowledge effects.

INFORMATION AND SIGNS AS COMMODITIES: THE BIRTH OF A POLITICAL ICONOMY

The shape of knowledge in post-industrialized societies has been radically altered in the last half-century (Lyotard 1984). Knowledge has become a routinely exchanged commodity. Digitalized and honed commercial management practices and manufacturing techniques are now used in the mass production, licensing and regulation of signs, symbols and intellectual products (Zuboff 1988). Consequently, there's an accelerating pervasiveness of forms of mass electronic communication in everyday activities. These have material and semiotic effects. For example, I work at my PC for a variety of reasons. I prepare and print my lecture notes, compose exams, do research on *OSTRICH,* dial-up the University Library, write and post e-mail to friends, colleagues and BITNET/INTERNET conferences, send faxes via my fax/modem and balance my checkbook. Also, I administrate, quarter-time, Digital Community College's "virtual classrooms."[3] Virtual classrooms exist in an ambiguous realm between a PC, a modem, a phone line and a minicomputer. Students relate to instructors and each other not in the "real space-time" of a classroom but on-screen via an Electronic Forum. The Community College district calls it "an alternative delivery service" and "distance learning," but it's closer to a production of a new social field. It exhibits a new textuality and literacy, not just an extension of an older one. This is just a brief sketch of how two forms of electronic communication - the telephone and the PC - shape what I do, how I perceive and what my objects of knowledge are becoming. I haven't even mentioned the ensembles of signs and procedures that are part of TV, VCR's, satellite communications, voice mail, automated bank account services or the compilation, rental and circulation of credit and consumer histories (Poster 1990). These bureaucratized activities, enabled by a hardware/software infrastructure increasingly dominated by a handful of transnational corporate behemoths, are grounded in complex webs of security and commodity logics.

Commodities are customarily defined as objects or services that are bought, sold and traded in negotiated transactions. All cultures create fields of objects/services as exchangeable. Historically, the marketing of commodities is contingent and variable. It does depend on supply and demand. But apart from the basic human needs, appetites for material goods, cultural signs and information are shaped by marketing and advertising technologies that link the channeling of desire (demand) with the act of consumption (supply) (Ewen 1988). New commodities such as digitalized information are significant because they signify and partially form complex, unpredictable and often contestable vectors of moral codes and behavior embedded in patterns of exchange. An active consumption and recodification of commodity signs by marginalized populations can, at times, become a productive political resource in the respeaking of selves and worlds (Coombe 1991).

To say an object/service is a commodity does not imply (except in ad campaigns for "the real thing," *ad nauseam*) a denotative claim about an item. Commodities signify a series of complex desire or object effects around activities and evaluative relations. These effects produce both material merchandise and semiotic strategies for "targeting" populations through technologies of persuasion and consent (Ewen 1988). In mining the flow of images, information, capital and *consumers-as-constituencies* into and through a vague but pervasive space known as "the market," I want to trace some productive forces and signs that make up management practices and corporate signifying strategies. Together, these provide us with key features of contemporary *regimes of detail.* For Foucault, *regimes of detail* or *the political anatomy of detail* are those disciplinary discourses and security apparatuses that produce and closely attend to the production of normative "useful individuals" (Foucault 1977, 1979, 1991). These security and administrative formats are designed to generate compelling fields (of behavior and identity). When the shape and boundaries of these fields take-on the convincing character of a naturalized social reality, prediction and control of predispositional thought and behavior for "all and each" becomes possible. When "all and each" perceive and act in the world only through habitual consumer or regulative logics and categories, we are witnessing "a power that insidiously objectifies those whom it is applied . . . [as it] forms (detailed) knowledge about these individuals" (Foucault 1977; Bernauer 1988).

Postmodern regimes of detail are marked by digital webs (or networks) of knowledge-collection activities. The digitalization of everyday activities has created qualitative changes in the scope, speed, deployment and depth of historic practices of surveillance and risk-management strategies (Virilio 1986; Poster 1990). Mundane and even banal activities of subjects are now encoded into networked databases. These can be linked together when economic or regulative transactions are mediated by such items as a credit card, drivers license or social security card. According to Foucault, it's part of "the politics of ourselves" that

> categorizes the individual, marks him by his individuality, attaches him to his identity, imposes a law of truth on him that he must recognize [making] individuals subjects...[Present struggles] must revolve around the question: Who are we? [Such a question] is a refusal of these abstractions, of economic...violence that ignores who we are...[we must] refuse scientific or administrative inquisitions...[by inventing] new forms of subjectivity (Foucault, pp. 212, 216).

There are three broad features to processes of digital commodification. The first set of effects is portrayed by K.'s story. We see exclusions to digitalized knowledge databases and the concurrent production of *information officers,* a new category of worker. By *information officer,* I mean an occupation that is broader than the mainframe information specialists that have managed corporate information for the last thirty-five years. Microcomputer *information officers* teach and troubleshoot the technical interaction of approved users with software/hardware packages and services. Simultaneously, we are asked to police the boundaries of legitimate access to digitalized knowledge resources.

K.'s exclusion also depicts an effect of (what I call) *political iconomy.* In another piece, I define political iconomy as the processes, products and effects of information that commodify, deploy and circulate texts and images in a digitalized form. A viable political iconomy emerges in the social biography of commodities or "thing-effects" when the licensing of signs or information (icons) as commercial property becomes an integral part of market logic and activity (Dennis 1992). The conceptual birth of political iconomy comes from a critique of the global effects of recoding the personal, social and the cultural as subsets of "the Market" (Gordon 1991). When global redescriptions of all fields of social and cultural activity as but forms of the market become a major symbolic and political project (as happened the 1980's) semiosis and political economy are no longer separate objects of inquiry (Dennis 1992).

The second effect emerges from this mix of postmodern regimes of detail with the global recoding of the social as a subset of the market. When all human interaction is assumed to be governed by market-logics, then the identity of the citizen has been collapsed into that of the consumer. We now have the "political consumer" (Siegel 1991). The third effect is the complex meshing of the first two effects. In the next section, I'll explore how subjectivities are produced and constrained under digital regimes of detail in the world of political iconomy.

THE EMERGING INFOGARCHY: INSTITUTIONAL PRIVILEGE MEETS PRIVATE PROPERTY.[4]

Positionality and Guiding Logics

Here's another story from the bowels of PostModern U.: In the computer lab, housed in the basement of Scarlett O'Hara Hall, the Program Coordinator (PC) and I were training a few undergraduate Legitimacy Students in the use of *OSTRICH.* As I tutored an East Indian woman in the process of searching, saving and downloading articles, a Chicana sat across from us. Her large brown eyes shone with amazement. She was alert to the shaded effects of access and exclusion from *OSTRICH's* databases. She asked piercing questions: "Is this available to us when the term is over?" She paused, squinted at me, and continued: "What about the others on this campus?" As I began to respond, the PC sidled up and said in a confidential tone: "No, not yet, but it will be standard across postmodern megauniversities in the next decade. It's just a matter of time." He then walked away. I said, "I don't think so." I turned away to attend to my East Indian student. When next I pivoted away from the monitor, the Chicana was gone.

From a nearby terminal, another female voice emerged. A young white woman asked: "I'm investigating media coverage of Brewton's allegations of the CIA's role in the S&L scandal. Is *In These Times* on this database?" "No, it's not," I said. "What about *The Progressive* or *Mother Jones?* I mutely shook my head no. I said that much of that source material was available on another database, *PeaceNet.* She perked up when she heard this. "Ohhhh," she said. "What commands do I type in for that?" I said that the PC had access to *PeaceNet* but it was not part of the *OSTRICH* service. I told her that there were monthly subscription fees and charges for connect time. She calmly accepted her exclusion. Quickly mastering the software's logic, she downloaded examples of "mainstream" coverage of the S&L fiasco.

These students, in brief exchanges with *OSTRICH,* sensed the imposition of market logics onto education. *Gutenberg Two* coauthor David Godfrey

> is nervous that education may be privatized. "Public sector information are libraries...and any mode of information that is nonprofit. From a capitalistic viewpoint, you'd say, Wow, here's a wonderful new thing that can be mechanized..made large scale and have profits. What else accounts for ten percent of the economy that's not already mechanized? There'll be a huge push soon to take educational facilities out of the public sector and that is potentially dangerous (Godfrey 1985).

To say that *market signs and logics* are shaping knowledge-intensive fields begs some questions. What do I mean by *market signs and logics*? How do I measure their effects? And what assumptions shape my analyses?

In "What Is An Author?", Foucault correlates the emergence of the author-function (as sign of a foundational author-ity) to commodity logics and a denotative policing of meaning (Foucault 1984). He suggests that the author-function is an effect of capitalism. As I reflected on this piece, it made remarkably good sense to swap each use of the word *author* with the word *market.* After all, the Invisible Hand, as the metonymical principle busily inscribing legitimate social orders, is the meta-sign of recent socio-political discourse. Below is a sample of my reinscription:

> [The sign of the Market] is the principle of thrift in the proliferation of meaning. We must reverse the idea of [the Invisible Hand] that says it is the genial creator of an inexhaustible [bounty]... We are used to thinking that the [Market] is transcendent ...proliferating endlessly.
>
> The truth is the opposite...[the Market] is the functional principle by which one limits, excludes and chooses, in short, by which one impedes the free circulation, the free manipulation, the free composition, decomposition and recomposition [of goods and

> services]. If we present [the Market] as a perpetual surging of invention, it is because it functions in an opposite manner. [This sign] is an ideological product, since it functions [as sign] as the opposite of its historical function. It is [the regulative trope] marking the manner in which we fear proliferation [of goods and services] (adapted from Foucault 1984).

Contemporary neo-liberalism (those projects that redefine social spheres as subsets of the Market) and current arguments for denotative readings of *author-itative* texts (such as the U.S. Constitution or Shakespearean plays) share a common impulse (Boyle 1988; Gordon 1991). Advocates of a strict constructionism or original intent frankly admit that they mean to impede or exclude multiple and connotative readings of *authori-tative* texts. These literalists claim knowledge of some transparent, uniform textual descent, such as "the Founding Fathers" or "the Genius." When this claim is enforced, the policing of meaning in the name of freedom is possible. The possibility for creative dialogism may give way to a prolific but poverty-struck monologism (Foucault 1970; Bahktin 1981). To appreciate how this form of textual/juridical monologism resonates with market logics, we must examine one aspect of how the everyday form of property has changed in the last half-century.

Traditionally, property has meant exclusive ownership of objects and bodies. Possession by one party precluded the possibility of use by others. With the spread of mass merchandising and advertising, electronic media and computers, new forms of property have emerged. Property is now often a matter of establishing and enforcing the right to license a body of trademarks, images, sounds and texts transnationally. Ownership is no longer a fixed exclusionary and spatial claim of a body or object. It is a *regulative* claim. Licensors manage the forms and degrees of access. They set the financial and material terms of circulation. They police the use of images, texts and data. Whether it's a dispute over microchip production masks or Mickey Mouse, clashes to establish the perimeters of denotative texts are implicated. Transnational licensors spend enormous sums and enlist armies of lawyers, agencies and corporate detectives. Their task is to harass and suppress un-authorized variations of corporate sign-properties. Like discursive literalism, these moves are intended to impede the creative redeployment of signs. They work to exclude those who cannot pay the license-fee. They tend to co-opt and narrow the range of image, text, sign and world needed for resistance and creative self-reconstructions. And they function, in "the market," to destroy nascent competition while carving up sections of public life as a subset of mass markets (Ewen 1988; Coombe 1991).

Foucault, in *Discipline and Punish,* noted the disparities between claims of juridic equality and the birth of regimes of biopower in the 19th Century

(Foucault 1977). Today we are observing comparable events. Under the sign of "democracy, self-determination and the market," we are subjects of and subjected to a digital intensification of webs of administrative technologies and procedural logics. (These include cost/benefit analysis, time/motion studies, potent survelliance techniques, focus-group research and risk-management procedures). The geometric and global amplification of these psycho-political techniques in the last twenty-five years renders aspects of habitual notions of public/private, property, sovereignty, nation/state and identity as juridic, theoretical and cultural antiques (Holstein 1990).

In a late formulation, Foucault called these psycho-political techniques *governmentalities*. Governmentalities are those repetitive, routinized activities that shape the "conduct of conduct" (Foucault 1991). Regimes of governmentalities are those productive, organized and emergent series of interactive procedures, instruments and languages that effectively shape, guide, prescribe or proscribe the conduct of humans. These signs and enabling practices are the crux of both "state" and "private" commercial, educational, military, health and related corporatist forms. They are versatile, portable discourses and technologies that move between "public" and "private" and render the supposedly self-evident boundary of each questionable.

Total Quality Management, as a historical set of standardized industrial quality-control techniques, is just such a redeployed governmentality. Connotations of the sign "quality" display several facets. First, when goods from luxury cars to colas are marketed, a quality-claim is often made about the inherent nature of any commercial item "X." That is, quality-claims are often essentialist. A Cadillac, a Sony TV or a Lexus auto, as sign, is constructed as an inherent signifier of quality. The work of corporatist symbolic workers, or *iconocrats,* is to naturalize these constructed sign-functions, in the minds of targeted consumers, for their clients' products. Secondly, when such claims cannot be accepted *prima facie,* iconocrats may then actively depict "new and improved" industrial quality-control manufacturing processes as heralding a commodity that will emerge as a signifier of quality. For example: By the late 1980's, Ford's subcompact, the *Escort,* acquired a reputation as an unreliable, problem-prone auto.[5] When Ford decided to retain the *Escort* name on a redesigned subcompact, their ads had a dual focus. The ads repetitively displayed U.S. Ford Motor workers in Japanese-style "quality circles." Sound and visual clips of enthusiastic, articulate and personable assembly-line workers were often woven into the TV ads. The second strategic ploy portrayed focus-group participants (as prototypical consumers) voicing surprise, amazement and wonder about the high quality of Ford's new *Escort.*

Despite the variation in marketing strategies represented in these examples, the sign that is quality remained focused on its traditional objects. These are claims made about tangible goods or about the standardization, at high performance levels, of industrial procedures used in commodity production. However, when sounds, speech, images and information are mechanized and commodified, *governmentalities* that emerged from the industrial factory are now ported, with adaptations, to service and information sectors. The object of quality-control processes is no longer merely the policing of the necessary conditions for the production of durable goods. The objects of "quality-control" are now the communicative fields that shape expressions of cultural life. As TQM becomes part of educational and corporatist routines, employees may be given, to paraphrase TQM guru W. Edwards Deming, the choice to love TQM or leave an institution. There is a danger that TQM may enable a process that promotes self-policing and censorship in the name of "uncovering resistance." And the master trope that legitimizes TQM is the competitive marketplace.

To show that my reinscription and condensation of the author-function with the market-function has empirical usefulness, an exemplar is offered. We'll follow *Digital Community College* as they embrace corporatist signs and procedures. In an in-house document, *Integrating Total Quality Management into the Educational Continuum,* the top-down vogue for *Total Quality Management* (TQM) at Digital becomes a strategy for disciplining faculty, administrators, workers and students into intensifying corporatist governmentalities.

ICONOMY OF MARKET IDEOLOGY: TQM AND THE REINSCRIPTION OF EDUCATIONAL DISCOURSE

What is Total Quality Management?

Although the acronym TQM proliferates throughout bureaucracies, its definition is not stable. As a corporate sign, TQM has a standard aspect. It is ambiguous and infinitely recodable. Yet, the core of TQM's geneaology, practice and ideology are recognizable. TQM's descent was from statistical process control techniques developed at Western Electric's Hawthorne plant in the `20's and `30's. TQM eventually became identified with management techniques in industrial and high-tech firms (such as Xerox, IBM, Kodak and Motorola). According to an article in *Financial Times of London,* TQM's core consists of "an emphasis on customer services (internal and external) and on changes emphasizing teamwork...while reorienting production processes so that they deliver products or services of consistent quality."

On first pass, TQM refers to the standardization of commodities and services signified within the usual corporate/sport metaphors. "Why the fuss?" you may ask. Because U.S. students, schools and workers are routinely perceived as competitive international market failures, there is pressure to convert curricular and administrative practices toward corporatist/market models. And for several reasons, TQM is the premier model. One zealous promoter of TQM was David Kearns, an ex-CEO of Xerox and former Undersecretary of Education in the Bush Administration. Kearns leads a cadre of Fortune 100 CEO's pressing for TQM-based management practices and cirricula in higher education. *Quality* is already a well-established discursive object. It has a magazine, *Quality Progress.* It has a professional organization - *The American Society of Quality Control.* There are conventions such as *The Total Quality Forum.* There's a contentious academic BITNET/INTERNET Listserv group, TQM-L. On the state level, ad campaigns for economic redevelopment such as "Forward Wisconsin" declare that the state is "an oasis of quality." And there are dozens of TQM pilot programs in full-swing in state universities and community colleges. With administrators in the Department of Education vowing to reshape the public schools in the direction of TQM, Digital's President recently pledged to reorganize along the TQM model.

> Let me share with you some thoughts about "the student as consumer." Digital has borrowed a concept called Total Quality Management (TQM) from our corporate friends who know that "quality" is just another way of saying "customer satisfaction." TQM, a system of constant improvement, will find us continously examining every process -- from registration to instruction -- for the purpose of perfecting the educational product you receive (Digital News (1):(2) 1991).

Concurrently, IBM announced a major grant program designed to assist (with money and hardware) colleges and universities that adopted TQM concepts in teaching, research and administrative activities. Digital Community College has applied for such a grant from IBM.[6]

Iconomy of Market Ideology: Digital's TQM Grant Proposal and Workshop

The grant proposal embraces a "five-year district-wide plan" (1992-1997) for the adoption of TQM practices. (Digital is one of the thirteen schools in the District). Implementation across the district has been delegated to the *Commission on Quantum Quality - The System Integrator* (est. 2/92). Apart from chronic hyperbole and the use of biologic metaphors that are the marks of truly bad writing, the draft grant-proposal - *Integrating Total Quality*

Management Into the Educational Continuum - has some intriguing and bizarre logics. For example:

> TQM requires that service and product be customer-driven. [Digital] treats students as customers and not as research guinea pigs... Community Colleges are living systems and consistently exchange vital fluids with local businesses and the citizenry.[!]
>
> We are motivated to make our community competitive because its survival is directly related to our own. We measure our success by customer feedback. Our missions are driven by our customers and by environmental analyses of future needs....Digital believes that TQM training will create added value for all students...who can learn from the marketplace.
>
> While universities approach course offerings like a chess game, [Digital] meets its customers' needs through a structure like an interactive video game....
>
> Every [tenured] faculty member is scheduled for specific TQM training tailored to increase student achievement...Once they have adopted TQM, they, *as Discipline Specialists,* will be empowered to provide continuous training to adjunct faculty.

These excerpts from the TQM grant proposal are transparent and even cartoonish examples of what Foucault called *biopower.*

> A power whose task is to [manage] life needs continuous regulatory and corrective mechanisms...to distribute the living in the domain of value and utility. [It must] qualify, measure, appraise and hierarchize by
> effecting distributions around the norm (Foucault, p. 144).

As an object for analysis, portions of this text raise some provocative questions. For example: What are the effects upon the students, service personnel and the faculty of recoding the identities of public-sector employees and students as producer/customer/consumer? Actual effects are complex; in fact, they're more elaborate than a surface reading could imagine. However, some interpretive avenues do seem auspicious.

First, Digital is a public site where proponents of market signs and practices, their status enhanced by resource inducements and corporatist monies, vow to broadly reshape management practices and curricular development. Digital is a locality busily reinscribing its populations - students, faculty and staff - as *homo economicus.* By *homo economicus,* I mean that subject-position that fuses Adam Smith's 18th Century economic subject, as he whose unique capacity is choice and whose activity must remain forever external to governments, with *homo manipulus*, the Watsonian-Skinnerian S-O-R subject who is predictably responsive to controllable alterations in local fields. As Colin Gordon notes: "Economic government here joins hands with Behaviorism" (Gordon 1991). This is the same logic that enables the PR firm of Sawyer-Miller to work normatively to produce docile subjects. They claim that

> If you can treat the voter as a consumer, why not the consumer as a voter? We sell candidates as products, so why not products as candidates?' Sawyer [says he's] in the service of `the new electronic democracy...by controlling the agenda through the people. With research, you begin to understand and manage people's attitudes and behaviors. We design strategies to affect [these] particular [corporate] constituencies (Siegel 1991).

If this political-consumer or student-consumer is *homo economicus/ manipulus*, then a notable facet of this TQM text is the production of ideological rhetoric that mimics the author/market-function. After all, most humans will not proudly claim that they are easily and transparently manipulable dupes. The implementation of power relations requires a legitimating mask that effaces power-effects. Through deconstructing the claims made in the name of TQM, the inversions that characterize one local variant of TQM discourse become comprehensible. For example, a Barthian analysis along the lines of the *Toys* piece in *Mythologies* is instructive (Barthes 1972). *Toys* is a short essay in which Barthes, when contrasting mass produced toys with older, simpler wooden toys, finds that plastic toys are a distressingly accurate isomorph of post-WWII French bureaucratic and consumer life. For Barthes, "French toys are based on imitation, they are meant to produce children who are users, not creators" (Barthes 1972).

I use a comparable deconstructive strategy to sections of the TQM text. What does it mean, for example, when the claim is made that

> While universities approach course offerings like a chess game, Digital meets its customer's needs through a structure like an interactive video game.

Denotatively, the claim is that chess (as a metaphor for the university) is a slow, confusing and difficult game with an uncertain outcome. While, on the other hand, interactive video games (as a metaphor for Digital) are quick, easy and painless. Outcomes are predictable and certain. But a more thorough analysis unpacks some useful dichotomies. These are below:

Table 1: A Connotative Analysis of Chess and Interactive Video Games as Signifiers in Digital's TQM Draft Proposal

Chess	Interactive Video
Low tech	High tech
Low cash outlay - Game in the public domain Missing pieces & parts replaceable	Higher cash outlay Proprietary software & hardware ensemble required
Social - played in a dyad often w/groups & in tournaments	Asocial - solo activity
Public venue - played in coffee-shops & parks	Private, played at home or in remote arcade malls
Relatively leisurely pace	Frenetic pace
Contemplative	Reactive
Proactive & Strategic w/high cognitive element	S-O-R model & cognitive skills irrevelant
Absorption (Concentration)	Distraction

Chess teaches the necessity and value of permanent habits of strategic resistances. It encourages participants to contemplate consequences, to anticipate moves and countermoves. It requires that players step back and actively assess and then reengage in fields where ultimate outcomes are uncertain and contingencies are always present. Unwittingly, this TQM text claims that universities will produce resistant and undocile subjects. This is not the goal of TQM. Digital's TQM is intended as a technology of obedience. It is designed to produce docile, efficient and (inexpensively) constituted subjects. Digital wants subjects who obey and are always striving to do it better. Whether "it," the activity, is worth doing, or what the consequences of any activity are, well, these questions are better left unasked.[7]

Digital is continually reshaped by forces busily encoding and opposing signs and procedures. TQM practices face tangible passive and active resistances throughout the district. (This is a theme for a later piece). However, it would be misleading to leave even a trace of an impression that

Digital ever resembled a "pure" space. Digital, like all bureaucracies, has always had a history of "governmentalities." What TQM represents, at Digital and at other sites, is an intensification of historical governmentalities.

CONCLUSION

Self-described anthropologist of science Bruno Latour once said that "science is politics by other means" (Latour 1984). By that, he meant that the adoption of technoscience instruments and techniques into routine activities generates profound displacements of networks of power/knowledge relations. These fresh sources of power are often external to standard political discourses. For example, while the content of TV programs is grist for the political mill, dialogues on the pivotal cultural, economic and political shifts associated with the spread of TV seem marginalized. *Technoscience is politics by other means*. Example Two: Conflict over an intractable issue, abortion, may end with a single shot. A reversible anti-pregnancy vaccine may soon make the abortion issue moot. New technological ensembles produce new social arrangements.

No one has voted on the digitalization and commodification of information, images and sounds. The selling of TQM and its intensification of surveillance and confessional technologies will never be on the ballot. As Foucault said, there are complex and productive, if disjunctive relationships between juridical and disciplinary fields of subjectivity (Foucault 1977). My conclusion is that we need to ask new questions about the shape of emerging practices of unfreedom. What are the effects, for example, when condensed identities such as citizen-as-consumer, student-as-customer, speech-image-sign as licensable commodity are constructed and then reenacted? What does it mean when the president of the on-line information utility *Dialog*, Roger Summit, says: "We can't afford an investment in databases that are not going to earn their keep and pay back their development cost...such as Humanities" (Schiller 1986)? Critical journals might vanish under such logic. Does the sign of the Market mask an authorless, but deeply political censorship process? What happens when a commodity-driven policing of the meaning of cultural signs, sounds, images saturates our imaginable universes of self-constructions? (I want my MTV....)

Late in his life, Foucault proposed that we are governed under security thematics (Gordon 1991). Historically, security concerns are correlated with an increased valuation of property rights. They are linked with problems of population, migration and demographic explosions. They accompany the rise of mass production machines and techniques. When the digital traces of those signs, images, and speech that form the banal choreography of our daily interactions are routinely encoded and commodified, our lives are impoverished. Is it any wonder, then, that regimes like TQM emerge within informational organizations when signs become policed commodities?

A marketplace of ideas (images, speech) is not the same as ideas (images, speech) in the marketplace. The former connotes a Bahktinian carnival of free play, negotiation and circulation. The latter denotes the restriction of access and deployment on the basis of wealth or affiliation. Increasingly, who gets to play and how (fields of play are formed) is dictated by the governmentalities of a few of transnational corporations. This is not a necessary or inevitable result. Digitalization processes are complex ensembles that often invite a creative play of selves and worlds. They are also part of security ensembles used in the rebirth of a neo-liberal Market Fundamentalism. Market Fundamentalism reinscribes all human activity as subsets of "an Invisible Hand" as it deploys intensifications of classification, risk-management and behavioral technologies onto public life. It deserves our attention as an emergent and influential "object of knowledge."

* *Dion Dennis is Visiting Assistant Professor of Criminal Justice, Political Science and History at Texas A & M International University.*

NOTES

1. This is part of a larger project called *The Subject Under the Sign of the Market. It has multiple foci:*

    a. examining the effect of the product, licensing, deployment and circulation of digitalized sounds, images and information. I call the economic production, circulation and licensing of information, images and signs *political iconomy*. The word *icon* in iconomy is a metonym for computerization. The (mouse-driven) icon is a function-symbol in the Apple-IBM PC-Compatible Windows world. Also, the term icon, as defined by the semiotician C.S. peirce, is any conventional symbolic meaning of a sign. Many icons are now licensed commercial signs whose realms of meaning are vigilantly guarded, through legal and extra-legal means.

b. A second research sphere looks at the effects surrounding the collection of and access to data as forms of social control. As parts of *regimes of detail*, our lives are intensively and digitally inscribed.

c. A third area apppraises the wide-ranging socio-economic, political and educational (research) impact of non-print based textualities known as hypertext.

d. A fourth zone of inquiry assesses the effects of the first three zones on traditional notions of sovereignity, identity, speech and political activity.

e. The master trope that serves as a discursive umbrella for all these changes is that of the market. It is my contention that, through the (so far) underexamined trope of the Market, all aspects of social life are now inscribed as subsets of market logics. A critique of the effects of such radical reinscriptions of our social world has not been sufficiently developed.

2. *OSTRICH* is a pseudonym. The corporation that OSTRICH stands for (in this text) has had an astonishing growth rate. For example: 1977 Revenues were reported as $11 million. Revenue estimates for 1990 were $500 million (plus).

3. *Digital Community College* is a pseudonym for a Phoenix metro institution.

4. *Infogarchy* is a condensation of the words information and oligarchy. By infogarchy, I mean that new forms of privilege and power are emerging for those that have a knowledge of computerized formats and databases. It is a ruling class based on the ability to penetrate electronic textualities. The word appears here (to my knowledge) for the first time.

5. See *Consumer Reports Buyers' Guide*, subcompact car section, for the years 1986-1989. New and used *Escorts* are ranked below Toyota Tercels, Nissan Sentras, Dodge Colts, etc.

6. A few weeks later (11/27/91), a consortium of Fortune 100

corporations (Motoral, IBM, Xerox, and Proctor & Gamble) announced that they were accepting applications for a joint educational program called *Total Quality Management - the University Challenge*. At a time of budgetary revertments for many state universities, this is the carrot to the disciplinary stick. To the university, as institution, this offering says: Accept this considerable financial and infrastructure support from our transnational corporate giants and be prpared to shape the university still further in the direction of an uncritical and dependent player to corporatist models and practices. Or be prepared to deal with the unknown (reduced resources and competition). The consortium hosted nearly a hundred engineering and business faculty from two universities. These faculty members received a week of on-site training and indoctrination about TQM. After that event, the universities have been encouraged to implement TQM curriculum and administrative practice. "All the participating companies will provide [financial] support to their chosen institutions" (from the *PR Newswire*, 11/27/91).

7. One aspect of TQM implementation at Digital is the production of week-long EST-like seminars for staff and management employees. Under the gaze of recycled Esalen-type trainers, the staff is segregated in a hotel or resort, given limited access to the outside world and urged (coerced) to make their innermost thoughts and feelings about their work world visible. The flushing out of "resistances" is given a high priority. Like many human potential formats, the production of a group consensus is desired. But that "consensus" is shaped by the expectations of upper management and the employees' desires to be "politically correct." Weeks later, in the face of a bond referendum defeat, Digital held a "Driving Out fear Seminar" at a Quality Inn (no joke, this was the name of the hotel!) in South Central Phoenix. These "TQM coaches rounds" continue.

REFERENCES

Barthes, Roland. 1972. *Mythologies*. Trans. Annette Lavers. New York: Noonday.

Bahktin. M.M. 1981. *The Dialogic Imagination*. Edited by Holquist, M. Trans. by A. Emerson and M. Holquist. Austin. University of Texas Press.

Barringer, Felicity. 1989. "Education; Information Tug of War; Consumers vs.

Creators." *New York Times*, 08/16/89; Section B; pg. 10, Col. 3.

Bernauer, James. 1988. "Beyond Life and Death: on Foucault's post-Auschwitz ethic." *Philosophy Today* 32 (2): 128-142.

_____. 1988. "Foucault's Ecstatic Thinking." Pps. 45-82 in *The Final Foucault*, edited by J. Bernauer and D. Rasmussen. Cambridge: The MIT Press.

Boyle, James D. A. 1988. "The Search for an Author: Shakespeare and the Framers." *The American University Law Review* 37: 625-643.

Coombe, Rosemary J. 1991. "Objects of Property and Subjects of Politics: Intellectual Property Laws and Democratic Dialogue." *Texas Law Review* 69: 1853-1880.

Dennis, Dion. 1992. *Under the Sign of Saturn: An Exemplar of Political Icomony*. Unpublished paper under revision.

Denvir, John. 1991. "Commercial Speech as Political Propaganda; `the electronic marketplace of ideas' is a seller's market rigged in favor of an ideology of unlimited personal consumption." *American Lawyer Media, L.P. The Recorder* 12/11/91; Media and Society: 6.

Dietrich, Jeff. 1990. "In the Dumps with Human Discards; Skid Row: The Wave of Technology and Economic Change has left stragglers who will never catch up. It's like expecting a non-swimmer to learn to surf." *Los Angeles Times*, 05/05/90; Metro, Part B.

Ditlea, Steve. 1990. "HyperTed: Hypertext inventor Ted Nelson." *PC-Computing*, 3 (10): 200-207.

Duggan, Mary Kay. 1991. Copyright of electronic information: issues and questions. *Online* 15 (3): 20-41.

Ewen, Stuart. 1988. All Consuming Images: The Politics of Style in *Contemporary Culture*. New York: Basic Books.

Ewick, Patricia. 1990. *The Commodification of Social Control*. Unpublished paper delivered at the 1990 Law and Society Convention. Berkeley.

Fawcett, Brian. 1990. *Public Eye: An Investigation into the Disappearance of the World*. New York: Grove Weidenfeld.

Foucault, Michel. 1970. *The Order of Things: An Archeology of the Human Sciences*. New York: Vintage Books.

____. 1978. *Discipline and Punish: The Birth of the Prison*. Trans. Alan Sheridan. New York: Vintage Books.

____. 1983. "The Subject and Power." Pps. 208-226 in *Beyond Structuralism and Hermeneutics*, edited by H. Dreyfus and P. Rabinow. Chicago: University of Chicago Press.

____. 1984. "What is an Author?" Pps. 101-140 in *The Foucault Reader*, edited by P. Rabinow. New York: Pantheon.

____. 1990. *The History of Sexuality, Volume I: An Introduction*. Trans. Robert Hurley. New York: Vintage Books.

____. 1991. "Governmentality." Pps. 87-104 in *The Foucault Effect*, edited by G. Burchell, C.Gordon and P. Miller. Chicago: University of Chicago Press.

Gordon, Colin. 1991. "Government Rationality: An Introduction." Pps. 1-52 in *The Foucault Effect*, edited by G. Burchell, C. Gordon and P. Miller. Chicago. University of Chicago Press.

Holstein, William J.; Read, Stanley; Weber, Joseph. 1990. "The Stateless Corporation." *Business Week*, 05/14/90; Vol. 3159.

Jackall, Robert. 1988. *Moral Mazes: The World of Corporate Managers*. New York: Oxford University Press.

Jaszi, Peter. 1991. "Toward a Theory of Copyright: The Metamorphoses of `Authorship'." *Duke Law Journal*, 2: 455-502.

Landow, George P. 1992. *Hypertext: The Convergence of Contemporary Critical Theory and Technology*. Baltimore: Johns Hopkins University Press.

Latour, Bruno. 1984. "Give Me a Laboratory and I Will Raise the World." Pps. 141-170 in *Science Observed*, edited by K. Knorr-Cetina and M. Mulkay. Beverly Hills: Sage.

____. 1987. *Science in Action. How to Follow Scientists and Engineers Through Society*. Cambridge: Harvard University Press.

Lyotard, Jean-Francois. 1984. *The Postmodern Condition: A Report on Knowledge*. Trans. G. Bennington and B. Massumi. Minneapolis: University of Minnesota Press.

McDonald, James H. 1993. "Te(k)knowledge: Technology, Education and the New Student Subject." (Forthcoming in the *National Association of Practicing Anthropologists (NAPA) Bulletin* Series).

McDonald, James H. and Dubinskas, Frank. 1993. "Electronic Technologies and Instruction: Tools, Users and Power." (Forthcoming in the *National Association of Practicing Anthropologists (NAPA) Bulletin* Series).

Poster, Mark. 1990. *The Mode of Information: Poststructuralism and Social Context*. Chicago: University of Chicago Press.

Schiller, Anita. R. and Schiller, Herbert I. "The Library as Emporium: Commercializing Information." *The Nation* 243: 306-312.

Schiller, Herbert I. 1989. *Culture, Inc.* New York: Oxford University Press.

Siegel, Barry. 1991. "Spin Doctors to the World: The Sawyer-Miller Group uses the tricks of political campaigns to change the way you think about foreign governments, big business and any client in need of an image lift." *Los Angeles Times*, 11/24/91, Magazine.

Virilio, Paul. 1986. *Speed and Politics*. Trans. M. Polizzotti. New York: Semiotexte.

Zuboff, Shoshana. 1988. *In the Age of the Smart Machine: The Future of Work and Power*. New York: Basic Books.

Chapter VIII

THE VALUE OF POSTMODERN THEORY TO CRITICAL CRIMINOLOGY: VIOLENCE AGAINST WOMEN AND CORPORATE VIOLENCE*

David O. Friedrichs** and Martin D. Schwartz***

There are many ways to characterize critical criminology over the past 20 years, but certainly much of this work emerged as part of a reaction against mainstream criminology's primary concern with conventional forms of violence. Thus, one prime focus of critical criminologists has been crimes of the state and the ruling class[1], with a more limited concern (particularly in the U.S.) with "street crimes."[2] More recently, feminist researchers have developed a rich literature on many different forms of violence against women: stranger rape, rape by intimates and acquaintances, woman battering, child sexual and physical abuse, pornography and sexual harassment.[3] Other newer forms of critical criminology include left realism, peacemaking and postmodernism (Schwartz, 1991). Left realism has been extensively covered in the literature,[4] and there has been a lengthy discussion of the peacemaking position (e.g., Pepinsky and Quinney, 1991), but to date less has been done on the relevance of the postmodern critique to critical criminology (Smart, 1990; Hunt, 1991; Milovanovic, 1991; Manning, 1991).

As we shall see, there is a great deal of tension between these latter two positions. The major problem, we argue, is that critical criminology is explicitly committed to a progressive social transformation and virtually by definition must be founded in some notion of social justice (de Haan, 1991; Reiman, 1990). The same is true for a related perspective, critical legal studies (Seaton, 1991). By contrast, the areas in which postmodernists have generally been most skeptical are those which are arguably most central to the critical criminologists' agenda. For example, postmodernists reject totalizing concepts, such as "state," "capitalism," and "working class," and usually reject the potential of collective action to transform society (to complete the process of modernization) (Carlen, 1992; Henry, 1991; Hunt, 1991). The rejection of all such paradigms for understanding the world means that there are no guidelines for determining what is an appropriate depiction of social reality; we have what is often termed a "crisis of representation" (Richardson, 1988).

This is not to argue that there are no points of intersection. There are many areas of shared heritage, perhaps the most important of which is that both critical criminology and postmodern thought are rooted in a critique of modern positivistic social science. However, critical criminologists, while increasingly aware of postmodernist thought, have for the most part not attempted to master this difficult literature and incorporate it into their writings (Matthews and Young, 1992). Indeed, some even question whether it has relevance at all: Agger (1991: 117-118) insists that "Postmodernism remains a largely French perspective on cultural and historical analysis that bears little explicit relationship to French or American sociology."

In this paper we will at least provisionally explore some of the tensions between these points of intersection and conflict. To move from the completely theoretical toward the concrete, we will pay special attention to the implications for formulating progressive responses to the problems of violence against women and corporate violence, two of the most important issues for critical criminologists in the early 1990s. Although we will make occasional reference to violence in relevant places throughout the paper, we will pay special attention to these problems later.

THE POSTMODERNIST CONCEPTUAL CHALLENGE

To many social observers, we have already entered a postmodern world and need to change our analyses to recognize that fact. A major problem, unfortunately, is that there seem to be an almost infinite number of postmodern perspectives. As a young Ph.D. remarked to us recently, when we noted that he had been studying with some of America's premier postmodernists and asked for his definition of postmodernism: "If you ask a question like that, then you don't understand what postmodernism is." This may sound pompous (and no doubt was), but it actually is a very good answer. If postmodernism can only be characterized in terms of a somewhat loose collection of themes and tendencies (Dews, 1987), it may well be a fundamental contradiction to attempt any coherent definition.[5] Huyssen (1986) explains: "the amorphous and politically volatile nature of postmodernism makes the phenomenon itself remarkably elusive, and the definition of its boundaries exceedingly difficult, if not *per se* impossible. Furthermore, one critic's postmodernism is another critic's modernism...." Perhaps making the term still more difficult is that it is commonly used to refer to different things. Dowd (1991: 191) has noted that:

> At a minimum, postmodernism refers to three separate but related phenomena: (1) post-1960 movements in art, cinema, architecture, literature and music; (2) a group of social theories, associated with French writers such as Baudrillard and Lyotard; and (3) the present historical epoch that began following the Second World War and which is associated with a restructuring of the world system, the increasing centrality of the electronics industry, and the greater penetration into all spheres of life of means-end, or technical, rationality.

The concern here is not with cultural tradition, but rather with interpretations of contemporary society and social theories inspired by French writers including not only Baudrillard and Lyotard, but also Derrida, Deleuze, Foucault, Barthes and others.[6] Rather than attempting to explain the complex work of each of these writers, we will try to identify some common themes inspired by their works which have some relevance to criminology. The exception is Baudrillard, who in Sociology has generally been one of the most important postmodern theorists. His argument is that new technologies have become the guiding forces that shape the world. What has happened is that there have been a number of major breaks from the modern to the postmodern, including representation to simulation, reproduction to replication, sex to genetic engineering, and mind to artificial intelligence (Haraway, 1990). Although modernity is based on a belief that people can have control over objects, nature and each other, Baudrillard finds that objects now have more and more control over us. For those who can grope their way through the fog of a semiotic theory based on Saussure, Baudrillard (1983) argues that commodities in a consumer society acquire use values so that we consume them for the *signs* and statements rather than the exchange value of their utility. When the simulations constructed for us by technology (mostly TV) conceal that the real no longer exists, when we cannot tell the difference between simulations and reality, we have entered *hyperreality*. Our primary experience now is to live and respond to simulations (Glassner, 1992). Accordingly, Willis (1991: 162) asserts that "We have no way to experience or conceptualize relationships between people except as these are defined by the exchange of commodities."

Quite literally, the postmodernist critique challenges the system of values and priorities that sustain contemporary life. It contends that modernity is no longer liberating, but rather has become a force for subjugation, oppression and repression. Postmodernists are disillusioned with liberal notions of progress and radical expectations of emancipation (Kellner, 1990). There are certainly points in favor of this argument. Clearly the forces of modernism (e.g., industrialism) have extended and amplified the scope of corporate violence, and have produced an environment conducive to various forms of direct and indirect violence against women. What is even worse, according to the postmodern critique, is that the major form of response to this violence is through rational organizations (e.g., the court system and the regulatory bureaucracies), with a great reliance upon specialists and experts. Such a response simply reproduces domination, the critique suggests, perhaps in new but no less pernicious forms.

Within critical criminology, the theorist who probably deserves the largest measure of credit for applying concepts and insights produced by postmodernist thought to the concerns of criminology is Dragan Milovanovic (e.g., 1986, 1988, 1989, 1991, 1992). He is not the only player on this field: Stephen Pfohl (1990) has promoted a postmodernist perspective on, for example, state crime, although his focus extends considerably beyond the specific concerns of criminologists. Peter Manning (1991) has been developing a critical semiotics which can be applied to an understanding of criminal justice communication. Milovanovic, however, has been developing a form of semiotic analysis which can be applied as a novel interpretation of the legal process. For example, Stuart Henry and Milovanovic (1991) have produced a pioneering effort - which they call constitutive criminology -- to integrate elements of postmodernist thought with the critical criminological project. They are especially concerned with highlighting the role of ideology, discursive practices, symbols and sense data in the production of meaning in the realm of crime. Crime, in their view (1991:293) "should be reconsidered as the coterminous discursive production by human agents of an ideology of crime that sustains it as a concrete reality." We must, in other words, understand how those who engage in crime, who seek to control it, and who study it "co-produce" its meaning.

Still, there remain a number of reasons to be cautious about the project of finding insights within postmodernism that can be adopted by critical criminologists. A major strength of postmodernist thought is that it tends to challenge "boundaries" of all types, including traditional boundaries between academic disciplines (Kellner, 1990). It incorporates (critically and selectively) elements of French structuralism, Romanticism, Phenomenology, Nihilism, Populism, Existentialism, Hermeneutics, Western Marxism, Critical Theory, and Anarchism (Rosenau, 1992). To the extent that such eclecticism is defensible, though, it should be expected to achieve some level of coherence, although some postmodernists would challenge the very notion of coherence.[7] On this view truth claims are a "form of terrorism," modern truth is "fragmentary, discontinuous, and changing," theory "conceals, distorts and obfuscates," and human experience has to be understood in terms of inconsistencies and contradictions (Rosenau, 1992: 78-82). These postmodernists invite us to consider the possibility - very much at odds with our professional socialization - that such concepts as violence against women and corporate violence cannot be "coherently" understood. Further, they argue that we should not even attempt to achieve such an understanding.

Postmodernist thought challenges the attempt to develop "totalizing" theories which reveal the fundamental "truth" about and "explain" violence against women, and corporate violence (Currie and Kline, 1991). Foucault's proposition, advanced in *Discipline and Punish* (1977), that criminology is a discourse/practice which in some sense creates the category of criminality,[8] can be extended to the notion of violence against women and corporate violence as products of discourse (Agger, 1991). The thrust of the postmodernist endeavor is to explore how images and meanings pertaining to such violence are constituted, giving privilege to the experience and perspective of the victimized over the victimizers, and attending to the marginal rather than the "representative" cases. Sociological and criminological scholarship has, in the postmodernist view, not succeeded in providing us with a penetrating understanding of how ordinary people experience a postmodern world increasingly dominated by a media-generated "virtual" reality (Denzin, 1986; Pfohl, 1992). The guiding premise here is that a postmodernist approach enables us to achieve a more appropriate level of comprehension of our knowledge of a dynamic and complex human environment. It looks to different layers of "texts"[9] which are interrelated with each other as the locus of social reality, and discounts the notion of some separate, "factual" reality.

Postmodernism addresses some of the enduring fundamental questions - on such matters as causality, determinism, egalitarianism, humanism, liberal democracy, necessity, objectivity and subjectivity, rationality, responsibility and truth - and rejects most if not all of the conventional epistemological assumptions pertaining to these questions. As part of an attack on all aspects of positivism, postmodernism calls for empirically-oriented social scientists to be reflexive and to confront "the ways in which their own analytical and literary practices encode and conceal value positions that need to be brought to light" (Agger, 1991: 121). Conventional positivist sociology is regarded as biased in a fundamental way, and engaged in a distorted misrepresentation of social reality.

Unfortunately, the problem still remains as to whether the discourse now being recommended advances our understanding of the suffering of real people, or whether it becomes increasingly irrelevant to us (Tong, 1989). Rosenau (1992: 111) points out the other side:

> Critics argue that debate over issues such as the existence of an independent reality are of interest only to post-modernists (and other intellectuals) who, insulated from reality, never personally experience the violence, terror, and degradation prevalent in modern society.

Here, in a nutshell, we have one of the most forceful reservations about the postmodernist enterprise, and one with potent relevance for our concern with violence against women and corporate violence.[10]

THE POSTMODERNIST SEMANTIC CHALLENGE

Postmodernist thought is intensely focused on the central role of language in human experience, and is somewhat infamous for its own tendency to invoke a specialized jargon, to invent and discard terms, and "play" with words (Rosenau, 1992). This postmodernist approach may sensitize us to the importance of language in the creation of our understanding of violence in all its many guises. The power of the word can not only be exposed as creating domination, but one means of resistance for those who are oppressed is to recapture the meaning of words (Freire, 1970) or at least "bringing into awareness suppressed, alternate meanings which are subversive to the established order" (Currie and Kline, 1991: 15). The problem is that these arguments have not been convincing to many students of violence (to say nothing of its victims). Those who do not agree with postmodernists tend to find the core experience outside the realm of language, and to find that "word games" tend to trivialize or diminish their view of the essential nature of violence.[11]

Even without word games, however, there remains the problem of the dense nature of the prose too often preferred by postmodernists. There is no virtue, they argue, in catering to the least common denominator in understanding. Postmodern readers, coming across the quote (Schwartz, 1991: 121): "Reading Lacan or Luhmann is like reading Cervantes in the original when you cannot read Spanish" make responses like: "So, you learn Spanish." The problem, however, is not that it is impossible to decipher what Lacan, Derrida or Luhmann are saying. Rather, it is the difficulty of imagining how a body of work will ever attain broad influence when the "style" of writing - in the work of postmodernism's seminal figures (Derrida, Lacan, Lyotard, Baudrillard) and those directly influenced by them - is so dense and obscure that it is largely inaccessible to all but the exceptionally dedicated or masochistic, and ultimately the "inner circle" or self-identified students of this body of work (Ritzer, 1990). Even when reaching out to broaden its influence, the self-characterization of the project is frequently obscure, as exemplified by Pfohl (1992: 34): "If postmodernism is about anything it is about the materiality of language as a dynamic force in the ritual social transformation of an indeterminate range of human possibilities into the restricted moral economy of a given order of things in time." Although feminist postmodernism can be seen as a different field, these criticisms apply there as well. Tong, for example, (1989: 231) recently noted the complaint that "postmodernist feminists apparently delight in their opacity, viewing clarity as one of the seven deadly sins of the phallologocentric order."

All of this raises some basic questions about the nature of intellectual influence and intellectual elitism. There is a paradox involved in the postmodernist insistence on not "privileging" the voices of the powerful over the voices of the powerless (including the victims of corporate and family violence) but then writing in a form and style largely inaccessible to the powerless as well as most of those positioned to act on their behalf (See, e.g., Weinstein and Weinstein, 1993). At the same time, the decision by some postmodernists (e.g., Baudrillard, not Foucault) to focus purposefully on the mundane (e.g., shopping malls) may also raise questions about their relevance for critical criminologists, who tend to favor topics such as conflict and violence. Accordingly, the focus by some key postmodernists on surfaces, imagery and the mundane rather than on violence and suffering can be seen as coming from a very privileged position. In a world filled with extraordinary starvation and bloodshed on mass scales, and then malnutrition and terrible suffering on individual scales, to find the most relevant objects of study the superficial images portrayed in suburban shopping malls is a powerful statement. This is not to say these are not objects worthy of study; the question is whether one claims they are the most important objects of study.

Arguments in favor of the dense and abstruse postmodernist style include: (a) it is more responsive to the complexity of what is being addressed, or, alternatively, (b) it is a worthy enterprise to be deliberately playful, as this enables readers to assume the central and appropriate role of making their own sense of the writing. The idea of the latter is to loosen the subject from the prison of language, to provide the opportunity to construct/read the text differently as a method of discovery. Thus, the question: is postmodernist work gratuitously obscure, incoherent, and undisciplined? Alternatively, is the problem that the rest of us are having a problem in liberating ourselves from the constraints of interpreting the world in the familiar idiom of rational, contemporary social science? If we reoriented ourselves would we find modes and styles of understanding which are ultimately more valid and revealing in a changing, endlessly complex world? Certainly if the latter is the case, a great deal more work is left to be done in constructing mediating "bridges" to this new form of discourse.

Despite our reservations with such stylistic obfuscation, we are open to the argument that the substance of postmodernist themes can be separated from the style in which they are originally formulated (undoubtedly this possibility is not universally acceptable), and we will attempt some small conceptualization of this sort here.

POSTMODERNIST POSSIBILITIES FOR UNDERSTANDING VIOLENCE

Postmodernism might be said to challenge the prevailing value system which sustains corporate violence.[12] If much of this violence is committed in the name of "progress," postmodernism challenges the basic notion of progress. At least the more extreme version of postmodernism questions the possibility of changing society, and compels us to consider whether the commonplace calls for reform (e.g., regulating and controlling corporations) are a self-indulgent fantasy and illusion, and largely meaningless. This is not the call more familiar in Marxist literature (e.g., Collins, 1982; Lynch and Groves, 1987) to ignore reform in favor of revolution; the postmodernist skepticism applies if anything even more fully toward calls for revolutionary transformation (e.g., Fish, 1989). We can only engage in personal local efforts of "resistance." Postmodernism challenges, as well, faith in "expertise" and rational organizations, and in this sense anticipates corporate violence. It calls for a shift of focus to the ordinary, "local," daily experience of corporate violence, rather than its broad and large-scale dimensions. Postmodernism challenges tendencies to produce categories, and at least implicitly rejects conflating very different forms or dimensions of corporate violence for the purpose of advancing broad propositions.

At the same time postmodernism promotes a greater sensitivity to the "intertextuality" of different forms of violence. This is a difficult maneuver for anyone who is attempting to avoid the creation of new categories, but it is particularly difficult for someone attempting a relativist approach to a social problem which incorporates some objectivist presuppositions (Woolgar and Pawluch, 1985). Here it is possible to raise questions about interconnections between corporate violence and violence against women. There has been little investigation into the interaction between corporatism and patriarchism in the generation of the "texts" of both types of violence. For example, in his response to the Woolgar and Pawluch charge of "ontological gerrymandering," Pfohl (1985: 230) argued that the principal objective of his work was deconstructive:

> It was to open a space for wondering why child beating is today most commonly read as a story of determinate pathology rather than, for instance, as the indeterminate effect of a bloody domestic drama - a powerful play of violence behind the closed doors of privatized power -- performed by people denied access to a script of public power and embedded in the text of corporate capitalism.

The same logic, of course, can be applied as well to any category of violence against women or corporate violence.

Somewhat independently of the postmodernist perspective one can ask how males' attitudes in the corporate context and in relation to women are interrelated, and whether victimization of corporate violence affects violence in the domestic forum. Some recent scholarship (e.g., DeKeseredy and Hinch, 1991; Gerber and Weeks, 1992) suggests how corporations engage in violence against women in the domestic context. "Institutionalized" sexual harassment, on the other hand, may be conceived of as a form of violence against women in a corporate context.

Finally, postmodernism refutes any "necessary" reading of the "texts" concerning corporate violence. It raises the possibility that authors in the realm of corporate crime impose "truths" on readers in inherently authoritarian ways. It also at least suggests - very controversially - that the pain and suffering associated with corporate violence resides principally in the domination of a particular meaning of such violence. Do policies intended to challenge and "punish" corporate violence and violence against women "reproduce" the structures of dominance? Do they lead to the diffusion of violence in new forms? Fish (1989) argues that there is no difference between being forced into an act by a gunman and being forced by law.

Postmodernism suggests that it is more liberating to empower "victims" (an imposed category?) of violence (an imposed category?) against women and corporate violence (an imposed category?) to reconstitute the meaning of the violence they experience, rather than imposing a critical interpretation of this violence on them (Rosenau, 1992). Of course, critical and progressive sociological and criminological analysis has traditionally championed the oppressed, including at least some classes of victims. But one criticism of progressive analysis is that it presumes to speak *for* the oppressed rather than allowing the oppressed to speak for themselves. Norman Denzin (1990: 4), in writing of C. Wright Mills' famous book, *The Sociological Imagination*, asserts:

> But nowhere in the pages of his work(s) do these little people and their personal troubles speak. Mills speaks for them; he quotes others who have written about them...his 'nowadays' sentence reflects either what he imagines men (and women) nowadays feel about their lives, or what others have written about men nowadays.

In Denzin's revisionist reading, this type of progressive analysis is hypocritical, and the metanarrative it advances is inappropriate for the late capitalist, postmodern era. At the same time, it is not entirely clear that the postmodern approach - which includes the rejection of all metanarratives - is not vulnerable to the similar claim (whatever its stated intentions) that it is even more removed from the experienced reality of ordinary people than is Mills' allegedly patronizing approach.

Indeed, some of this dispute is over *which* approach is more elitist. Is it elitist to presume that as researchers and theoreticians we have something to offer in terms of explaining how the world operates? Are we imposing our categories of explanation on the oppressed peoples of the world with our analyses, silencing their voices in favor of our own? Certainly it is not hard to find examples of this within critical criminology for finger-pointing purposes.[13] Yet, the opposite approach may be just as elitist. It has become a common sight at some sociology and criminology conferences to see panelists at a session on postmodernism carefully excluding from the discussion anyone who is not a member of a clique well versed in a special vocabulary, delivering papers that critique modernists for excluding the voices of the oppressed from their narratives. At the same time, the nihilism of denying the legitimacy of all categories (racism, sexism, classism) without proposing a replacement can be seen, despite claims to the contrary, as providing a justification for lack of political action (Matthews and Young, 1992; Schwartz, 1989). Relatedly, we have the enduring question of what should be the primary mission of scholars and academics.[14]

POSTMODERNISM AND THE SOCIAL POLICY DILEMMA

A major question for progressive social policy is what to do about corporate violence and violence against women, assuming that we have agreed that it exists and is not the imposition of a category by critical criminologists on innocent people. As we have seen, postmodernism calls upon critical criminologists to consider whether their calls for fundamental transformation of social policies, and the structures which create oppression, are either illusionary in terms of what can be accomplished, or in fact end up reproducing an unequal distribution of power.

Interestingly, it is difficult to see whether this inherently boils down to a position that comes from the left, or is a conservative position that supports the status quo (Agger, 1991). At least one strand of postmodernism has sunk so deeply into its epistemological relativism that it denies the legitimacy of any political views, sincc any such views necessarily imply a foundational basis (Rosenau, 1992). These postmodernists often urge withdrawal from political participation on the basis that the struggle for social change is meaningless, and individual human beings are powerless to influence government and society. At the least, they urge Baudrillard's "ironic detachment," where the jaded and bored theorist stands above it all.

Of course, there are many varieties of postmodernism, most of which are "internally inconsistent" (Rosenau, 1992) both with each other and within themselves. Some argue for a retreat from politics in favor of searching out the lost years of Jesus or beating drums in the woods, while others argue that the only worthwhile change is in the individual, not society. In general, though, Handler (1992) argues that all postmodernists lack foundationalism, which means a politics without moral judgments, leading only to unbridled relativism. A social movement based mainly on vague attacks on a dominant rationality, he argues, does not make for a feasible transformative strategy. More likely is that postmodernists will be co-opted, Handler argues, which means that they will be contributing to the status quo, not changing it.

Where this can be most frustrating is not to the person sitting out in a rustic but luxurious lodge on a $2500 five day New Age retreat, or to the host of a $375 entrepreneurial seminar on Postfeminist Male Parenting. For survivors of corporate violence and violence against women, and the front line workers who work with these survivors, it has been very easy to feel for the past two decades that criminologists are, in the evocative Texas phrase, all hat and no cattle. Today, it is even harder to avoid feeling that the latest philosophy is to make fun of front line workers for trying to help. Certainly there are postmodernist theorists with a strong political agenda (as contradictory as this sounds; see Lather (1991) for an example), but as Malcolm Bradbury (1988: 4) points out, while earlier theorists were strong on plight and anguish, altogether too much postmodernism "in keeping with the times, is clean absurdism or cool philosophy; it is laid back, requires no weighty black gear, and goes very well with Perrier water and skiing."

Responding to Violence Against Women

The problematic of whether to attempt reform by engaging the state has been most heavily debated within feminist theory, especially as it involves the problem of battered women. If does not take a particularly sophisticated political analysis to understand that to work with the criminal justice system is to run the risk of being co-opted by it (Smart, 1989). For example, many feminist authors argue that it is essential for the state to step in and deal with men who commit violence against women by arresting them and sending them to prison for long terms (e.g., Edwards, 1989; Box-Grainger, 1986; Gregory, 1986). Much more than in most countries, the battered women's movement in the U.S. and Canada has been successful in making changes in criminal justice system practice. Police departments across North America have moved to a pro-arrest of mandatory arrest policy, and quite a broad variety of other changes such as protection orders, streamlined prosecution, and increased use of jail are being widely implemented (Hirschel et al., 1992). Although these policies are far from being universally accepted, they are increasingly common (Dobash and Dobash, 1992).

Yet, a great many women are progressively worried about increasing the power of the state and widening the net of social control (Smart, 1989; Bannister and Milovanovic, 1990; Henry and Milovanovic, 1991). At the very time that critical criminology generally is arguing that the state is using the criminal justice system as the strongest element of a social control system designed to blunt social protest against an unjust political system, some of us are arguing that we must increase our use of this very system to serve our own ends. The dilemma is not to be trivialized. Although some theorists argue that legal reform has been advantageous for women (e.g., Agger, 1991), others have come to the conclusion that law reform only changes the nature of patriarchal state oppression of women, rather than lessening it (Currie and Kline, 1991). Dobash and Dobash (1992) remain convinced that in an advanced industrial society we have as yet few workable strategies for addressing social injustices other than the mechanisms of the state, and for that reason the imbalance of power within the family must be addressed by the law and the justice system. Still, they point out (1992: 209):

> Entering criminal justice machinery may mean yielding to the exigencies of that system. Once encapsulated within criminal justice, reform movements must inevitably serve the needs of that system and potentially assist its expansion into more areas of civil society. The CJS may embrace the movement and yet subvert its demands, particularly within a law and order agenda, as a means of gaining greater resources and of widening the net of its response. An absorbent state may be able to incorporate the pragmatic concerns of the movement while ignoring or even rejecting its politics.

The call by activists such as the Dobashes for the intervention of the state also speaks to another dilemma brought about by some forms of postmodern analysis. Many feminist theorists have argued for an emancipatory agenda that incorporates postmodernist thought with a praxis (e.g., Lather, 1991). This would include allowing women to define what is best for themselves, the ways they want help, and what they think will help them. As Hutchinson (1992: 780) puts it: "By abandoning the search to recover or fix a unified and pristine self, the hope is to empower subjects by making them individually aware of their capacity for self-(re)creation and their collective responsibility for establishing a mode of social life that multiplies the opportunities for transformative action." This empowering of women may have some theoretical advantages but simultaneously may often be fairly meaningless. It may be assuming a degree of agency that battered women do not have when they are living in frightful circumstances with all of their energies focused on getting out alive and protecting their children (Horley, 1991). It is admirable to be anti-hegemonic, but we may need to take some time out from patting ourselves on the back to wonder how much responsibility we are placing on women in crisis to solve their own problems.

Responding to Corporate Crime

The question of how to respond to corporate violence confronts critical and progressive criminologists with some conundrums. Corporate violence -- e.g., polluting the environment, dangerous working conditions, unsafe products -- is primarily a consequence (with the specific harm unintended) of efforts to enhance corporate profit making. The purely radical strain of critical criminology obviously views corporate violence as an absolutely inevitable feature of a modern capitalist society, which cannot be obliterated or even significantly diminished without a revolutionary, structural transformation of the political economy (Lynch and Groves, 1989). Furthermore, the state is viewed as an important source of violence, and is deeply imbricated with corporations in some of the most substantial forms of violence. State-based reform efforts directed at corporate violence are seen largely, in this view, as means of enhancing the legitimacy of the political economy without substantially reducing corporate violence. Most critical criminologists, however, concede that revolution is hardly imminent in the United States and other Western developed nations, and probably most critical criminologists do not regard revolution as the solution to oppressive social conditions. If critical criminologists are quite united in their hostility to the traditional functions of the state in a capitalist political economy, many nevertheless promote a tougher state attack on corporate violence. As is the case with violence against women, there has been an overall movement toward more state intervention with corporate violence since the 1970s. Parallel to the feminist response, critical or progressive criminologists tend to be divided between those who favor strong state intervention against corporate violence and those who favor alternative tactics which avoid reliance upon the state. Mokhiber (1988) and Snider (1990) are among those who argue for a strongly punitive approach to corporate violence, while Simon and Eitzen (1993) for example, recommend a centrally planned economy, state takeover of certain industries and government legislated change in the power structure of corporations. On the other hand, Pepinsky and Jesilow (1984) want the seriousness of corporate violence to be recognized by the state but favor a stress on community-rooted solutions. All camps, however, are likely to be united in a skepticism toward a postmodern perspective which at least implicitly defers to the victims of corporate violence - citizens, workers and customers - the prerogative of assigning their own meaning to it. As is the case with battered women, there are some serious concerns about the meaning of "agency" in this context, more importantly as victims of corporate violence in particular are often not even aware of their victimization in the short run.

Postmodernism and Policy

Obviously, the strands of postmodernism opposed to broad and wide scale resistance to problems are the least likely to provide extensive guidance on the policy conundrum outlined above. More likely, it offers a basis for exposing possible pretenses and illusions in the pursuit of a just policy. At least one major strand of postmodernist thought seems to promote empowerment of victims, enabling them to engage more fully in a process of reconstituting the meaning of violence. At the same time, however, postmodernists such as Baudrillard seem to be echoing the romantic early days of critical criminology in seeing terrorism, violence and insurrection as laudatory efforts to deny legitimacy to the state (Baudrillard, 1983). The victims of terrorism, one presumes, are not the ones being empowered here. In general, an approach that argues against direct action in favor of semantic groundwork opens itself, at the least, to criticism as being idealist and utterly insensitive to the very direct, concrete experience and needs of victims and survivors.

Still, Baudrillard is correct in many ways about the effect of media imagery. Indeed, it has been a standard and central focus of critical criminology for close to 20 years that the public's attitude toward crime is shaped by the media. What he has failed to analyze, however, is that the media is a battleground that does not have to be automatically won by the forces of corporate capitalism. It is, perhaps, the most common critique of Baudrillard that his theory depends on a stronger break with modernity than in fact is the case.

> Baudrillard's insistence on the hermetic nature of postmodern simulacra is better seen as the introjection and projection of the capitalist imaginary -- the dram of seamless closure, complete mystification, and perfected hegemony -- than an accurately descriptive thesis, a super-implosive postmodernism which confuses *tendencies* of contemporary society with a *finalized state* of affairs (Best, 1989: 48).

Society today might be better described as being in a state of modernity, while showing signs or tendencies in the direction that Baudrillard describes. This has important implications. This means that while it is possible to create a hyperreality that most people react to, it is also possible (although very difficult) to create a counter-hyperreality. Loseke (1992), for example, describes in detail the process by which women in the battered women's movement have created the image of the "battered woman," an image that may actually fit the lived realities of few of the real women who show up at the doors of shelter houses, but which dovetails into other U.S. ideologies. "Since Americans tend to define as social problems those conditions defined as morally intolerable, since we tend to withhold sympathy from all but pure victims in desperate situations, viable claims will construct problems and people in ways comparable with these underlying interpretive schemes" (Loseke, 1992: 46). In other words, just as we have constructed the concept of "battered woman" as a wife and mother severely abused, morally pure and not complicit in her plight, grass roots claimsmakers rooted firmly within the project of modernity have the ability to create other definitions and realities, just as postmodernists have claimed can only be done outside these boundaries.

The postmodern society not only isn't the seamless and completed society that Baudrillard describes, but in many ways its current condition *depends* on modernity for its vitality; the attack on modernity is the entire project of postmodernist theory. At the same time, of course, the essential justification of modernity -- the opposition to the forces of feudalism -- is long dead. Thus, Ferraris (1992: 25) argues:

> I believe, therefore, that modernists should be very grateful to postmodernists, because their ostracism of postmodernism now constitutes the only *point* of the discourse on the reconstruction of modernism. What could Habermas write without Derrida? How topical would his program for the reconstruction of modernism be?

Postmodernism serves to remind modernity of the reason for modernity's existence. It is not to serve progress, in the sense of rushing the technical hyperreality of the postmodern world ever faster and ever closer. It is not to extend domination. The reminder delivered by postmodernism is that "progress" and domination are exactly the ends now being served modern solutions.

The key point of modernity is that it believes in human agency and reason: that we can, through our will and hard work, change society for the better. What postmodernism has done is to remind modernity that it has too often failed in this task. Paulo Freire and Henry Giroux (1989: vii) make just this argument:

> The task of modernity, with its faith in reason and emancipation, is perhaps then to renew a sense of urgency in a postmodern world, the world where difference, contingency, and power increasingly challenge the boundaries of nationalism, sexism, racism, and class oppression.

The various criticisms of postmodernist thought, especially as applied to criminological concerns, inevitably raises the question: why bother with it at all? We have been quite persuaded that exposure to this literature is in fact worthwhile and stimulating. First, it sensitizes us to certain ephemeral, fragmentary and chaotic emergent tendencies in contemporary society, although we need not accept the claim that contemporary society as a whole is more postmodern than modern. Second, it exposes some of the pretenses of both mainstream and critical forms of criminological analysis, although we need not embrace deconstructive analysis in its totality. And third, it provides us with some striking concepts (e.g., hypperreality), metaphors and analytical tools (e.g., semiotics) which at least potentially enable us to achieve a richer understanding of contemporary social and criminological phenomena, although we need not adopt these concepts, metaphors and analytical tools uncritically.

The task for critical criminology is to renew a sense of urgency that we can change the direction of the world, and to energize people into working toward that goal. It is impossible in a short paper to lay out all of the directions in which we would move to accomplish this goal, but it is essential that we read Baudrillard as the parable Charles Dickens found in the Ghost of Christmas Future. If we ignore the warning of the postmodernists, our future may be the seamless technological hyperreality that Baudrillard describes.

* *An earlier version of this paper was presented at the annual meeting of the Society for the Study of Social Problems, August, 1992. A later, quite different version of this paper was published as: Martin D. Schwartz and David Friedrichs (1994) "Postmodern Thought and Criminological Discontent: New Metaphors for Understanding Violence," Criminology, 32: 221-246. Grateful thanks are given to Jody Miller and Leon Anderson for their help on a number of crucial*

points, and to a University of Scranton faculty research grant to help with work on this paper.

** *David O. Friedrichs is Professor of Sociology/Criminal Justice at the University of Scranton.*

*** *Martin D. Schwartz is chair of the Department of Sociology and Anthropology at Ohio University.*

NOTES

1. See, e.g., Barak, 1990; Michalowski, 1985; Reiman, 1990; Simon and Eitzen, 1993. For some representative work in and commentary on the radical criminological tradition see Beirne and Quinney, 1982; Chambliss and Mankoff, 1976;
Greenberg, 1981; Inciardi, 1980; Lynch and Groves, 1989; Quinney, 1980.

2. However, see for example Currie, 1985, 1989; Iadicola, 1986; Lea and Young, 1984; MacLean, 1986; Michalowski, 1983; Platt, 1978; or Schwartz and DeKeseredy, 1991a.

3. See, e.g., Daly and Chesney-Lind, 1988; Dobash and Dobash, 1992; Dworkin, 1981; Gelsthorpe and Morris, 1990; Gordon, 1988; Loseke, 1992; Pleck, 1987; Renzetti, 1992; Russell, 1984; Sanday, 1990; Segal and McIntosh, 1993; Smart, 1990, and many more.

4. See, for example, DeKeseredy and Schwartz, 1991; Matthews and Young, 1992; Schwartz and Dekeseredy, 1991; and Young and Matthews, 1992.

5. This is not to suggest that such an introduction has not been tried. There is a rapidly growing literature which provides explications of postmodernist thought. Two of the most helpful are Rosenau (1992) and Sarup (1989). Some other (there are many more) recent books of special relevance to the themes discussed in this piece include Bauman, 1991; Boyne, 1990; Callinicos, 1989; Carty, 1990; Conner, 1989; Denzin, 1991; Frug, 1992; Gane, 1991; Giddens, 1990; Harvey, 1989; Jameson, 1991; Lash, 1990; Nicholson, 1989; Rose, 1991; Seidman and Wagner, 1991; Smart, 1993; Turner, 1990; and Woodiwiss, 1990.

6. There are some who would argue that these theorists all represent the field of post-structuralism, which is but a part of postmodernism (Smart, 1993). However, as seen above, boundary lines are notoriously difficult to draw.

7. However, in at least one reading it is a contradiction (or oxymoronic) to write a postmodern sociology, or to attempt to integrate postmodernist propositions into a conventional sociological framework, insofar as such an attempt at integration is completely at odds with the inherently anarchic character of postmodernism (Agger, 1991).

8. Of the postmodernist thinkers, Foucault's work, especially *Discipline and Punish*, has probably attracted the most attention from criminologists. For some recent illustrative examples of discussion of Foucault's work for criminological concerns see Forsythe (1990) on penal practice, Bell (1991) on sexual assault, and Hunt (1992) on law. But we regard Foucault as a somewhat special case in postmodernist tradition, and we have chosen to focus on other strands as more central to contemporary postmodernist thought.

9. Everything in life can be considered a text in postmodernist thought, including people, events or even writings.

10. It may be worth noting that critical and progressive criminologists have hardly been immune from similar attacks. Boehringer et al. (1983), for example, has chastised the left for preaching irrelevant theory to the masses, suggesting that "the customary working class victim is understandably unimpressed by heady talk of the socialist millennium and this fact has played into the hands of the Right."

11. This is a very difficult area to analyze. Sociologists would not deny that language is a crucial medium through which we filter experience and structure our motivation. Words, then, ARE very important. However, although the postmodernist discourse has been very helpful in keeping this insight at the forefront of social science analysis, it is hardly a unique or new insight.

12. Although corporate violence was not the focus of Edwin Sutherland's early writing on white collar crime it has

attracted a substantial amount of attention in more recent years. Some of the books which provide a theoretical grounding for understanding the origins of corporate violence as well as the growing (if still limited) criminal justice response to it, and some illustrative cases, include: Braithwaite, 1984; Cullen, Maakestad, and Cavender, 1987; Goff and Reasons, 1978; Hills, 1987; Mokhiber, 1988; Reiman, 1990; Simon and Eitzen, 1993; and Snider, 1993.

13. Just as one example, not chosen because it is the worst, one can look at the debates within feminist literature on pornography and prostitution. When we label sex trade workers as oppressed, do we simply add another layer to their oppression by thus labeling them as helpless women when they might not view themselves in this manner (see, e.g., Bell, 1987)? If we follow Patti Lather's advice (1991) to only engage in fully collaborative research, do we work with women who claim to be victimized by men who read pornography? Or do we collaborate with women who make pornography and claim it is not at all harmful?

14. Twitchell (1992: 269) sets the basic argument for a return to the principles of modernity:

> The purposeful obscurity of much contemporary criticism may well prove salutary, may well turn us from the ditzy theories du jour we have hidden behind and return us to what the preprofessional generation (roughly 1890 to 1980) or modern academic gatekeepers did: explain the world around them to the world around them.

REFERENCES

Agger, Ben, 1991, Critical theory, poststructuralism, post-modernism: Their sociological relevance. In W. R. Scott and J. Blake (eds.) *Annual Review of Sociology*. Palo Alto: Annual Reviews.

Bannister, Shelley and Dragan Milovanovic, 1990, The Necessity Defense, Substantive Justice and Oppositional Linguistic Praxis. *International Journal of the Sociology of Law* 18: 179-198.

Barak, Gregg (ed.), 1990, *Crimes By the Capitalist State*. Albany: SUNY Press.

Baudrillard, J., 1983, *In the Shadow of the Silent Majorities*. New York: Semiotext(e).

Bauman, Zygmunt, 1991, *Intimations of Postmodernity*. New York: Routledge.

Beirne, Piers and Richard Quinney (eds.), 1982, *Marxism and Law*. New York: John Wiley.

Bell, Laurie, 1987, *Good Girls, Bad Girls: Sex Trade Workers & Feminists Face to Face*. Toronto: The Women's Press.

Bell, Vikki, 1991, Beyond the "thorny question": Feminism, Foucault and Desexualization of Rape, *International Journal of the Sociology of Law* 19: 83-100.

Best, Steven, 1989, The Commodification of Reality and the Reality of Commodification: Jean Baudrillard and Post-Modernism. *Current Perspectives in Social Theory* 9: 23-51.

Boehringer, Gill, Dave Brown, Brendan Edgeworth, Russell Hogg, and Ian Ramsey, 1983, "Law and Order" for Progressives?: An Australian Response. *Crime and Social Justice* 19: 2-12.

Box-Grainger, Jill, 1986, Sentencing Rapists. In Roger Matthews and Jock Young (eds.), *Confronting Crime*. Beverly Hills: Sage.

Boyne, Roy, 1990, *Foucault and Derrida: The Other Side of Reason*. Winchester, MA: Unwin and Hyman.

Bradbury, Malcolm, 1988, *My Strange Quest for Mensonge*. London: Penguin.

Braithwaite, John, 1984, *Corporate Crime in the Pharmaceutical Industry*. London: Routledge and Kegan Paul.

Callinicos, Alex, 1989, *Against Postmodernism: A Marxist Critique*. New York: St. Martin's Press.

Carlen, Pat, 1992, Criminal Women and Criminal Justice: The Limits to, and

Potentials of, Feminist and Left Realism Perspectives. In Roger Matthews and Jock Young (eds.), *Issues in Realist Criminology*. London: Sage.

Carty, Anthony (ed.), 1990, *Post-Modern Law*. Edinburgh: Edinburgh University Press.

Chambliss, William and Milton Mankoff, 1976, *Whose Law? What Order?* New York: John Wiley.

Collins, Hugh, 1982, *Marxism and Law*. Oxford: Clarendon Press.

Connor, Steven, 1989, *Postmodernist Culture: An Introduction to Theories of the Contemporary*. Cambridge, MA: Blackwell.

Cullen, Francis, T., William J. Maakestad, and Gray Cavender, 1987, *Corporate Crime Under Attack*. Cincinnati: Anderson.

Currie, Dawn H. and Marlee Kline, 1991, Challenging Privilege: Women, Knowledge and Feminist Struggles. *Journal of Human Justice* 2: 1-36.

Currie, Elliott, 1985, *Confronting Crime: An American Challenge*. New York; Pantheon.

____, 1989, Confronting Crime: Looking toward the twenty-first century. *Justice Quarterly* 6: 5-26.

Daly, Kathleen and Meda Chesney-Lind, 1988, Feminism and Criminology. *Justice Quarterly* 5(4): 497-538.

DeKeseredy, Walter S. and Ronald Hinch, 1991, *Woman Abuse: Sociological Perspectives*. Toronto: Thompson Educational Publications.

____ and Martin D. Schwartz, 1991a, Left Realism and Woman Abuse: A Critical Analysis. In Harold E. Pepinsky and Richard Quinney (eds.), *Criminology as Peacemaking*. Bloomington: Indiana University Press.

____ and Martin D. Schwartz, 1991b, U. S. and British Left Realism: A Critical Comparison, *Journal of Offender Rehabilitation and Comparative Criminology* 35(3): 248-262.

Denzin, Norman K., 1986, Postmodern Social Theory. *Sociological Theory* 4: 194-204.

____, 1990, Presidential Address on the Sociological Imagination Revisited. *The Sociological Quarterly* 31: 1-22.

____, 1991, *Images of Postmodern Society - Social Theory and Contemporary Cinema*. Newbury Park, CA: Sage.

Dobash, R. Emerson and Russell P. Dobash, 1992, *Women, Violence and Social Change*. London: Routledge.

Dowd, James J., 1991, Social Psychology in a Postmodern Age: A Discipline Without a Subject. *The American Sociologist* 22: 188-209.

Dworkin, Andrea, 1981, *Pornography: Men Possessing Women*. New York: Perigee.

Edwards, Susan S. M., 1989, *Policing "Domestic" Violence: Women, the Law and the State*. London: Sage.

Ferraris, Maurizio, 1992, Postmodernism and the Deconstruction of Modernism. In Marco Diani (ed.), *The Immaterial Society: Design, Culture, and Technology in the Postmodern World*. Englewood Cliffs: Prentice-Hall.

Fish, Stanley, 1989, *Doing What Comes Naturally: Change, Rhetoric, and the Practice of Theory in Literary and Legal Studies*. Durham, NC: Duke University Press.

Forsythe, Bill, 1990, Foucault's Careceral and Ignatieff's Pentonville - English Prisons and the Revisionist Analysis of Control and Penality. *Policing and Society* 1: 141-158.

Foucault, Michel, 1977, *Discipline and Punish: The Birth of the Prison*. New York: Pantheon.

Freire, Paulo, 1970, *Pedagogy of the Oppressed*. New York: Herder and Herder.

____ and Henry A. Giroux, 1989, Pedagogy, Popular Culture, and Public Life: An Introduction. In Henry Giroux, Roger I. Simon and contributors, *Popular Culture, Schooling and Everyday Life*. Granby: Bergin and Garvey Publishers.

Frug, Mary Joe, 1992, *Postmodern Legal Feminism*. New York: Routledge.

Gane, Mike, 1991, *Baudrillard: Critical and Fatal Theory*. New York:

Routledge.

Gelsthorpe, Loraine, and Allison Morris (eds.), 1990, *Feminist Perspectives in Criminology*. Philadelphia: Open University Press.

Giddens, Anthony, 1990, *Consequences of Modernity*. Stanford, CA: Stanford University Press.

Glassner, Barry, 1992, *Bodies: Overcoming the Tyranny of Perfection*. Los Angeles: Lowell House.

Goff, Colin H. and Charles E. Reasons, 1978, *Corporate Crime in Canada: A Critical Analysis of Anti-Combines Legislation*. Scarborough: Prentice-Hall.

Gordon, Linda, 1988, *Heroes of Their Own Lives*. New York: Viking.

Greenberg, David F., 1981, *Crime and Capitalism*. Palo Alto: Mayfield.

Gregory, Jeanne, 1966, Sex, Class and Crime: Toward a Non-sexist Criminology. In Roger Matthews and Jock Young, (eds.), *Confronting Crime*. Beverly Hills: Sage.

de Haan, Willem, 1991, Universalism and Relativism in Critical Criminology. *The Critical Criminologist* 4(1): 1-2, 7-8.

Handler, Joel, 1992, Postmodernism, Protest, and the New Social Movements. *Law & Society Review* 26: 796-731.

Haraway, Donna, 1990, A Manifesto for Cyborgs: Science, Technology, and Socialist Feminism in the 1980s. In Linda Nicholson (ed.), *Feminism/Postmodernism*. New York: Routledge.

Harvey, David, 1989, *The Condition of Postmodernity - An Enquiry into the Origins of Cultural Change*. Cambridge, MA: Blackwell.

Henry, Stuart, 1991, Introduction: The Post-Modern Perspective in Criminology. In Brian D. MacLean and Dragan Milovanovic (eds.), *New Directions in Critical Criminology*. Vancouver, B.C.: Collective Press.

____ and Dragan Milovanovic, 1991, Constitutive Criminology: The Maturation of Critical Theory. *Criminology* 29: 293-316.

Hills, Stuart L., ed., 1987, *Corporate Violence: Injury and Death for Profit*,

Totowa, NJ: Rowman and Littlefield.

Hirschel, J. David, Ira W. Hutchison, Charles W. Dean and Anne-Marie Mills, 1992, Review Essay on the Law Enforcement Response to Spouse Abuse: Past, Present, and Future. *Justice Quarterly* 9: 247-283.

Horley, Sandra, 1991, *The Charm Syndrome*. London: Harper Papermac.

Hunt, Alan, 1991, Postmodernism and Critical Criminology. In Brian D. MacLean and Dragan Milovanovic (eds.), *New Directions in Critical Criminology*. Vancouver, B.C.: Collective Press.

____, 1992, Foucault's Expulsion of Law: Toward a Retrieval. *Law & Social Inquiry* 17: 1-38.

Hutchinson, Allan C., 1992, Doing the Right Thing? Toward a Postmodern Politics. *Law & Society Review* 26: 773-787.

Huyssen, Andreas, 1986, Mass Culture As Woman: Modernism's Other. In Tania Modleski (ed.), *Studies in Entertainment: Critical Approaches to Mass Culture*. Bloomington: Indiana University Press.

Iadicola, Peter, 1986, Community crime control strategies. *Crime and Social Justice* 25: 140-165.

Inciardi, James A. (ed.), *Radical Criminology: The Coming Crises*. Beverly Hills, CA: Sage.

Jameson, Fredric, 1991, *Postmodernism: Or, The Cultural Logic of Late Capitalism*. Durham, NC: Duke University Press.

Kellner, Douglas, 1990, The Postmodern Turn: Positions, Problems and Prospects. In George Ritzer (ed.), *Frontiers of Social Theory: The New Synthesis*. New York: Columbia University Press.

Lash, Scott, 1990, *Sociology of Postmodernism*. New York: Routledge.

Lather, Patti, 1991, *Getting Smart*. London: Routledge.

Lea, John and Jock Young, 1984, *What is to be Done about Law and Order?* London: Penguin/Pluto.

Loseke, Donileen R., 1992, *The Battered Women and Shelters: The Social*

Construction of Wife Abuse. Albany: State University of New York Press.

Lynch, Michael J. and W. Byron Groves, 1989, *A Primer in Radical Criminology, Second Edition*. New York: Harrow and Heston.

MacLean, Brian D., 1986, *The Political Economy of Crime*. Toronto: Prentice Hall.

____ and Dragan Milovanovic (eds.), 1991, *New Directions in Critical Criminology*. Vancouver, Canada: The Collective Press.

Manning, Peter K., 1991, *New Directions in Critical Criminology*. Vancouver, Canada: The Collective Press.

Matthews, Roger and Jock Young, 1992, Reflections on Realism. In Jock Young and Roger Matthews (eds.), *Rethinking Criminology: The Realist Debate*. London: Sage.

Michalowski, Raymond, 1983, Crime Control in the 1980s: A Progressive Agenda. *Crime and Social Justice* 19: 13-23.

Milovanovic, Dragan, 1986, Juridico-linguistic Communicative Markets: Toward a Semiotic Analysis. *Contemporary Crises* 10: 281-304.

____, 1988, *Primer in the Sociology of Law*. Albany, NY: Harrow & Heston

____, 1989, Critical Criminology and the Challenge of Post Modernism. *The Critical Criminologist* 1 (Winter): 9-10, 17.

____, 1991, Images of Unity and Disunity in the Juridic Subject and the Movement to the Peacemaking Community." In Harold Pepinsky and Richard Quinney (eds.), *Criminology as Peacemaking*. Bloomington: Indiana University Press.

____, 1992, *Postmodern Law and Disorder-Psychoanalytic Semiotics, Chaos and Juridic Exegeses*. Liverpool: Deborah Charles Publications.

Mokhiber, Russell, 1988, *Corporate Crime and Violence -- Big Business Power and the Abuse of the Public Trust*. San Francisco: Sierra Books.

Nicholson, Linda (ed.), 1989, *Feminism/Postmodernism*. New York: Routledge.

Pepinsky, Harold E. and Paul Jesilow, 1984, *Myths That Cause Crime*. Cabin John, MD: Seven Locks Press.

Pfohl, Stephen, 1985, Toward a Sociological Deconstruction of Social Problems. *Social Problems* 32: 228-231.

____, 1990, Terror of the Simulacra: Struggles for Justice and the Postmodern. In School of Justice Studies (ed.), *New Directions in the Study of Justice*. New York: Plenum.

____, 1992, Postmodernity as a social problem: Race, class, gender and the new social order. *Preliminary Program: Annual Meeting of the Society for the Study of Social Problems*.

Platt, Tony, 1978, Street crime: A view from the left. *Crime and Social Justice* 9: 26-34.

Pleck, Elizabeth, 1987, *Domestic Tyranny*. New York: Oxford University Press.

Quinney, Richard, 1980, *Class, State and Crime*. New York: Longman.

Reiman, Jeffrey, 1990, *Justice and Modern Moral Philosophy*. New Haven: Yale University Press.

Renzetti, Claire M., 1992, *Violent Betrayal*. Newbury Park, CA: Sage.

Richardson, Laurel, 1988, The Collective Story: Postmodernism and the Writing of Sociology. *Sociological Focus* 21(3): 199-208.

Ritzer, George, 1990, *Frontiers of Social Theory: The New Syntheses*. New York: Columbia University Press.

Rose, Margaret, 1991, *The Post-Modern and the Post-Industrial*. Cambridge: Cambridge University Press.

Rosenau, Pauline Marie, 1992, *Post-Modernism and the Social Sciences - Insights, Inroads, and Intrusions*. Princeton: Princeton University Press.

Russell, Diana E. H., 1984, *Sexual Exploitation*. Beverly Hills, CA: Sage.

Salyer, Lucy E., 1991, The Constitutive Nature of Law in American History. *Legal Studies Forum* 15: 61-64.

Sanday, Peggy Reeves, 1990, *Fraternity Gang Rape*. New York: New York University Press.

Sarup, Madan, 1989, *An Introductory Guide to Post-Structuralism and Postmodernism*. Athens: University of Georgia Press.

Schwartz, Martin D., 1989, The Undercutting Edge in Critical Criminology. *Critical Criminologist* 1(2): 1-5.

____, 1991, The Future of Critical Criminology. In Brian D. MacLean and Dragan Milovanovic (eds.), *New Directions in Critical Criminology*. Vancouver, B.C.: Collective Press.

____ and Walter S. DeKeseredy, 1991, Left Realist Criminology: Strengths, Weaknesses and the Feminist Critique. *Law, Crime and Social Change: An International Journal* 15 (1): 51-72.

Seaton, James, 1991, The Two Branches of the Law and Literature Movement: A Critique of Stanley Fish. *Legal Studies Forum* 15: 65-74.

Segal, Lynne and Mary McIntosh (eds.), 1993, *Sex Exposed: Sexuality and the Pornography Debate*. New Brunswick, NJ: Rutgers University Press.

Seidman, Steven and David Wagner, 1991, *Postmodernism and Social Theory*. New York: Cambridge, MA: Blackwell.

Simon, David R. and D. Stanley Eitzen, 1993, *Elite Deviance, 4th ed.* Boston: Allyn and Bacon.

Smart, Barry, 1993, *Postmodernity*. London: Routledge.

Smart, Carol, 1989, *Feminism and the Power of Law*. London: Routledge.

____, 1990, Feminist Approaches to Criminology or Postmodern Woman Meets Atavistic Man. In Loraine Gelsthorpe and Alison Morris (eds.), *Feminist Perspectives in Criminology*. Philadelphia: Open University Press.

Snider, Laureen, 1990, Cooperative Models and Corporate Crime: Panacea or Cop-Out? *Crime & Delinquency* 36: 373-390.

____, 1993, *Bad Business - Corporate Crime in Canada*. Scarborough, Ont.: Nelson.

Tong, Rosemary, 1989, *Feminist Thought*. Boulder: Westview.

Turner, Bryan S. (ed.), 1990, *Theories of Modernity and Postmodernity*. Newbury Park, CA: Sage.

Twitchell, James B., 1992, *Carnival Culture: The Trashing of Taste in America*. New York: Columbia University Press.

Weinstein, Deena and Michael A. Weinstein, 1993, Postmodernizing (Macro)sociology. *Sociological Inquiry* 63: 224-238.

Willis, Susan, 1991, *A Primer for Daily Life*. London: Routledge.

Woodiwiss, Anthony, 1990, *Social Theory After Postmodernism: Rethinking Production, Law and Class*. Winchester, MA: Unwin and Hyman.

Woolgar, Steve and Dorothy Pawluch, 1985, Ontological Gerrymandering: The Anatomy of Social Problems Explanations. *Social Problems* 32: 214-227.

Young, Jock and Roger Matthews (eds.), 1992, *Rethinking Criminology: The Realist Debate*. Newbury Park, CA: Sage.

Chapter IX

THE DISCURSIVE CONSTRUCTION OF 'DELINQUENT' GIRLS: RACE, CLASS, SEXUALITY AND GENERATION IN PROBATION INVESTIGATION REPORTS

Jody Miller*

While feminist researchers have extensively documented gender bias within the field of criminology (Cain, 1989b; Campbel, 1981; Chesney-Lind, 1977, 1978, 1988; Daly and Chesney-Lind, 1988; Gelsthorpe and Morris, 1990; Leonard, 1982; Smart, 1976, 1977), we have rarely examined our own theories and research for biases related to race, class and ethnicity. Instead, feminist scholarship about gender and criminal justice has tended to examine gender discrimination extracted from its race and class contexts. Only recently have debates among feminist criminologists expanded to include critiques of our own universalizing tendencies (Daly, 1991; Hudson, 1989, 1990; Klein, 1991; Rice, 1990).

The goals of the current research are to examine the ways that race and class shape the treatment of delinquent girls, and in doing so, to contribute to a theoretical alternative to unitary explanations of gender discrimination--one which recognizes the interconnected dynamics of race, class, age, sexuality and gender. To do so, I will examine investigation reports written to provide judges with recommendations for deciding upon girls' dispositions. Specifically, I will provide a detailed analysis of the discursive frameworks drawn upon to describe delinquent girls and to justify the court's decisions about their handling. The handling of delinquent girls is based not just on their actions, but also on their ways of being in the world. I will reveal how the interpretive frameworks used by juvenile court officials are shaped by hegemonic understandings of race, class, gender, sexuality and generation.

The most widely accepted theoretical framework used by feminists to explain the treatment of girls within the juvenile justice system is the thesis of judicial paternalism. According to this perspective, female offenders are treated more severely than male offenders at all levels of the juvenile justice system. This is a consequence of two factors. First, it is theorized that female criminals are treated harshly in order to punish them for violating normative gender expectations (Armstrong, 1977; Cain 1989b; Figueria-McDonough, 1985; Mann, 1979; Parisi, 1982). Second, it is argued that punitiveness is a consequence of attempts to protect girls "from 'temptation' and their own sexuality" (Chesney-Lind, 1977: 128, 1978, 1988; Chesney-Lind and Sheldon, 1992).

A large number of studies have documented the existence of gender discrimination within the juvenile justice system (Alder, 1984, Cain, 1989a, 1989b; Canter, 1982: 388; Chesney-Lind, 1977, 1978, 1988; Chesney-Lind and Shelden, 1992; Figueira-McDonough, 1985: 279-280; Gelsthorpe, 1986, 1989; Gelsthorpe and Morris, 1990; Hudson, 1989, 1990; Kersten, 1989; Krohn, et. al., 1983; Mann, 1979, 1984; Sarri, 1976; Visher, 1983, but see Teilmann and Landry, 1981). Discriminatory treatment has been reported in varying degrees at all levels of the system: police arrest and diversion decisions, police decisions to forward cases to court, adjudication and disposition decisions, and treatment received within placement facilities. Often these findings are drawn upon to offer support for the judicial paternalism thesis.

However, the notion of "paternalism" as an explanatory tool for the treatment of females is race and class bound (Collins, 1990; Davis, 1981; Rice, 1990; Smith and Stewart; 1983; White, 1985; Woodward, 1988). In the United States, protection has been extended to middle class and white women, to the exclusion of poor and working class women and women of color. Judicial paternalism may contribute to our understanding of the types of discriminatory treatment faced by middle class white status offenders. However, it provides limited theoretical usefulness for explaining the variations in girls' treatment by race and class.

While it is sometimes mentioned in passing in their analyses (Chesney-Lind and Shelden, 1992; Gelsthorpe, 1989), there has been little attempt by researchers to analyze in depth the impact of race and class on the types of treatment girls face within the juvenile justice system. This is despite the fact that much research within the field of criminology reveals the existence of widespread racial and class bias within the criminal and juvenile justice systems (Bondavalli and Bondavalli, 1981: 55-56; Chesney-Lind and Shelden, 1992; Dannefer and Schutt, 1982; Empey and Stafford, 1991; Feyerherm, 1981; Krisberg, et al., 1986; Krohn, et. al., 1980 Laub and McDermott, 1985; Quinney, 1974; Rice, 1990; Sarri, 1983; Schuster, 1981; Scott, 1982; Visher,

1983; although for contradictory findings, see Empey and Stafford, 1991: 315). These studies reveal that the investigation of gender discrimination divorced from the contexts of discrimination based on race and class is problematic, and provides a limited picture of the true and complex dynamics of girls' experiences within the juvenile justice system.

METHOD

Data for this project were gathered from the case files of girls on probation in an area office of the Los Angeles County Probation Department. The area office was chosen because it was a racially mixed region within the county, with significant populations of whites, Latino/a, and African Americans, and therefore provides a useful means of comparative analysis. Approximately 200 girls were on probation in the region when the investigation began in May 1992. For the current research, I stratified the population of girls by race, then randomly selected 30 case files for close content analysis: these included 10 African American girls, 10 Latina girls and 10 white girls.[1] In addition, I analyzed these cases by subdividing them into four categories: AFDC recipients, non-AFDC recipients with family income under $20,000, family income between $20,000 and $45,000. This allowed me to also explore within group differences by class.[2]

Within the Los Angeles juvenile justice system, probation officers do not only function in supervisory positions; instead, there are officers whose primary role is that of investigator. When a juvenile is arrested and the case is pursued for further action, her file ends up assigned to an investigating probation officer, who, based on interviews with the girl, family member(s), and other interested parties such as school personnel, creates an investigation report. This document includes all information deemed pertinent for decision-making, as well as the probation officer's disposition recommendation. The report is forwarded to the judge hearing the case, who then makes a disposition decision. In most cases, the judges do not deviate from the disposition recommendations put forth by probation investigators.

Information included in the probation officer's report includes: sex, age and birthdate, ethnic origin, religion, natural parents' marital status and legal custody of the juvenile, stepparents, a description of the offense and companion(s) in the offense, a victim's report, and a description of the juvenile's prior record. In addition, there is a section in the report for discussion of the juvenile's personal history, including the following: type of residence, length of occupancy, mortgage/rent, occupants in the home, parents' and minor's employment statuses, occupations and incomes, other sources of income (such as AFDC), the juvenile's physical, mental and emotional health, substance abuse, gang activity, and behavior in school (including grades, attendance, conduct and suspensions). The next section of the report includes the minor's statement, parent(s)'s statement, and the statements of any interested parties (such as counselors or teachers). The report concludes with the probation officer's analysis and plan. This is the section I have analyzed most carefully (though not exclusively), because this is where officers' make inferences about the youths' demeanor, behavior, dangerousness, and rehabilitative needs, based on all of the information listed previously in the report.

Critiques have been raised regarding methodological problems in choosing data from case files, because the information contained therein may be incomplete for the purposes of social science research (Garfinkel, 1967; Gelsthorpe, 1989). However, these files are uniquely suited for the current research specifically because they are not being examined for "accurate" information. Investigative officers draw upon and help create discursive frameworks in their reports in order to convince judges that their recommendations are correct. I am not making claims about the truthfulness of the information in investigation reports, but am instead interested in what these discursive frameworks look like, and what they imply about juvenile court understandings of race, class, age and sexuality in the handling of girls.

In the sections that follow, I will examine the discursive constructions of delinquent girls, beginning by discussing age and generation.[3] These issues revealed themselves in several ways: first, in probation officers' reinforcement of adult and parental authority; second, in probation officers' commentaries on the parents' adequacy as parents and accountability in their daughters' behavior. The latter commentaries were situated in varied race and class contests. After discussing generational dynamics, I will discuss the construction of sexuality, pregnancy and motherhood in investigative reports. Finally, I will discuss strategies for describing girls' behaviors and demeanor. These strategies involved individualizing, and in some cases pathologizing girls' behavior. In addition, several patterns of discursive constructions emerged that categorized white, Latina and African American girls in varying ways.

GENERATIONAL DYNAMICS

Parental Authority

The creation of the juvenile justice system was grounded in the development of the doctrine of *parens patriae* and the construction of the delinquent child as in need of protection and guidance (Chesney-Lind, 1978; Chesney-Lind and Shelden, 1992; Empey and Stafford, 1991; Mann, 1984). According to Platt, "[m]any of the child savers' reforms were aimed at imposing sanctions on conduct unbecoming youth and disqualifying youth from the benefit of adult privileges" (in Chesney-Lind, 1978: 172). This concern with the control and development of children's morality led to a commitment by the court to uphold parental authority. This commitment remains, and many girls find entry into the juvenile justice system through complaints initiated by their parents (Chesney-Lind, 1982, 1988; Chesney-Lind and Shelden, 1992; Hudson, 1989, 1990; Teilmann and Landry, 1981).

Not surprisingly, probation officers often discussed girls within the investigation reports by examining their relationships to their parents, particularly in terms of their willingness to accept both parental and adult authority. To begin with, hierarchical relationships between adults and juveniles were emphasized in the reports by consistently referring to the individual in question as "minor" or "the minor" rather than by name. In addition, parents were not referred to throughout by name, but were categorized as "the father" or "the mother." This treatment was consistent within all of the investigative reports. Likewise, the investigating officers did not call themselves by name, but, in the context of the reports were "this officer." These linguistic constructs functioned to diminish the individuality of girls, as well as their parents and probation officers, and highlight and mark the girls' lack of full adulthood, while reinforcing the power relations of adults over them.

Girls were spoken of harshly in the case files when they challenged these generational power relations. One way some girls challenged this relationship was by not accepting the definition of the situation offered by their parents, probation officer, or other authority figure. Tonia,[4] for example, was an upper middle income African American girl arrested for shoplifting. The probation officer, mother and a counselor attempted to situate her shoplifting in a framework of emotional problems requiring counseling. Tonia rejected this definition, and as a result, the probation officer concluded, "minor denies that there is a problem. She has very little insight into her own behavior." Likewise, another probation officer expressed concern about Amber, an

African American girl, because she "refused all help" from the adults around her.

More frequently, girls were criticized for what was seen as more direct defiance of parental authority. Marsha, a middle income white girl, was arrested after a fight with her mother. According to the investigative report, when "the minor became belligerent towards her...the victim felt that the minor was beyond her control and she was taken into custody...." Later in the report, the probation officer continued: "the minor acted in a defiant and disobedient manner toward the mother....Minor refuses to adhere to any parental instructions and has had absolutely no concept to the seriousness of her behavior....[She] flat out refuses her mother's control." As a result, part of the probation officers' concept of their role was to help restore parental authority.

For example, Dora, an upper middle income Latina, was arrested after taking her parents' car without permission. While the offense was not deemed serious, the probation officer recommended formal probation because "she seems to be having difficulties in following the directions of her mother and may be beyond her control." The definition of juveniles as "beyond parental control" was frequently called upon to justify official intervention, as in Dora's case, where it was used to "provide her mother with a certain amount of support and guidance in helping to control her." This goal of restoring parental authority sometimes came as a result of explicitly rejecting the girl's definition of her relationship with her parents.

Finally, girls were critiqued for attempting to exert their adulthood. Diana, a middle income African American girl, was harshly described by the probation officer because she was perceived as "insistent upon having her way at all costs. She shows no respect to her mother and does nothing [she] does not want to do." According to the probation officer, Diana "talks to her mother as a peer. She responds to the probation officer in much the same manner." As a result, the probation officer stated, "this is the consummate spoiled brat. One who has decided she is running her own world." Diana's attempt to exert her adulthood by interacting with adults without proper deference was used to justify the recommendation that she receive counseling. At the end of the report, the officer softened, but remained paternalistic in recommending that "[t]he minor is not lost, she just needs a lot of help."

Diana's case was not unique, instead there was a tendency to view early adulthood negatively. Amber, for example, was critiqued because "she thinks she is grown." And Vanessa, an African American AFDC recipient, was described as a "young lad[y] with a desire to grow up fast and be on [her] own." The probation officer recommended that "minor needs to become involved in a counseling program so that she can explore the problems of growing up into adulthood in a more mature fashion."

Class, Gender and Parental Accountability

While girls from all class and racial classifications were expected to respect parental authority, many files secondarily assessed the competence of parents, labelling some more fit than others. These labels tended to emerge in specific class contexts. Probation officers' constructions of parental abilities and responsibilities revealed greater approval of middle class mothers, parents who were married and living together and fathers who took the initiative to be interviewed. Disapproval of the family environment tended to be expressed more harshly against working class and single parents. Because the majority of parents interviewed at the probation department were mothers, these constructs were most frequently levied at mothers.

In fact, it was not assumed that fathers had a responsibility to be interviewed for the probation report. Fathers' absences from the investigation interview were never commented on in the probation reports, but mothers' absences were perceived as indicative of family problems, for example, one probation officer "suspect[ed]" that Leanne, a working class Latina, had "serious problem in the home," in part because of "the *failure* of the mother to attend the interview..." [my emphasis]. No such expectations of fathers' behavior emerged. All of the fathers who came for interviews with investigating officers were described positively as parents. For example, Maria's father, a working class Latino, was described as "making an honest effort to provide effective parental supervision." According to the probation officer, he "appears to be a concerned parent who has had difficulty controlling minor's behavior both in and outside the home." However, he "feels capable of controlling minor's behavior with probation assistance."

Harsher language was used to describe Rochelle's mother, an African American woman receiving AFDC to support her family. She was described as "cooperative...but this officer's impression was that mother had little in the way of parenting skills and has allowed her daughter to become a school dropout, which contributed to her involvement in a delinquent act." In this instance, in contrast to Maria's, Rochelle is not just out of her mother's control, but her mother is conceived as partially responsible for this by having *allowed* her inappropriate behavior. Likewise, Becky's participation in school vandalism was explained by the probation officer as stemming in part from emotional problems, but there was implicit mother-blaming in the officer's discussion of her mother, a white AFDC recipient who had a number of children and a husband with a long term illness: "It is believed that this situation rendered the mother relatively non-nurturing, if ever she was, and it is highly unlikely that minor or anyone else in the family was ever aware or able to express the frustrations created by unfulfilled needs."

Middle class parents tended not to be held responsible for their children's behavior in the ways that working class and poor parents were. Vickie's mother, a middle class Latina, "impressed the probation officer as being a caring and supportive parent." Similarly, while Rochelle and Becky's mothers had been implicitly held accountable for their daughter's behaviors, Linda's middle class Latino parents were not held responsible for her assault on another girl:

> The minor seems impulsive and she had been having some problems getting along at home and in school. The reasons for these problems are not really known as she has a united family, but apparently she had the need to feel more important that was satisfied by her negative associations and behavior.

This notion of the traditional middle class nuclear family was common. Something about being middle class and/or dual parent provided many families with an air of legitimacy that allowed them to escape discursive frameworks which held them accountable for their children's actions. Tonia's upper middle income African American parents "have provided her with a stable home and financial security that she has taken for granted." Similarly, Susan's family was described as an all-American white middle class family: "The minor comes from a united family and they appear interested and concerned in her welfare." In general then, working class parents, especially mothers, were held accountable for their children's involvement in delinquent activities, while middle class parents were perceived as having provided their children with "the good life," which their children refused or were unable to accept.

SEXUALITY, PREGNANCY AND MOTHERHOOD

Much of the research on the treatment of girls within the juvenile justice system focuses on the treatment of female status offenders, because their handling often provides the clearest examples of the system's preoccupation with the protection and control of juvenile morality, particularly the sexual morality of girls (Chesney-Lind, 1977, 1978; Hudson, 1989, 1990; Sarri, 1976). In addition, evidence on the impact of deinstitutionalization and diversion programs point to a continued preoccupation with the "morality" of delinquent girls (Alder, 1984; Chesney-Lind, 1988; Chesney-Lind and Shelden, 1992).

Interestingly, this was not an issue dwelt upon for very many of the girls in the current investigation. This may be due to the fact that these were girls on probation for criminal offenses rather than status offenses, and may also be reflective of the more punitive approach to delinquency that has shaped juvenile justice in the last decade (Krisbery, et al., 1986). Nevertheless, the handful of girls who probation officers discussed in terms of their sexual experiences and/or maternity are worth investigation for what they reveal about normative standards of morality and definitions of appropriate motherhood. In all, there were four cases in which sexuality, pregnancy and/or motherhood constituted the framework in which probation officers discussed girls. They included two African American girls, both of whose families were in higher income brackets (one $20,000 to $45,000; one over $45,000), one white girl whose family was on AFDC, and one lower income/non AFDC Latina.

The first case involved Angela, a middle income African American girl, arrested for bringing a gun to school. According to the report, Angela was threatened by a female classmate who claimed that Angela had let the girl's brother and two other boys fondle her. The girl was physically larger than Angela and according to Angela, "there were all sorts of rumors of what I did. I was going to scare her....The deans are afraid of the kids and you have to take it up on [sic.] yourself when there are problems." Angela's mother agreed with her daughter that "the school has very poor control of students" and felt this was why her daughter "overreacted" and brought a gun to school. While Angela and her mother situated the event in terms of her daughter's personal safety in the school environment, the probation officer resituated the event with a focus on Angela's alleged sexual behavior:

> The initial incident...involved the allegation that the minor had allowed other boys to fondle her inappropriately. Minor claims these are just rumors. Counseling should focus on this area and on the minor's ability to maintain social relationships at school....Given the aggravating circumstances surrounding the present offense it is felt that the minor should go home under a stayed placement order rather than straight home on probation.

Two issues are significant in the probation officer's framing of events. First, the minor was not believed. Her testimony that the girl who threatened her was spreading rumors was discounted, and instead was seen as further evidence that she needed treatment to uncover the underlying causes of her sexual behavior and her denial of its existence. Second, the probation officer was placing a value judgment on Angela's alleged sexual behavior, labeling it "inappropriate" and recommending that her disposition be more severe as a result.[5] The "aggravating circumstances" surrounding the offense were not that the school environment was not safe, but that the minor was allegedly sexually active; and as a result, this was used as evidence of her need to receive "appropriate counseling."

Angela's case was unique in the manner that she was framed sexually. Three other girls were framed by probation officers in related ways, but in reference to pregnancy and motherhood rather than specifically sexuality. Stacy, an upper middle income African American girl, and Heather, a white AFDC recipient, both were framed by probation officers in terms of the need to protect their "unborn children." Heather was arrested for shoplifting, and was pregnant at the time of the investigation. Although it was her first arrest and she was nearly of age, the probation officer chose to recommend a more restrictive treatment than often recommended under such circumstances, in order to monitor the "safety" of Heather's fetus:

> Probation officer feels that minor is too irresponsible to be expected to function adequately on an informal probation program and it is felt that formal probation services will be required to monitor subject's future behavior if only for her unborn child's benefit.

Similarly, Stacy was pregnant at the time of her arrest. Her parents were divorced, and her father, who was wealthy, accused her of having an adult boyfriend and of using drugs. Both Stacy and her mother, who was lower income, denied that she was using drugs. The probation officer believed the father rather than Stacy and her mother, and concluded:

> The minor is pregnant and possibly involved with drugs....[She] should be committed to the California Youth Authority (CYA) where they have a unit for pregnant girls. They would be able to provide for the safety of the fetus within this minor. She would not be able to use drugs during her pregnancy.

Further, the probation officer stated, "She has made irresponsible decisions about boyfriends and pregnancy. The minor is in need of counseling." While the probation officer had no evidence of drug abuse, she recommended the harshest sentence available for juvenile offenders because of her perception that the fetus needed protection. In both Stacy's and Heather's cases, the social control imposed upon them was more intense specifically because they were pregnant. The sanctions recommended by the probation officers were less about their delinquent acts than about the desire to monitor their pregnancies, "unborn babies," and motherhood.

In a similar case, Sylvia, a lower income Latina girl, was framed by the probation officer in very negative terms due in part to the probation officer's perception of her as a bad mother. Arrested for a stolen vehicle charge, "the minor has set a pattern of living on the streets generally abandoning her child to associate with car thieves." It was stressed several times in the report that she had "left her child," who remained in the care of Sylvia's mother. According to the probation officer, Sylvia "generally rationalized her socially deviant behavior...[and] failed to acknowledge the seriousness of her actions...." It is significant that the only minor who was described as deviant in any of the reports I investigated was one whose "deviance" was clearly linked to being a bad mother and abandoning her child.

These four cases point to the fact that, for at least some girls, sexuality, pregnancy and motherhood are drawn upon to wield greater social control over their lives. The interesting question that remains, however, is why this treatment was the exception rather than the rule, particularly given the fact that these were not the only girls who were sexually active and/or mothers. In the following section, I will explore the more frequent discursive frameworks drawn upon to construct delinquent girls.

RACE, CLASS AND THE CONSTRUCTION OF FEMALE DELINQUENCY

Premise of Individualized Causation

Within the investigation reports, there was a consistent discursive pattern among probation officers of emphasizing individualized causes of girls' delinquent behaviors, removed from their social contexts and wider social, political or economic causes. Officers did not attempt to search for answers to the question of why girls committed offenses beyond the individuals' emotional health, family dynamics or peer group influences. Evidence of the wider social influences on delinquent activities, particularly among African American girls, was frequently deemed unimportant or incorrect, and girls' behaviors were resituated in a discursive framework emphasizing individualized solutions. Girls who attempted to call upon wider social influences to explain their behavior faced harsher interpretations of their behavior and attitudes because they were perceived as not taking responsibility for their actions.

Amber was an African American girl whose family received AFDC. Involved in a fight with a school official, she was put in a choke-hold that she and her mother both claimed left her "foaming at the mouth." As a result, she became "very loud and aggressive...extremely uncooperative and violent," shouting threats and obscenities at school officials and the officers who arrested her. While the minor framed her behavior in terms of the outrage caused by her treatment by school personnel, the probation officer and school officials deemed her anger an inappropriate way of responding, and even argued that it might be a sign of mental illness. While admitting that one-on-one, she "was pleasant, cooperative, and promised to do better," the probation officer argued that Amber didn't act "as a normal person would" when she was angry:

> Minor has severe problems controlling her emotions when upset. Whether this is indicative of severe mental disorder or simply immaturity and rage, is not known....she needs to have a psychological evaluation....A counseling program...coupled with a psychological evaluation should help minor gain insight into her self and her behavior.

Gloria's experience provided the most vivid example of the lengths to which probation officers would go in order to reinscribe juveniles' behavior as an individual trouble. A lower income African American girl, Gloria was arrested after taking a gun to school. According to the minor, she "had been threatened and told she would be 'jumped' after school by...gang members" and therefore borrowed the gun to protect herself. She had "told the assistant principal...about the threats against her" and explained that "she would not have taken the gun to school if they, the school, had taken care of the problem she had reported to them."

Gloria was placed in a violent school environment, and attempted to protect herself by brandishing a weapon. Rather than examine the dangerous environment she was expected to survive in, the probation officer deemed her response not just inappropriate but indicative of deeper mental health problems: "Due to threats against the minor, she feels she was justified in bringing a loaded gun to school. This type of thinking concerns this officer and feels the minor needs and would benefit from a program of counseling." This case reveals the lengths juvenile justice officers will go to in ignoring the social causes of delinquent acts.

Roots of Delinquent Behavior

The most striking difference in the framing of delinquent girls by race was in the discursive constructs used to describe the roots of their delinquent activities. African American girls' behavior was sometimes pathologized, as seen above in Amber's (and to a certain extent Gloria's) case; it was also framed in terms of inappropriate "lifestyle" choices. On the other hand, white girls' delinquent acts were frequently described as resulting from their being "easily influenced" by "negative peer influences," or, less frequently, as a result of "abandonment issues" having to do with their relationships with their fathers. Significantly, these discursive constructs were not used in *any* of the analyses of African American girls. Latina girls were framed using both those constructs typically used to describe African American girls, and those used to describe white girls.

Janice, an African American AFDC recipient, was arrested after she lied to the police "in order to protect her brother." In making recommendations to the judge, the probation officer stated: "She needs to participate in counseling so that she can explore her current lifestyle and set positive goals for her future." These discursive constructs--"positive goals" and "lifestyle"--seem to function as codes for class expectations. In a more blatant example, Diana, a middle income African American girl, was harshly criticized for failing to assimilate into a middle class lifestyle when provided with the opportunity. According to the probation officer, Diana resented her mother for divorcing her father. However, the officer was very critical of Diana's feelings, and her criticism was steeped in class-based value judgments:

> [Minor] knows that when her mother and father were together the family was on welfare and living in the inner city. In the process of *lifting her family up*, the mother has found that she is not at all in touch with minor's stated desires, which seem to be to return to the *insidious place* they left [my emphases].

In both Diana's and Janice's cases, social class was reflected in the probation officers' recommendations. For Diana, non-conformity to proper class and age positions (see above) were at the heart of the sanctions the probation officer recommended. Diana was defined as "manipulative" and "self-centered," and the officer stated that "the minor needs to delve into why she finds it necessary to behave as she does." The probation officer pathologized her behavior, rather than examining what values or relationships her mother may have left behind in the "inner city" that Diana might legitimately choose not to abandon.

Like Diana, Tonia, an African-American girl, was judged harshly for rejecting the upper-middle class expectations that came with her family's position: "Minor is spoiled and immature. She lives for the moment and is not goal oriented." According to Tonia's mother, she "gravitates toward losers." However, the twist in Tonia's case, which was not found in the descriptions of lower income African American girls, but was found consistently among white and Latina girls of all income levels, was the label "self destructive" rather than having negative "lifestyle" choices. In being framed as "self destructive," she was in need of help and protection. On the other hand, girls with poor "lifestyle" choices were framed instead as deviant, as when Leanne, a lower income Latina, was described as "devoid of values" for her participation in a gang.

Except for the label "self destructive," even Tonia was not afforded the explanations frequently drawn upon to describe white girls' actions. In contrast to the above examples, the delinquent acts of a number of white girls were framed in ways that emphasized their vulnerability to the "corrupting" influences of others, or their fragility as a result of emotional problems. In these cases, the girls weren't delinquent because of some "badness" within them, but from some weakness or from external sources. Becky, an AFDC recipient arrested for vandalism, was described as having a difficult time "withstand[ing] the negative influence" of her peers. In addition, the probation officer theorized that Becky had "an unhealthy blocking of feelings and growing rage." As a result, the officer concluded:

> It is very doubtful that she would commit this type of offense of society again but probation officer believes that she is very capable of becoming self-destructive without intense therapy. This destruction might begin as simply as failing her classes but would then progress into poor, destructive relationships and any negative activity that might result from those relationships.

In addition to negative peer influences and self destructive tendencies, several white girls were described as also having low self images. Nowhere did such a construct appear to describe African American girls. Cathy, a lower income white girl, was characterized as "easily influenced by others." She has "a tendency to pick the wrong kind of friends, but she does not seem to be delinquently sophisticated." As a result, the probation officer recommended that "participation in counseling might help her develop a more positive self-image and ability to think for herself." Cathy's behavior was not characterized as originating from her own delinquent proclivities, but rather from those of negative peers.

Similarly, Marsha, a middle income white girl "does not appear inordinately delinquent...[but] can best be described as a teenager unable to set limits for herself....Minor has low self-esteem and has continually re-involved herself with less than positive peers." Her need for help was framed as stemming from "low-esteem" rather than from lifestyle choices; the discourse drawn upon described her as influenced by negative peers, rather than being inherently delinquent herself. Likewise, Karen was a middle income white girl arrested for shoplifting. While Leanne was described as "devoid of values" for her gang involvement (see above), Karen's gang involvement was framed as a consequence of "family dysfunction":

> Although in a relative sense, this is not a serious offense, there are numerous severe problems in this minor's life which need ongoing supervision. Her stepfather is an alcoholic and her mother is an enabler....Minor denies that she is self-destructing by her ongoing truancy, gang associations et cetera....Minor must become involved in some type of self-help group to deal with her feelings regarding her alcoholic stepfather, her natural father's abandonment of her and her anger towards her mother for her own codependency.

Interestingly, Latina girls were framed in ways that paralleled those found in the descriptions of both African American and white girls. Some Latina girls were characterized by drawing upon paternalistic discursive constructs similar to those describing white girls, as "self-destructive," having a "negative self-image," and "negative peers." For example, of Dora, the probation officer said, "[a]lthough this offense should not be taken lightly, it appears as though she may have been acting from emotions rather than in a delinquent manner." Other Latina girls were framed in more punitive ways (see Leanne and Sylvia above).

This dichotomized treatment of Latina girls may be related to probation officers' interpretations of gender norms in Latino culture. Perhaps girls who violate gender norms by participating in offenses deemed particularly masculine (in the above cases, car theft, burglary and gang membership) face harsher treatment than Latina girls who commit offenses perceived as feminine, or commit offenses as a result of their involvement with a boyfriend. These findings point to the need for further investigation of the treatment of delinquents from Latino communities, an area of research that is currently lacking (Bondavalli and Bondavalli, 1981; 50-51; Empey and Stafford, 1991).

DISCUSSION

Unitary analyses of gender discrimination, based on comparisons between the treatment of delinquent boys and girls, miss the intersecting dimensions of race, class, age and gender. Through detailed content analyses of investigation reports, I have attempted to explore the variations and nuances which exist in the construction of delinquent girls. While the analysis in this paper was based on a relatively small number of cases, it reveals many complexities in the discursive construction of female delinquency. The interpretive frameworks used by juvenile court officials are shaped, not simply by assumptions about gender, but by hegemonic understandings of race, class and generational power relations as well.

The discursive shifts that took place within specific race and class contexts were often quite subtle, but revealed themselves in significant ways. Girls were expected to recognize and accept parental and adult authority, as well as the definitions of their experiences as presented by adults (and specifically by probation officers). Challenges to this generational authority structure were not taken lightly. Similarly, middle class girls were expected to appreciate their class privilege and behave accordingly, and lower income girls were expected to aspire to middle class values and goals. Paternalistic discursive frameworks were frequently called upon to explain the behavior of white and Latina girls, while punitive constructs were more likely to be used to describe African American girls. These findings represent general patterns in the data, rather than universals.

The significance of my findings lie in their challenge to the universalizing tendencies of feminist criminology. The differences in probation officers' constructs of delinquent girls may be the result of several factors. First, some researchers have indicated differences in girls' gender ideologies by race (Dill,

1987; Ladner, 1987; Malson, 1983; Rice, 1990). According to Rice:

> black girls develop early on a particular set of subcultural values which stress strength, independence, resilience and perseverance and which are necessary in the face of a racist and sex-segregated labor market....However, these qualities, when judged by ethnocentric standards, are viewed as 'unfeminine' (1990: 60).

Differences in girls displays of gender may account for some of the variation in probation officers' constructions of their behavior. Given evidence that reveals the tendency to punish females for violating normative gender expectations, and given the fact that these normative expectations specifically reflect white middle class values, African American girls and lower income girls are less likely to "measure up."

In addition, however, cultural stereotypes about women and girls differently depict girls by race and class, and may be drawn upon by probation officers, consciously or unconsciously, in their attempts to analyze the "needs" of the girls they interview and report on. Cultural stereotypes of white females depict them as "tender, warm, quiet and gentle" while depicting African American females as "aggressive, rebellious, rude and loud" (Smith and Stewart, 1983: 2). Likewise, popular images of Latina women present them as submissive and dependent, a counterpart to Latino men's machismo (Sanchez, 1990; Zinn, 1982). It is likely that girls' treatment is partially rooted in these stereotypes.

Feminist analyses of the treatment of delinquent girls must take into account the complexities and variations in the constructs used to describe the girls and make decisions about them. Analyses which seek only to examine judicial paternalism in the handling of girls are theoretically limited. We must continue to examine more carefully the relationships between race, class, age and gender at all levels of the juvenile justice systems. Only by examining the interactive effects of these constructs can we begin to truly understand the multiple and contradictory experiences of delinquent girls.

* *Jody Miller is at the University of Southern California.*

NOTES

1. While I had hoped to include Asian girls in my comparative analysis,

I could only locate six girls on active probation in the area. Of these, two had unique extenuating circumstances which would make them problematic to use for the analysis. This left only four girls, which I did not feel provided enough cases for inclusion in the sample.

2. While this does not provide a comprehensive definition of social class, it provided a fruitful way of examining disparities in the ways that girls are discussed by income levels, and allowed me to examine the possible stigmatizing effects of being welfare recipients.

3. This is not to imply that my findings apply uniquely to girls. Most likely, some constructions apply to both girls and boys in varying degrees, and some apply only to girls. This is an empirical question open for further investigation. My study is not meant to be a comparative analysis of girls and boys, but rather to explore the complexities in the handling of girls.

4. Names used throughout this paper are fictitious.

5. Suitable placement orders are not technically defined as more "severe." They are recommended for those juveniles who are believed to have emotional problems which contribute to their delinquent behavior, for which "treatment" in a placement facility can "help" them. However, in that they are taken out of the home (in Angela's case a stayed placement was recommended, not removing her from the home immediately but leaving the probation officer the power to do so at a later date), it is a disposition that involves greater intervention on the juvenile's life than probation does, and in that sense is more severe.

REFERENCES

Alder, Christine. 1984. "Gender Bias in Juvenile Diversion." *Crime & Delinquency*, 30(3): 400-414.

Armstrong, Gail. 1977. "Females under the Law-Protected buy Unequal." *Crime & Delinquency*, 14(1): 61-76.

Bondavalli, Bonnie J. and Bruno Bondavalli. 1981. "Spanish-Speaking People and the North American Criminal Justice System," In R. L. McNeely and Carl E. Pope, eds. *Race, Crime and Criminal Justice*. Beverly Hills: Sage

Press.

Cain, Maureen, ed. 1989a. *Growing Up Good: Policing the Behavior of Girls in Europe*. London: Sage Publications.

____. 1989b. "Feminists Transgress Criminology." In Maureen Cain, ed. *Growing Up Good: Policing the Behavior of Girls in Europe*. London: Sage Publications.

Campbell, Anne. 1981. *Girl Delinquents*. New York: St. Martins Press.

Canter, Rachelle J. 1982. "Sex Differences in Self-Report Delinquency." *Criminology*, 20: 373-393.

Chesney-Lind, Meda. 1977. "Judicial Paternalism and the Female Status Offender: Training Women to Know Their Place." *Crime & Delinquency* 23: 121-130.

___. 1978. "Young Women in the Arms of the Law." In Lee H. Bowker, ed. *Women, Crime and the Criminal Justice System*, Lexington, Massachusetts: Lexington Books.

___. 1988. "Girls and Status Offenses: Is Juvenile Justice Still Sexist?" *Criminal Justice Abstracts* 20(1): 144-65.

___ and Randall G. Shelden. 1992. *Girls, Delinquency and Juvenile Justice*. Pacific Grove, California: Brooks/Cole Publishing Company.

Collins, Patricia Hill. 1990. *Black Feminist Thought*. Boston: Unwin Hyman.

Davis, Angela Y. 1981. *Women, Race & Class*. New York: Vintage Books.

DeFleur, Lois B. 1975. "Biasing Influences on Drug Arrest Records: Implications for Deviance Research." *American Sociological Review*. 40: 88-103.

Daly, Kathleen. 1991. "Impact of Feminist Theory on Studies of Law and Crime." Paper presented at the American Society of Criminology annual meeting.

Daly, Kathleen and Meda Chesney-Lind. 1988. "Feminism and Criminology." *Justice Quarterly* 5(4): 497-538.

Dannefer, Dale and Russell K. Schutt, 1982. "Race and Juvenile Justice Processing in Court and Police Agencies." *American Journal of Sociology*. 87: 1113-1132.

Dill, Bonnie Thornton. 1987. "The Dialectics of Black Womanhood." In Sandra Harding, ed. *Feminism and Methodology*. Bloomington, Indiana: Indiana University Press.

Empey, LaMar T. and Mark C. Stafford, 1991. *American Delinquency: Its Meaning & Construction*, Belmont, California: Wadsworth Publishing Company.

Feyerherm, William. 1981. "Juvenile Court Dispositions of Status Offenders: An Analysis of Case Decisions." In R. L. McNeely and Carl E. Pope, eds. *Race, Crime and Criminal Justice*. Beverly Hills: Sage Press.

Figueira,-McDonough, Josephina. 1985. "Are Girls Different? Gender Discrepancies Between Delinquent Behavior and Control." *Child Welfare*. 64: 273-289.

Garfinkel, Harold. 1967. *Studies in Ethnomethodology*. Englewood Cliffs, New Jersey: Prentice-Hall.

Gelsthorpe, Loraine. 1986. "Towards a Skeptical Look at Sexism." *International Journal of the Sociology of Law*. 14: 125-152.

___. 1989. *Sexism and the Female Offender: An Organizational Analysis*. Aldershot, England: Gower.

___ and Allison Morris, eds. 1990. *Feminist Perspectives in Criminology*, Milton Keynes/Philadelphia: Open University Press.

Hudson, Annie, 1990. "Elusive subjects': Researching Young Women in Trouble." In Loraine Gelsthorpe and Allison Morris, eds. *Feminist Perspectives in Criminology*. Milton Keynes/Philadelphia: Open University Press.

Kersten, Joachim, 1989. "The Institutional Control of Girls and Boys: An Attempt at a Gender-specific Approach." In Maureen Cain, ed. *Growing Up Good: Policing the Behavior of Girls in Europe*. London: Sage Publications.

Klein, Dorie, 1991. "Dilemmas of Diversity for Feminist Criminology." paper presented at the American Society of Criminology annual meeting.

Krisberg, Barry, Ira M. Schwartz, Paul Litsky, and James Austin. 1986. "The Watershed of Juvenile Justice Reform." *Crime & Delinquency*, 32: 5-38.

Krohn, Marvin, Ronald Akers, Marcia Radosevich, and Lonn Lanza-Kaduce. 1980. "Social Status and Deviance: Class Context of School, Social Status, and Delinquent Behavior", *Criminology*. 18: 303-318.

___, James P. Curry, and Shirley Nelson-Kilger, 1983. "Is Chivalry Dead?" *Criminology*. 21: 417-439.

Ladner, Joyce, 1987. "Introduction to *Tomorrow's Tomorrow: The Black Woman*." In Sandra Harding, ed. *Feminism & Methodology*. Bloomington, Indiana: Indiana University Press.

Laub, John H. and M. Joan McDermott, 1985. "An Analysis of Serious Crime by Young Black Women." *Criminology*. 23: 31-98.

Leonard, Eileen. 1982. *Women, Crime and Society: A Critique of Theoretical Criminology*. New York: Longman.

Malson, Michelene Ridley. 1983. "Black Women's Sex Roles: The Social Context for a New Ideology." *Journal of Social Issues*. 39(3): 101-113.

Mann, Coramae Richey. 1979. "Making Jail the Hard Way: Law and the Female Offender." *Corrections Today*. 41: 35-41.

Mann, Coramae Richey. 1984. *Female Crime and Delinquency*. University, Alabama: University of Alabama Press.

Parisi, Nicolette. 1982. "Are Females Treated Differently? A Review of the Theories and Evidence on Sentencing and Parole Decisions." In Nicole Rafter and Elizabeth Anne Stanko, eds. *Judge, Lawyer, Victim, Thief: Woman, Gender Roles and Criminal Justice*. Boston: Northeastern University Press.

Quinney, Richard. 1974. *Critique of Legal Order: Crime Control in Capitalist Society*. Boston: Little, Brown and Company.

Rice, Marcia. 1990. "Challenging Orthodoxies in Feminist Theory: A Black Feminist Critique." In Loraine Gelsthorpe and Allison Morris, eds. *Feminist Perspectives in Criminology*. Milton Keynes/Philadelphia: Open University Press.

Sarri, Rosemary. 1976. "Juvenile Law: How It Penalizes Females." In Laura

Crites, ed. *The Female Offender.* Lexington, Massachusetts: Lexington Books.

___. 1983. "Gender Issues in Juvenile Justice." *Crime and Delinquency.* 29: 381-397.

Smart, Carol. 1976. *Women, Crime and Criminology: A Feminist Critique.* London: Routledge & Kegan Paul.

___. 1977. "Criminological Theory: Its Ideology and Implications Concerning Women." *British Journal of Sociology.* 28(1): 89-100.

Smith, Althea and Abigail J. Stewart, 1983. "Approaches to Studying Racism and Sexism in Black Women's Lives." *Journal of Social Issues.* 39(3): 1-15.

Teilmann, Katherine S. and Pierre H. Landry, Jr. 1981. "Gender Bias in Juvenile Justice." *Journal of Research in Crime and Delinquency.* 18: 47-80.

Visher, Christy A. 1983. "Gender, Police Arrest Decisions, and Notions of Chivalry." *Criminology.* 21: 5-28.

White, Deborah Gray. 1985. *Ar'n't I a Woman*? New York: W. W. Norton & Company.

Woodward, Carolyn. 1988. "Real Women and the Cult of True Womanhood." In Jo Whitehorse Cochran, Donna Langston and Carolyn Woodward, eds. *Changing Our Power: An Introduction to Women's Studies.* Dubuque, Iowa: Kendall/Hunt Publishing Company.

Chapter X

DECONSTRUCTION AND RADICAL CRIMINOLOGY: AN ANALYSIS OF POST-MODERNISM AND ITS POSSIBLE USES IN CRIMINOLOGY[1]

Michael J. Lynch*, Richard A. Lynch**
& Dragan Milovanovic***

During the 1980s post-structuralism made inroads in a number of disciplines including criminology (Pfohl and Gordon 1985; Manning 1988, 1990a,b), and several recent works (Schwartz 1989; Thomas and O'Maochatha 1989; Henry and Milovanovic 1991) suggest that post-structural thought might inspire future developments within radical criminology. This article assesses this possibility by analyzing deconstruction's (and related forms of post-modern thought) compatibility with radical criminology's assumptions, and the prospect of generating an integrated critical analysis. Toward this end, Section I reviews the deconstructionist tradition. Section II examines similarities and dissimilarities between deconstruction and radical thought. Section III reviews contemporary contributions to critically oriented deconstructionist thought that can be integrated with the perspective taken by radical criminologists. Section IV describes some difficulties in applying deconstruction to criminology. Finally, in Section V we suggest how critical deconstruction might be applied to criminology, addressing the advantages and disadvantages of so doing.

I
BACKGROUND

Deconstruction is a form of post-structural analysis that emerged from the work of Jacques Derrida in the mid-1960s. This perspective owes an intellectual debt to structuralism and semiotics, and to a diverse range of philosophers including Hegel, Nietzsche and deSaussure. Recently, alternative deconstructive approaches based upon critical-materialistic, psychoanalytic semiotics (what we call *critical deconstruction*; e.g., see Deleuze and Guattari 1987; Kristeva 1984; Pecheaux 1979; Zizek 1989; and Section III), have added new directions to post-modern analysis. As a result, deconstruction cannot be discussed as a wholly developed, unified or isolated theoretical tradition, and must be discussed in relation to its prehistory as well as its own history.

Defining or characterizing deconstructionism in a precise manner is difficult for several reasons. First, those subscribing to this approach view it as "without form." Second, given the tremendous growth and rapid transformation of deconstructionist thought, attempts to specify the structure of this theory are generally dismissed as inaccurate, ill-conceived and inconsistent with the logic of the theory. Deconstruction's proponents dismiss classification as a banal attempt to apply the terminology and logic of older theories to a new order of thinking (Ellis 1989:4). This inability to describe deconstructionism in a precise manner, while problematic (see Ryan 1982:144; Ellis 1989: 4,7) could be viewed as one of deconstruction's strengths, insofar as deconstruction's emerging conceptions are dynamic and offer the potential for fundamentally reorienting critical thought when the two are integrated.

Given deconstruction's "formlessness" and rapid transformation, we could easily forego a discussion of its basic assumptions. However, such a discussion is central to our critique and synthesis (Section V), and, in the following section, we attempt to capture some of deconstruction's more undisputed points.

A) Deconstruction: A Description?

Deconstructionism emerged as a critique and response to traditional (metaphysical, ontological, epistemic and logocentric) assumptions of Western philosophy that emphasizes reason, the centered subject, rationality, truth, Logos, linear progress (science) and binary opposition (see: Melichar 1988:370; Shaw 1986:260; Culler 1979:155; Ryan 1982:9-11, 33: Sarup 1989; Flax 1990; Milovanovic 1990a, 1991a). As a critique of traditional philosophy, deconstruction rejects the foundational elements of western philosophy, and has been used to rebuke a variety of approaches including structuralism (Flynn 1989), empiricism (Berman 1988:199-200) and Marxism (Fish 1982, 1984).

Derrida's deconstruction rejects all of Western philosophy: from external validation of knowledge to the human ability to Know or discover Truth or Being, (which we interpret as shared assumptions/interpretations that act as the foundation for a (rational?) philosophy of knowledge). This rejection goes beyond a simple disbelief in Western philosophical "truth claims," and argues that the human ability to Know (discover "Truth"[2] or Being) is restricted by the boundaries and structure of language. There is, in short, an irreconcilable split between reality (Truth) and the human ability to represent reality in a linguistic/symbolic format. This leads to the paradoxical conclusion that while Truth cannot be understood apart from language,the structure of language makes the discovery of Truth impossible, which means that the "being" of an object is viewed as a relationship between objects and language (Ryan 1982:22).

In many western philosophies, the inability to discover Truth or Being is conceptualized as an ontological, metaphysical or empirical problem. For deconstructionists, however, the problem is linguistic and symbolic. This means that there is no "real truth" -- no metaphysical or ontological or empirical "being" -- to be reflected by language. What is "real" is always a human construction. And, because the real is a human construction, meaning is in a constant state of flux. For deconstructionists, therefore, the relationship between objects and language are not inherent, natural or stable, but emerge through human agents' attempts to communicate relationships between objects using symbols. Thus, discovering Truth is problematic for two reasons.

First, language and symbols cannot capture or reflect Truth (i.e., they are separate entities). Second, language and symbols are multidimensional and unanchored, meaning that what is captured in language and symbols is not objective Truth but some subjective understanding or interpretation of Truth. Consequently, linguistic formats (symbols, writing and speech) are open to a variety of interpretations by the audience receiving the message. No interpretation is more valid or reliable (Truthful) than any other, since deconstruction has done away with the notion of external validation or the authority to make such judgments (see Fish's antifoundationist position, 1980, 1982, 1984). The text, in short, is inherently unstable, even though rules of grammar and logic provides a surface stability to meaning (de Man 1986).

Two other factors confound human attempts to understand reality. First language has its own independent history (Ryan 1982:23), meaning that the structure of language and Reality may develop independently of one another (the study of this relationship is referred to as the "Diacrohnic Function"). In this view, language (composed of signs, constituted by a diad signifier which stands for an acoustic image or psychological imprint, and the signified or concept referred to) increasingly takes on self-referentiality where each signifier refers to other signifiers, and so on in a self enclosed system of meaning (Jackson 1985, 1988). The extreme version of this position is captured by Baudrillard's (1983) term "hyper-reality."

Second, prevailing models argue that there is an inherent split between communicators and audiences (i.e., between authors of texts and readers/consumers of texts) that generates additional variations in text interpretations (Berman 1989:201; Ryan 1982:22-23), and gives the text "lateral reference," permitting "a text, against the conscious will of the author, to 'disseminate' meanings that are not consciously intended" (Ryan 1982:23-24; see also Silverman 1983). The text, in other words, takes on an autonomous, subjective existence. On one hand, producers of texts cannot present what they really intend to say, and consequently a variety of alternative meanings can be extracted from texts (Lacan 1977; Lecercle 1985, 1990). On the other hand, the text itself subverts congruent reading and the attribution of stable meaning to different readers (Derrida; Barthes 1974; Silverman 1983:237-283; de Man 1986). This view of text stands in direct opposition to traditional western philosophical traditions in which the text reflects the will or intent of the conscious, determining and centered subject's reflection of reality.

B) Deconstruction as Linguistic Theory

Deconstructionists define language as "an interwoven fabric...of signifiers, of language itself, with no demonstrable power of direct representation or reflection (mimesis) of reality external to it" (Berman 1988: 202; see also Jackson 1985; Zizek 1989:89-92; Lacan 1977). The text is reality, or as Derrida would say, "There is nothing outside of the text" (quoted in Berman 1988:201). This means that the "thing" to which the text refers has no independent reality -- it lives inside the text (i.e., it has self-referentiality).

Texts employ "signs" and "signifiers" to communicate the "referent" (the Real) to an "other." Written and spoken language are based upon interpretations of concepts into and out of symbols. However, as representations of concepts, symbols fail to capture the concept completely or accurately; they do not capture the world as binary opposite, as traditional philosophies suggest (Ryan 1982:25). Rather, signs are relations that simultaneously distinguish, relate and blur the distinction between things. For example, the individual letters that comprise words contain no meaning; they are signifiers of vowels and consonant sounds. Letters have no meaning in themselves beyond the sound they represent, but they can be combined to form complex sound sets that represent verbal interpretations of written symbols. Letters represent sounds; sounds represent letters; complex sounds (words) represent concepts. Letters/sounds are signifiers of concepts and meanings (for further discussion see Ryan 1982:12-13). However, the concepts and meanings signifiers refer to are not inseparable.

Further, signs and signifiers (letters/sounds/words) are incapable of capturing the referent accurately. Three assumptions support this assertion. First, words are not the concepts themselves, and thus are open to various individual interpretations. Second, when we move from concepts to words or from words to concepts, we institute a process in which a loss of meaning is part of the interpretive process. Third, there is an inherent alienation or split between the Real and language. Thus Truth, as defined by the Real, cannot be known, given the limits of language. This sets the stage for a theory that posits a deep schism between the Real and human ability to know the Real. This schism, coupled with the denouncement of Western philosophy's attempts to provide external validation, generates a philosophical system dominated by the predicament of inevitable human alienation and despair (Melichar 1988).[3]

The reader's role (the subject) is emphasized by deconstructionists who argue that it is the reader, not the author, who determines the text's meaning. This view of the reader reverses the traditional authoritative[4] hierarchy employed in western philosophies which place the author in a dominant position and the reader in a submissive (passive) role. In deconstruction, the author's role is diminished (for an alterative interpretation see Ryan 1982:24-25), and s/he is denied a voice in determining the meaning(s) extracted from the text by the reader. The text, in short, is "free" to stand on its own: no reading of the text is "wrong."

C) Deconstruction: Some General Criticisms

One of the primary drawbacks of Derriderean deconstruction is that it offers no solution to the problem of language and (MIS)interpretation; nor does it offer solutions to the general problems that emerge in the process of attempting to communicate reality and interpret texts. Having removed the possibility of external validation, deconstruction is left with a system based upon subjective validation; one based upon despair and human alienation that cannot be overcome by human action (Melichar 1988). They have, to paraphrase Marx's critique of philosophy (1982), merely interpreted the world when the point is to offer ways to change it.

In addition, problems such as the human inability to communicate the Real, the alienation of humans from the Real, etc., are accepted as the natural consequence of the state of human interaction and existence. The conclusion, in short, is that communication is always an alienating process that can never represent the Real universe. Humans are inherently isolated from the Real, and live in a world of limited capability. This is the message of deconstruction.

Consequently, critics argue that deconstruction is an anti-humanist "ideology of despair" (Melichar 1988:366) that results from a failure to ground deconstruction in a socio-political theory or to analyze "socio-historical movement" (Ryan 1982:35-36).

However, deconstructionist thought does not have to be interpreted in such a strict manner. A critical deconstruction, grounded in materialist assumptions, offers one alternative to these dilemmas. This approach is useful for explaining how a "loss of meaning" is instituted. To give an example grounded in critical deconstruction, Lacan (1977) argued that meaning is inherently unstable since, in the natural state, signifiers perpetually slide over the signified. However, "points de capiton" stabilize these relationships by tying particular signifiers to the signified. Other contemporary critical theorists have analyzed how political-economic structures affect this tying or knotting process (Laclau and Mouffe 1985; Giroux 1988; Zizek 1989; Volosinov 1986). Such a view is of particular importance in analyzing how ideology is constructed, stabilized and perpetuated in the form of hegemony. Particular discourses are said to convey value positions embedded in the signs that make up discursive regions tied to political economic formations (Milovanovic 1991a; Zizek 1989:45, 88, 90, 98-99; Pecheux 1982). Such a view, which combines radical, semiotic and deconstructive views, creates the potential for developing a more humanistic and praxis-oriented philosophy of the human condition which is liberating to the extent that human action can be relied upon to create meaning from despair. We will return to this theme when discussing how deconstruction and radical thought can be synthesized.

D) The Text: Objective and Subjective Dimensions

All exegeses/studies of text (regardless of how "text" is defined and regardless of the theoretical position employed) amount to an attempt to understand the text. There are five competing perspectives on text interpretation: (1) the text is assumed to be objective (justified in criminological traditions based on positivism); (2) the text is assumed to be subjective (e.g., deconstruction, existential, phenomenology); (3) the text is assumed to represent a unity of subjective and objective contexts (critical/radical/Marxian perspectives); (4) the text is assumed to be destabilizing or subversive (e.g., Nietzschean inspired theorists such as de Man; see discussion below); and (5) the text is assumed to be the site of struggle where the constitutive effects of political economic determinants circumscribing the particular discourse in use are of paramount importance (e.g., post-Frankfurt perspective). The first two approaches, in particular, include assumptions that limit their applicability, since they abstract the text from its historical context or make history unimportant in text analysis.

Clearly, objective and subjective interpretations of text treat history differently. In objective positions, the text is assumed to have transhistorical meaning, as in positivism, where the attempt is to construct general theory (Pfohl and Gordon 1986:597). Conversely, in subjective approaches -- such as deconstruction and existentialism -- the text has neither a transhistorical nor an historically specific meaning. Here the subjective content of the text is stressed; the individuality of interpretation is the foremost concern, and the individual struggles to create meaning from the text in an isolated, alienated atmosphere, free from structural constraints such as history. Both purely subjective or objective treatments of text-problems fail to examine the connection between language and other relevant phenomena. For example, such approaches neglect the structuring effect the material foundation of society has on language production and the historically contingent meanings language acquires.

This subjectivity/objectivity problem is somewhat remedied in author-text-history approaches (3 thru 5 above). Here, subjectivity and objectivity are seen as dialectically related: authors produce texts, texts produce authors -- and this occurs within given and definite historical circumstances that set the stage for certain types of text interpretations (i.e., the meanings the subject can extract or that the author can communicate are limited by the stage of historical development). For Marxists and post-Frankfurt (critical) theorists in particular, historical and structural factors are of great importance (e.g. Volosinov 1986). Yet, there is also a concern with subjectivity. Thus, for critical theorists, the text must be interpreted within a integrative framework emphasizing the dialectic nature of subjective and objective criteria. These criteria include class structure, domination, power/knowledge, the historically specific content of communication; language, and the interaction of the subject and object of communication (see: Milovanovic 1988, 1986; Henry and Milovanovic 1991; Zizek 1989; Deleuze and Guattari 1987; Pecheux 1982).

Within criminology, theories based in one dimension of the subjectivity/objectivity dualism are problematic (Groves and Lynch 1990), yet quite common. The meaning of crime cannot be fully understood by relying upon only one of these dimensions. Positivism's penchant for general theory, for example, attempts to create transhistorical objective meaning. Forms of criminal behavior, however, appear and disappear over time and change with structural circumstances (Michalowski 1985). Deeds such as "computer crime," "hijacking" or "auto theft" have historically specific meanings (Thomas and Meyer 1990); they cannot be comprehended by individuals living in societies that have not developed the types of technology (let alone language) conducive to these acts (Lynch and Groves 1989). Punishments such as banishment or transportation can no longer be practiced (have lost their meaning) given current levels of world population, social development and transportation capabilities (Rusche and Kirchheimer 1968; on corporal punishment see Foucault 1977b; Newman 1985). Further, objective approaches make it difficult to explain why some people perceive certain behaviors as serious, while others living within the same set of social circumstances do not (e.g. drug use, gambling, abortion, etc.).

Pure subjective approaches contain the reverse bias. Here, subjective experience and interpretation is assumed to be the only legitimate means of explaining perception/meanings. In such a view, any form of common experience or transhistorical meaning is coincidental.

In certain critical traditions (e.g., Foucault 1977b), pure subjective or objective (structural) understanding is impossible if not irrelevant to an analysis of social processes. In Foucault's (1970, 1973, 1977a, 1977b) view there is always an interaction between subjects and objects that takes place within the confines of a simultaneous historical-transhistorical construction of knowledge. This view, which has been applied to criminological concerns (Foucault 1977b), emphasizes the structuring effects of prevailing power relationships on the content and control of knowledge, bodies and minds of subjects in acts of communication, domination and submission. Such a view emphasizes the complicated, interactive process of constructing and asserting power. The relations constructed in this process, though ordered, have no beginning or end, but are part of a continual act of constructing and deconstructing power and control; of creating order and disorder.

E) Deconstructing The "Text": Closing Critical Comments

Deconstruction's attempt to demystify the text by granting the reader a greater voice in (MIS)interpretation, while noteworthy, falls short of a total critique of communication. We base our critique upon a materialistic interpretation of social relationships, which we believe has the ability to add a missing dimension to deconstruction. Viewed from the materialist perspective, deconstruction fails for several reasons.

First, it fails to examine the relation between social reality and communication. Attempts to communicate are constructed within the confines of definite social arraignments. The text, therefore, can only acquire a limited range of meanings, since meaning is historically contingent (Ryan 1982:41). Within criminology, as noted, this idea is supported by the fact that definitions of crime change over time, and that certain types of crime (e.g. auto theft, hijacking, computer crime, environmental crime, etc.,) are possible and meaningful only within social structures that obtain a specific level of technological sophistication.

Second, deconstruction fails to analyze power relations and the effect power relations have over interpretation (e.g., Foucault 1973; Deleuze 1988). Under certain power arraignments, for example, social reality is constructed by a limited segment of society, while under other power arraignments (e.g., a true democracy), broader or even narrower (e.g., in a monarchy) social segments have an input (Michalowski 1985). The only critique deconstructionists offer in this regard relates to rationality and the relationship of science to knowledge and meaning. These first two pitfalls, however, have largely been remedied by those supporting a more critical form of deconstruction (see Section III).

Third, deconstruction fails to ask critical questions about its primary concept, the text. For many deconstructionists, the text is written words. The irony here is that deconstructionists have failed to deconstruct the text, or analyze the traditional meaning associated with the linguistic symbol "text." This neglect may be related to one of the primary assumptions of deconstruction: that writing has a privileged position over speech (Derrida 1967), and apparently behavior. Speech, text and behavior when taken in their social context, however, are all interrelated elements of communication (Baskin 1986), and form the dialectic whole of communication. As forms of social discourse, speech, behavior and text serve as methods of communicating observations about behavior to others. Thus, behavior would appear to be the Real, and has primacy over speech and text. Deconstructionists have largely neglected behavior, though some have suggested that deconstruction can be extended to behavioral analysis (Henning 1982). The neglect of this problem becomes very apparent in behavioral science, and criminology in particular (see Section IV).

Despite the criticism we have noted above, it is possible that deconstruction may be useful in reorienting radical theories of crime and justice. Before discussing this possibility, we turn to a discussion of the similarities and differences between deconstructive and Marxian world views. This material is necessary to the integrationist effort we offer in section V.

II
SIMILARITY AND DIVERGENCE: DERRIDEREAN DECONSTRUCTION AND RADICAL THOUGHT

A) Similarities

The deconstructionist view of the text, while critical of the Marxian perspective, bears similarities to Marxian analyses of commodity production (Ryan 1982). Both: (a) analyze objects of study as misunderstood entities, and as dead labor; (b) make a distinction between theory and practice (Ryan 1982:34); and (c) offer a critique of ideology (Ryan 1982:38). This view of the similarities between deconstruction and Marxian analyses make sense if we conceptualize or (RE)interpret the text as a commodity. Doing so we are able to pinpoint certain features these approaches share. This may be an extreme liberty to take with the text as understood in the deconstructionist perspective. But, since we will argue for a view that integrates deconstructive and Marxian-oriented theory, this liberty is necessary to our argument.

Taking this staring point, in the Derriderean view, the text can be viewed as the dead, alienated labor of the author; it is controlled by the reader/subject. The voice/intention of the author is denied realization on the assumption that it is impossible for readers to grasp the author's intended meaning. The text thus becomes the property of the reader, and is free to stand on its own (as text) and to be interpreted by the reader/subject/consumer. Some (e.g., Barthes 1974; Giroux 1988) use this approach to provide a method through which repressed voices produced by the text can be recaptured. This method also produces subversive readings of texts that undermines hegemonic constructs, and overcomes the ultimate condition of alienation and despair that deconstructionist predict for humankind.

In contrast to many of the assumptions of Derriderean deconstructionists stand Marxian interpretations. In the Marxian view, the commodity (in this case, the text) is the dead, alienated labor of the worker, controlled by the owner of the means of production (Bannister and Milovanovic 1990). In either view (Derriderean or Marxian), however, the producer (author/worker) looses control over the product of their labor (commodity/text). In short, we suggest that there are four primary sources of alienation common to Derriderean and Marxian analysis (listed as dyads; deconstruction/Marxian) that can be used to unite these two approaches and demonstrate similarly in their concerns:

(1) the author from the audience/the worker from the consumer;
(2) the audience from the text/the consumer from the product;
(3) the writer from the text/the worker from the commodity; and
(4) the writer from the Real/the worker from the means of production.

These similarities, while meaningful and useful, should not be over-emphasized since they hide some potential problems or differences that need to be addressed before a synthesis can be attempted.

B) Divergence: Derrida's Deconstruction and Radical Thought

While deconstruction and Marxian perspectives share some common ground, the differences between these views are pronounced and meaningful. For example, Marx's analysis stripped commodities of their subjective content, and laid bare the objective basis of a commodity's value (this is the importance of the labor theory of value). It emphasizes that workers' alienation from the product of their labor is historically contingent on productive relations, and can be overcome under a different set of historical conditions. These insights have been employed in the post-Frankfurt perspective to reveal the "forced semiotic grids" by which initial desire and verbal/written texts are given form by political economy. The role of human action or praxis is paramount to this achievement.

Deconstruction, however, imposes no historically situated concerns, and views the alienation between producers (authors, communicators) and consumers (readers/audience) as an ever present problem. Thus alienation cannot be overcome under any circumstances -- and there is no mention of the idea of praxis. In short, Marxists hold out the optimistic hope that alienation can be eliminated or substantially reduced, while deconstructionist view alienation as part and parcel of human social interactions.

Another difference between these two approaches concerns the humanist orientation of radical theory (Grose and Groves 1988; Soper 1986) and the anti-humanist orientation of deconstruction (Melichar 1989); for opposing position see Ryan (1982) and Anderson (1990). To overcome this difference, radical theorists can (RE)structure the basic assumptions of deconstruction so that they are more consistent with Marxian theory (Ryan 1982). In fact, such a step must be taken if deconstruction is to contribute to radically oriented critiques and theories of society and social relationships. An emphasis on praxis in critical deconstruction drastically reorients the conclusion of

Derriderean deconstruction, especially the claim that despair and human alienation are part of the natural order of human relations (Melichar 1988). Critical deconstruction, by positing that human action can be liberating and a means of overcoming despair and alienation, transforms deconstruction into an action-based and optimistic theory of society and human relations.

With the summaries and critiques presented in Sections I and II in mind, let us turn to contemporary attempts to apply the deconstructionist view in a materialistic fashion. This material makes it clear that while many of the specific tenants of deconstruction may be questionable and inconsistent with Marxian theory, the overall approach argued by deconstructionists may be of use in helping us to interpret social problems and relations in a critical-materialistic fashion.

III
POST-FRANKFURT SCHOOL -- TOWARD A NEW SYNTHESIS

Given the limitations of Derriderean deconstruction, this section examines a few contemporary developments that provide the elements necessary for a critical deconstruction. Of particular interest is a post-Frankfurt perspective which attempts to synthesize Hegelian/Marxian analyses with Nietzsche and Lacan (Deleuze and Guattari 1987). Post-Frankfurt analysis is distinguished from the Frankfurt school (e.g., Sartre, Habermas, Marcuse, Fromm, Adorno, Horkheimer) through its focus on (1) the decentered subject, (2) differentially segmented discourses (linguistic coordinate systems) and their effects, (3) the gendered subject in the symbolic order, (4) the insights of Nietzsche, and (5) the political economic determinants of the "knotting" process. There are certainly significant internal differences among post-Frankfurt theorists. These differences aside, we briefly examine Nietzsche's and Lacan's fundamental ideas, show how they are applied in literary criticism and deconstruction, indicate a general Lacan-Nietzsche-Marx deconstructive synthesis, and point out some potential contributions for a radical/critical criminology.

A) Nietzsche's Heritage

The "return to Nietzsche" was a recent development traceable to France. While Hegel was central to French thought throughout the 1940s and 1950s (Bogue 1989:2), by the 1960s and 1970s Nietzsche's work became more dominant. Perhaps the disillusionment with certain forms of Marxism, made manifest by the 1968 uprisings in France, crystallized this changed emphasis. Some of Nietzsche's central and distinct ideas are his notion of genealogy (an alternative to Hegelian's linear model of the Absolute Spirit), the semiotic fictions of the subject, the will to power, and the movement to the "overman" by an affirmative action.

Nietzsche's view of genealogy fundamentally differs with Hegelian and Marxian inspired historical analyses (see Love 1986; Deleuze 1983; Bogue 1989; Foucault 1977a; Sarup 1989). For Hegel, the eternal working out of the logic of the Absolute Spirit drove historical development, while for Marx, the process of dialectical and historical materialism was the motor force of history (both were linear processes). In Nietzsche's genealogical view, however, modern people find themselves in a situation of "eternal return"; history is neither infinite nor finite (Love 1986: 85). As Sarup stated: "genealogical analysis attempts to establish and preserve the singularity of events, turns away from the spectacular in favour of the discredited, the neglected and a whole range of phenomena which have been denied history" (1989:64). Hence, genealogy

> is a form of critique. It rejects the pursuit of the origin in favour of a conception of historical beginnings as lowly, complex and contingent. It attempts to reveal the multiplicity of factors behind an event and the fragility of historical forms...there can be no constants, no essences, no immobile forms of uninterrupted continuities structuring the past (Sarup 1984:64; see also Foucault 1977a:139-164).

For Foucault (1977a:152), "the development of humanity is a series of interpretations. The role of genealogy is to record its history." Much like recent analysis in chaos theory (Milovanovic 1991), genealogical analysis views historical development as consisting of different centers of forces (finite) that undergo an infinite number of variations; these appear on the one hand as chaotic, and on the other, as predictable (the eternal return). All phenomena, including the will, are envisioned as "dynamic quanta" of energy in relation to other quanta of energy. As Nietzsche would say "[t]he total character of the world...is in all eternity chaos -- in the sense not of a lack of necessity but of a lack or order, arrangement, form, beauty, wisdom, and whatever other names there are for our aesthetic anthropomorphism" (in Love 1986:92).

In *Genealogy and Morals* Nietzsche argued that reacting and negating are inherently conservative and consequently an insufficient means for changing society. For Nietzsche only active negation creates transcendence ("transfiguration") -- a transpraxis rather than a praxis -- and the future man/woman or "overman."

Nietzsche also argued that we develop semiotic fictions that provide horizons that produce regularity and predictability (Nietzsche 1968: 494; see also Love 1986: 53; Milovanovic 1991a). In *Twilight of the Idols*, he argued that language provides the fiction for dualities, projected constructs of plenitude. In language, action and actor are fictitiously separated. Consequently the perception, given a deed, that (1) causality can be attributed to some determining, self-conscious actor; (2) events have an identifiable (verbalizable) causes; and (3) freedom of the will (the determining, centered subject) is the force that mobilizes the process. For Nietzsche however, "there is no 'being' behind doing, effecting, becoming; 'the doer' is merely a fiction added to the deed -- the deed is everything" (1968:481).

B) Lacan: Psychoanalytical Semiotics

The second major contribution to a post-Frankfurt perspective is Lacan's linguistic rereading of Freud's early writings (pre-1920s).[5] Lacan's central ideas revolved around the decentered subject, the effects of the signifier, speech production, and gender creation. Although influential in Europe, little Lacanian inspired analysis and integration has taken place in the United States outside of English and Language departments.

For Lacan, the subject is stretched out over four points on two axes: the unconscious and the "moi-other". The unconscious, has two polarities: "I" and Other. The "I" (the grammatical subject, or "I" of discourse), represents (signifies) absence (the signified, or the actual producer of the utterance). The Other is a repository of floating signifiers and desires (a felt lack-in-being). The conflict between the absence in "I" and the desires in the Other produces representatives of desire and the personal pronoun I. In other words, desire seeks objects (including words) which offer a sense of completeness. The "I" in discourse gives an outlet to desire's expression, or in Hegelian terms, externalizes inner states of being in objectified structures that once created now reflectively (consciously) give expression to being itself.

The second diagonal, the "moi-other" represents imaginative constructs. The moi, or ego (itself an illusory image of a complete being in control) is said to be caught up in illusory constructions of the other in discourse. The "other," for Lacan is the object of desire; much like in the Hegelian construct, the subject desires the desire of the other. It is these illusions that give stability to speech production. The two axes, one intersubjective, the other intra-subjective, constitute subjectivity.

Lacan also posits three main orders: the Real, the Symbolic and the Imaginary. The Real is lived experience. The Symbolic is constituted by language. Language and meaning are produced when the subject chooses a particular signifier from two dimensions: the metaphoric and the metonymic. The Imaginary is the sphere of images, of plentitude, of unity. These images are to be duplicated throughout life: the subject will develop a multitude of imagoes which give it a false sense of being unitary.

The three orders of Lacan along with the notion of the decentered subject are given a dynamic form in his notions of the "graphs of desire" depicting speech production. The subject periodically perceives gaps in their life (which mobilizes desire), which creates a drive for closure. To facilitate closure, the subject searches for an "objet petit a," (the object of desire), which "sutures" the gap, producing a sense of plenitude (a jouissance). The subject finds itself at the mercy of desire's search for signifiers that would give it expression; the Other, as a locus of signifiers, provides them. Metaphoric and metonymic displacements continue until a knotting (a "point de capiton") is established, fastening a particular signifier to a signified, giving temporary sense to a signifier. Signifiers placed in a linear grammatical utterance are only given final meaning by way of a retroactive glance after a punctuation whereby the whole utterance is grasped. The natural state of signifiers is that they float; they slide over signifieds -- it is the anchoring process that gives them a particular meaning.

Recent theorists have attempted to overcome some of the shortcomings of Lacan's approach (e.g., its logocentric, monolithic conception of the symbolic order and the imaginary structure; its lack of political economic determinants). Deleuze and Guattari, for example, indicated that specific stabilized discourses ("regimes of sign") are historically unique with effects (1987:111-148; see also: Foucault 1970; Laclau and Mouffe 1985; Pecheux 1982; Milovanovic 1991b; and Wittenstein 1983). Within discursive formations, subjects are viewed as "tenants" (Pecheux 1982; Smith 1988) and value-laden signifiers float, awaiting appropriation by subjects (Volosinov 1986; Lacan 1977). Discourse is a product of historically determined hegemonic practice, but is subject to destabilization and subversion that occurs when subjects construct alternative readings of texts. Alternative readings thus "anchor" signifiers to "new" concepts through both subjective struggle and changing material circumstances which also affected meaning production.

In this process, human desires become "territorialized" and inscribed on the body: flows of desire on the subject are segmented, coded, and recoded anew in system-supporting ways. Regimes of signs become the mechanisms by which inscription takes place (i.e., through what Deleuze and Guattari refer to as "mots d'ordre," order-words, that are authoritative). In short, a semiotically constituted subject is revealed, one who constructs her/himself, and is constructed by the text. The text's meaning and the subject's ability to act and react are, in turn, constrained by political economic determinants. In the end a "diagram of power" is constituted which reveals a territorialized subject (Deleuze and Guattari 1987; Deleuze 1988; Bogue 1989:130-149).

Critical legal theorists, for example, have recognized "juristic subjects" or actors who create their behavior by legal signifiers that are anchored to political-economic determinants (Milovanovic 1988). Another example is Foucault's (1977b) "disciplined subject." This "disciplined subject" is acted upon by law (law in action and law as linguistically constructed) and the penal apparatus in a way that turns it into a "docile body." In each case, the subject is territorialized by imposing structurally constructed diagrams of power that are system supporting over the subject's actions and desires. The subject's behavior is, in short, reinterpreted within a preconstructed hegemonic discourse. This minimizes the subject's desires and neutralizes the subject's behavior. The subject is fit into the straight-jacket of the existing power structure. In doing so, the subject is forced back into the time and space dimensions laid out by the hegemonic diagram of power (Foucault 1977b).

C) Deconstruction and Reconstruction (Transfiguration)

Nietzsche's and Lacan's (and for some, Hegel's) ideas are key ingredients to an alternative, critical deconstructionist perspective (e.g., Pecheux 1982; Zizek 1989; Deleuze and Guattari 1987; Kristeva 1980, 1984). A critical deconstructive strategy examines textual production, the production of the subject (as producer), the ways in which certain voices are denied expression, the role dominant discourses place in providing materials (i.e., signifiers that are value-laden) that limit what can be said, and how the subject as spoken is created by the text s/he interprets. Below, we briefly discuss an alternative critical deconstruction.

Critical deconstruction has been widely used to assess gender construction[6] (e.g., Barthes 1974; Silverman 1983:237-283; Kristeva 1980, 1984; Deleuze 1988; Lecercle 1985, 1990; MacCabe 1985; Irigaray 1985a, 1985b; Flax 1990). In developing these views, Barthes argues that two main strategies of reading the text exist. The first, the "readerly" text, reconstitutes dominant symbolic orders by concealing the origins of production while encouraging the reader to identify, uniformly, with the unfolding plot and key characters

(Silverman 1983:243-246; MacCabe 1985:47). The reader is interpellated (Althusser 1971), or sutured (Lacan) or forced to take a reading-position within a particular discursive formation that places the subject in a receptive position to the key signifiers provide in hegemonic discourse. Once the subject accepts this position, gaps in the text are sutured over with pre-existing and privileged signifiers ("objects petit a") that are readily available within discourse (Silverman 1983; Smith 1988:75-77). The subject, then, is spoken (Silverman 1983: 245; see also Pecheux 1982; Deleuze and Guattari 1987). In the readerly text, a consistent, stable, linear and hegemonic text is produced, along with a self-conscious, stable, determining/producing subject.

The second text, the "writerly" text, excavates hidden, repressed voices from the margins, and is *inherently subversive* because it provides provisional and contingent constructions (Silverman 1983:246-259; MacCabe 1985:47-55; Giroux 1988:138-146). Thus, the producer of texts is not permanently grounded in a privileged (hegemonic) position. In addition, the writerly text encourages non-linear production of the text and the subject. Instead of repetition (i.e., of the given cultural and symbolic, hegemonic messages) and passivity, what is encouraged is innovation and transcendence -- a transpraxis.

Giroux argued that the dominant culture emphasizes a "language of accountability," particularly in schools whereby "a major emphasis [is] on structuring both knowledge and pedagogy around interests grounded in that which is measurable, efficient, and standardized" (1988:158; see also Foucault 1977b). Textual production reflects these ideals, attempting to produce hegemonic discourse that (RE)produce social relations. However, subversive readings of the text can undermine hegemony. Struggles of all forms (not necessarily just "class" struggle, but antiracist, feminist, antiauthoritarian, etc.) do not work themselves out via Hegelian's Absolute Spirit, culminating in the transfiguration of society; rather, struggles need to be articulated in a specific discourse that gives them form and content. Laclau and Mouffe (1985) suggest that antidemocratic discourses of the Right can articulate floating signifiers and anchor them in a discursive formation in which the goals are outwardly at one with the Left. For example, under the banner of individualism, libertarianism, and distaste for the "oppressive" state, the Right has articulated a discourse for dismantling historical gains made by the disenfranchised (Laclau and Mouffe 1985:175-175); systems of inequalities and hierarchical arrangements are legitimized in the new discursive formation. Text construction in all forms reflect these new hegemonic discursive formations that articulate signifiers that stabilize and sustain the system.

To escape this problem, critical deconstruction has developed a "language of critique and possibility" or a replacement discourse that empowers subjects with knowledge about their own historical development and cultural traditions, and presents a language pregnant with a plurality of voices representing diverse segments of society (Giroux 1988:189; Smith 1988:56-69). Along with deconstruction of the text, then, we need to develop a *reconstructive strategy* -- a transformative discourse/politics -- that excavates disallowed voices and provides visions for an alternative society.

In the post-Frankfurt school view, the opportunity to undermine otherwise deterministic structures (e.g., whether the focus is the text, subjectivity, discursive subject positions, or institutional arrangements) exists. In this view, the text is an unstable articulation of a multiplicity of competing significations where one signification dominates (the hegemonic discourse). As Laclau and Moufee (1985:136) noted, "organic crises" periodically occur at the macrolevel of discursive formations which allow for alternative interpretation and hegemonic destruction. At the microlevel (subjectivity), symbolically/culturally constituted syntactical structures and privileged signifiers (i.e., logocentric, phallocentric in emphasis) imposed on the desires, drives, and somatic states are at best tenuous, and subject to collapse. In short, at both the macro and micro level, structures periodically undergo disruption which releases floating signifiers and requires that meanings be constructed anew. These represent moments of subversion.

Pecheux (1982) argued that "distantiation" can take place, whereby "bad subjects" distance themselves from the constraining structures of discursive subject-positions assumed for meaning-construction and communication within any discursive formation. This can happen in trial proceeding where alternative constructions of reality result (Bannister and Milovanovic 1990). Contemporary feminist analysis (Kristeva 1984; Irigaray 1985a, 1985b; Grosz 1990; Cicoux 1981) makes a similar claim. Irigaray, for example, argues for a replacement discourse that is feminist-based and moves away from maleness as a central (logocentric, phallocentric) standard (see also Cicoux 1981). Barthe's "writerly text" also is in accord here.

A critical deconstructive strategy embraces disruption and actively searches for writerly text readings. Within this subversive strategy, a replacement discourse has the potential to develop. In re-placement discourse, both floating and anchored signifiers can be "reanchored" to represent polyvocity, contingent meanings, multiplicity, diversity and interdependencies. A replacement discourse: (1) makes marginalized social groups visible; (2) supplies the marginalized with an alternative discourse reflecting their spatio-temporal existence; (3) legitimizes their cultural histories; (4) exposes transformative potentials located in these histories; and (5) prepares the way for conditions that can transfigure society and social relations (Giroux 1983:35, 1988; Smith 1988:64). Such replacement discourses have had some effect on criminology, resulting in suggestions for a "conciliatory style" of social control (Black 1976), diversifying narratives in law-finding (Gilsinan 1982), reconceptualizing crime and justice in term of redress (de Haan 1990), and reconceptualizing penology (Milovanovic and Henry 1991) and criminology (Henry and Milovanovic 1991).

IV
DECONSTRUCTION AND CRIMINOLOGY--SOME INITIAL PROBLEMS

Our purpose in this section is to review some of the potential problems encountered in applying traditional (Derriderean) deconstruction to criminology.[7] After reviewing these concerns, we will suggest some alternative strategies that help remedy these problems.

A) Traditional Derriderean Deconstruction and Criminology

Deconstruction views text as written documents, stories, articles, etc... This strict view of the text is of limited value in criminology or any other *behavioral* science because as criminologists our ultimate concern is behavior. This is not to say that we are uninterested in written documents such as laws, crime statistics, ethnomethodological, theoretical and biographical accounts of crime, criminals and social control agents. However, none of these written documents are meaningful without behavior (including action and acts of linguistic construction). For instance, law cannot be written without the behavior of legislators, a legal apparatus and in some cases mobilized interests (public or private interest groups). And law and crime certainly would not be an issue if no one behaved in a way that others did not disapprove of and labelled "criminal." Consequently, if we interpret the mission of deconstruction too strictly, criminology would become a field of study that is far removed from the behaviors that generate the materials criminologists study.

Criminology's text, in short, eclipses deconstruction's narrow definition of the text: criminology's text is behavior, from the behavior of law (law in action, or applied law), to the behavior of police, to the behavior of criminals and non-criminals; of the relationship of conforming and non-conforming behavior. Behavior, especially the behavior of law-breakers and the agents who seek to control them, is the single most important aspect of the criminological text.

What we argue for is a critical-deconstructive criminology that is interdiscursive and demonstrates how behavior and textual production are interconnected. In this view, text production is not only limited by behavior, but serves, in turn, to define and limit behavior. At the same time, both processes occur in a definite historical context which constrains behavior and the meanings attached to those behaviors by text.

B) Lack of Replacement Discourse

Traditional forms of deconstruction are limited in another sense as well; they fail to establish the criteria whereby a replacement discourse can be constructed. This is a severe problem in criminology, where criminally constituted subjects result largely from the efforts of agents empowered to defend the status quo and reproduce hegemonic discourse that reaffirms existing power relationships (Henry and Milovanovic 1991).

C) The Privileged Subject: Crimes, Criminals or Agents of the State?

Since criminology is the study of the actions of criminals and the reactions (behavior) criminal behavior elicits from police, the community, etc., criminology's formal, written text cannot be separated from the criminal. It can also not be separated from the actions of agents of social control. Thus, if deconstruction is to apply to criminology, it must expand its method of analysis.

There is an additional problem as well. Traditional deconstruction is a subject-centered concern. But, in criminology, where there is more than one subject, one needs to ask more probing questions. Is *one* subject (the criminal or the agent of social control) more *privileged* than the other when it comes to determining meaning? Further, in positing this concern for the subject, deconstruction also rejects traditional authoritative hierarchies. Does this imply, then, that the "real" (privileged) subject is the powerless criminal? Again, we must return to the question of behavior. If behavior is not part of the text (as traditional deconstruction implies), then we cannot concern ourselves with the criminal, since the criminal authors only the behavioral text that is interpreted by agents of social control. In other words, a distinction between "readerly" and "writerly" texts must be made. A traditional deconstructive criminology produces a readerly text that reproduces the status quo because it excludes consideration of behavior as text. A similar point has been made by Henry and Milovanovic (1991) who, in their "constitutive criminology," address this confusion between behavior and text. They argue -- and we agree -- that crime as a text is coproduced by agents of control, those who attempt to explain crime and the criminal. At the same time, then, the criminal must also be considered. Let us take this view a bit further.

D) The Criminal as Author

The criminal as the "author" of criminal behavior generates various texts, including a self-text. By self-text we mean the control agent's verbalizations about the criminal, which are intimately connected with a flow of desire (if not two flows of desire, the criminal's and the agent's of control) and how these desires are given concrete expression. The criminal's desires, often hidden, are "spoken" by the agents of control (lawyers, courts, court recorders, etc.,) who are located in a preexisting, value-laden symbolic order designed to reformat the criminal's behavior in accordance with hegemonic discourse. In this way, the behaviors of all criminals are reinterpreted and homogenized. In short, the criminal's "text" is interpreted by an audience of subjective "readers" consisting of the "scientific community" of criminologists, the police, court reporters, judges, jurors, etc., -- those in authority. But, here's the rub: deconstruction instructs us to value subjective (the audience's) interpretations. In criminology, however, the audience is the powerful, scientific, rational community of authority that, as previously noted, deconstructionist attack on the grounds that it constructs a hierarchy of power which denies the subject a role in communication. Consequently, if we follow the logic of deconstruction too closely, especially in criminology, we end up with a system of knowledge production designed to enhance the hegemonic control and authority of the powerful (the scientific, rational community) by discounting or excluding the acting subject, the powerless criminal. This process of interpretation denies the subjectivity of the criminal. Thus, the situation that deconstruction fights against in philosophy and literature -- in pure linguistic communication -- is undermined when behavior is considered as part of the communication process.

E) The Political-Economy of "Knotting"

One more point of criticism needs to be addressed with regards to applying traditional forms of deconstruction in criminology. That point, as we noted above in reviewing critically-informed alternatives to deconstruction, is that deconstruction fails to address important political-economic determinants behind "knotting" processes by which signifiers are connected with a particular content (the signified). Also unaddressed is the subcultural significance of language and behavior, and the connection between subcultural construction of reality (behaviorally or linguistically) as a by-product of class position (e.g., Thomas 1991).

In response to our criticisms, some might argue that deconstruction is not concerned with behavior, and that it is purely a study of linguistic communication processes and problems. If this is the case, then such a philosophy is of little use in criminology where the subject matter is real, acting agents who communicate through action and behavior, not solely through language. Within criminology, language and written text are the sole domain of the powerful -- of those who write law; of those who try cases and make case law; of those who write textbooks and chalkboard notes; of those who collect and disseminate information about the criminal. Thus a focus on the text, especially if it excludes the criminal's behavior -- is nothing less than elitist.

In sum, the primary impediments to doing deconstructive criminology is to ensure that the method of analysis does not produce a system of thought that is unreflexive and capable only of reproducing existing social relationships. This is why we argue in favor of critical deconstruction: critical deconstruction pays greater attention to the powerless and the meanings they are attempting to construct, and the intersection of language, subjective and structural concerns (see Milovanovic 1990a, 1990b, 1988b; Goodrich 1984; Thomas 1988; Coombe 1990).

V
DECONSTRUCTING CRIME? TOWARD A CRITICALLY INFORMED DECONSTRUCTION

In the criminological tradition, a crime is generally understood as behavior that violates law. To deconstruct crime or the text defining crime, we must look for the unspoken -- we must read the margins of the text to discover the meaning that the author/text hides from us.

A) Behavior as Text

Crime is not only a word or text, it is also behavior -- something hidden by traditional deconstructive accounts of the text. Crime is constructed by those who act and those who interpret the act. As behavior, crime defines the role or relationship between acting individuals: criminals and victims; lawmakers and criminals; lawmakers and lawbreakers; lawmakers and the public; lawmakers and the victim; criminals and the police; etc. In each of these relationships there is a winner and a loser, social processes that bestow honor, prestige and dishonor, and a process that inscribes signs on the body. Taken together, the total process promotes a hierarchy which allows individuals or groups to assert their will over others, thus reconstituting a powerful/powerless hierarchy. In this power confrontation, winners (sometimes criminals) exert their will over losers to gain prestige and honor in concrete materialistic terms and abstract terms (Newman and Lynch 1988). In either case, winners accumulate and losers forfeit. The loser is forcefully subjected to conform, is stripped and humiliated; this game dehumanizes the powerless and territorialized the criminal. This process is captured in court, police and correctional records, but how is it captured? Along with Barthes, we suggest that the "readerly" text produced by the defenders of law and order produces a subject who is forced into relations and roles that protect existing hierarchical structures and which denies the criminal expression, or turns that expression into something other than what is intended. In addition, the deconstruction of the criminal's behavior which occurs in such texts hides from view unwanted connections, such as a connection between the criminal's behavior and society's material structure. The reader of these readerly texts, unless using an uncritical eye, is compelled to accept the legal system's view; is interpellated or sutured into the discourse constructed by the state and its agents to accept key signifiers and their meanings as legally constructed in the world of law and order. The authority or interest behind such rule making and language construction lays hidden and unquestioned. This, we suggest, is not simply a discourse, it is a discourse with a motive -- a motive driven by material forces.

B) Power and the Law Deconstructed

As a power relationship, law always represses the lowest, marginalized social class most forcefully and completely (Rusche and Kircheimer 1939). Criminal law represses the spirit of the least powerful; controls their minds and bodies; renders them docile; makes them submit to the will of the powerful; controls the time and space in which powerless sexes, races, ages and classes can move, think, breath, feel and act (Foucault 1977b). In this context, crimes themselves can be viewed as acts of deconstruction -- the behavioral deconstruction of the power arrangements of society and a reconstruction of existing power relations in a way that segments and territorializes. Certain age, race, sex and class groups are more likely to commit such deconstructive acts of crime because they are impelled to do so by virtue of their structural location, or because they are denied a stabilized discourse that allows articulation of the "I". However, and again, the linguistic system constructed by law hides this possibility from our view by referring to the criminal's state of mind and culpability -- by its own act of deconstruction.

Legal labels, in short, act as means of deconstructing not only the act of crime, but the person who undertakes the behavior. And, it does so in a way that shovels aside the subjective perspective of the criminal, relying instead upon criminal expert testimony, evidence, eye-witnesses and a jury of peers.

C) Criminals: Deconstructing and Reconstructing Social Order

Criminals deconstructs social arraignments by using behavioral forms to assert their power over the body of a victim (for the law-breaker's point of view see Athens 1990; Katz 1986). This act defies prevailing power arraignments sanctioned by law and creates the appearance of disorder. Law is thus called into play and acts, according to its written mandate, to reconstruct the order that the criminal has deconstructed. Law acts to reconstruct prevailing, historically specific meaning, or prevailing forms of power and domination. Law is brought to bear upon the body of the offender and to reassert the power of the victim over the offender; of society over the power of the individual; over the power that transgression has created through the criminal's action. This text is produced continuously. During this process, the constructor of action (the criminal, the acting subject) is transformed into an object that law acts upon. The object (the victim) is also transformed into an object that law acts upon. The object (the victim) is also transformed, through her/his attachment to the state, into the subject of action who now attempts to construct a new course of action that legitimizes the old order. The new course of action is a reconstruction of previously existing power relations that the initial subject (the criminal) has transformed or deconstructed through his/her action and the reactions of the state.

There is, in this process, an ongoing act of communication between subjects-objects who attempt to construct, deconstruct and reconstruct power relations within a given structural context that involves the immediate level of legal language and procedures and the more distant backdrop of the material context of society. The power relations that are involved in this process take the form of text (law), speech (commands, e.g., from police, judges, etc.,) and behavior (the subject's, legal, punishment), that attempt to effect the form of power that will prevail.

By looking at crime, criminality, criminal behavior and criminal processing through the lens of a critically-informed deconstruction, the stage is set for a humanistic and materially grounded replacement discourse. This discourse not only reveals what is happening in the legal process, but connects the legal process and its reaffirmation of the status quo to social inequality and the political-economic context. It does so in order to overturn the status quo and to establish a replacement discourse (an hegemonic discourse) based on humanism (cf. Marx 1976, 1975; Marx and Engels 1955).

D) Deconstructing Legal Processes

While we have been critical of traditional deconstruction, arguing that it needs to be "reformed" to analyze the criminal as an agent and the law as behavior, orthodox deconstructive (linguistic) theory may be of use to criminologists attempting to understand the structural nuances inherent in courtroom procedures that legitimize power relations and instill power (Jackson 1985, 1988; Bennet and Feldman 1981; Bannister and Milovanovic 1990). The relation of judge and jury is a linguistic relation -- both listen to and interpret "the facts" presented by attorneys. Both sets of agents construct meaning within subjective and structural (historical, class, power, knowledge, etc.,) confines. Criminal cases are set forth in testimony of witness, in evidence, somewhat like the chapters of a book. These testimonies are pieced together by judge/jury, who arrive at a verdict in a coherent narrative construction. Before the final verdict is rendered, the judge charges the jury, the jury meets, discusses and interprets the case. The information that the judge/jury receives in a case is essentially a deconstructed reading of the criminal act; they reconstruct "the facts" and occurrences from information that at times is conflicting, incomplete or absent. To complicate matters, they may be faced with testimony from people of different social, economic and ethnic backgrounds. These testimonies may not be fully understood because of linguistic differences.

Deconstruction implies that the act of the criminal is subordinate to the language used to interpret the behavior and that language may not be able to represent the Real (the behavior). Here, deconstruction does not solve our problem, but merely becomes a method through which problems may be revealed. It offers no course of action. Deconstruction of court proceeding, law, etc., may do nothing more than show that the painstaking detail of law, its exactness of words and actions, may be vague in practice.

CONCLUSION

We have argued that the overall methods and goals of *traditional* deconstruction are inconsistent with a radical view. Radical theory is humanistic and materialistic; it focuses on the interaction of subjects and objects within specific historical contexts. Deconstruction is idealistic (based in philosophy) and anti-humanist; it constitutes an attempt to make readers and interpreters superior to authors and objects; it is subjectively oriented; it is not concerned with historical nor material contexts.

These observation, however, are not meant to imply that the insights derived from deconstruction are useless. Rather, our argument implies that deconstruction's insights should be placed into a material and historical context that examines the relationship between language, communication, meaning and power relations (class, gender and race). Without this context, deconstructive analysis is too abstract -- it separates the act of communication from the structural context in which agents act and construct meaning. Actions and text producing activity cannot be divorced from social structure. Social structure provides the confines, roles and relationships that impinge upon human acts, which in turn reconstitute the dominant form.

Language, communication and the construction of meaning should be viewed in relation to human culture and structures. We should, as Mills (1959) urged, view human relations within the structural context that humans are enmeshed. In criminology, the lessons derived from a critically informed deconstruction may help us fulfill this goal.

* *Michael Lynch is an Assistant Professor at Florida State University.*

** *Richard A. Lynch is an Assistant Professor at Niagara University.*

*** *Dragan Milovanovic is Professor of Criminal Justice at Northeastern Illinois University.*

NOTES

1. An earlier version of this paper was presented at the Annual Meeting of the Academy of Criminal Justice Sciences, March, 1990. We would like to thank Ray Michalowski for his helpful comments on an earlier

version of this manuscript.

2. This perspective suggests that while truth cannot be understood given the human predicament or condition, that there is still a provisional and historical contingent truth.

3. Those from the post-Frankfurt, critically informed psychoanalytic semiotic view, argue that alienation is inherent to the human condition, initially introduced in the inauguration of the subject into the symbolic order; it is constitutive of self-identity and all of its illusions produced to overcome them; it is also the form that is subsequently the basis of politically and economically determined objects of desire, offered as potentials for fulfillment in overcoming the inescapable primal alienation (See, Williamson 1987 for an application to advertisement).

4. Readers are directed to Pecheux's (1982:155-170) discussion of the "good" subject who identifies with discursive subject-positions and cheerfully reconstructs dominant conceptions of reality, and the "bad" subject who actively distances him/herself from the subject-position assumed (see also MacCabe 1985:100-109; Bannister and Milovanovic 1990).

5. Lacan's work synthesizes Saussure's linguistics, Levi Strausse's examination of symbolic structures, Jakobson's analysis discourse production, Benveniste's insights on personal pronouns, and Hegelian-Kojevian notions of human desire.

6. There are 5 types of feminist approaches, those: (1) in support of Lacan (see Mitchell 1974; Mitchell and Rose 1982; Ragland-Sullivan 1986), or (2) revisionist stances (Kristeva 1980, 1984), or (3) oppositional stances (an "essentialist position" concerning the female subject; Irigaray 1985a, 1985b; Cixous 1981a, 1981b), or (4) qualified support -- a more "tactical" feminist position (Grosz 1990; Smith 1988:132-151), or (5) a pessimistic stance concerning the possibility of the female subject being resurrected in a phallocentric order (Moi 1985; Flax 1990). This latter position is exemplified by Moi, who argues that "there is no space uncontaminated by patriarchy from which women can speak" (1985: 81). For Moi, feminist struggles are situated in the more general struggles of the oppressed and marginalized.

7. We employ a legal definition of crime here for the sake of simplicity.

We recognize that there are other ways to define crime that are also legitimate.

REFERENCES

Althuser, Louis. 1971. *Lenin, Philosophy and Other Essays*. London: New Left Books.

Athens, Lonnie. 1990. *The Creation of Dangerous Violent Criminals*. NY: Routledge.

Bakhtin, Mikael. 1986. *Speech Genres and Other Late Essays*. Austin, TX: University of Texas Press.

Bannister, Shelley and d. Milovanovic. 1990. "The Necessity Defense, Substantive Justice and Oppositional Linguistic Praxis" *International Journal of the Sociology of Law* 18(1): 179-198.

Barthes, Roland. 1974. *S/Z*. R.Miller (Trans.). NY: Hill and Wang.

Baskin, Deborah. 1988. "Community Mediation and the Public/Private Problem." *Social Justice* 15(1):98-115.

Baudrillard, Jean. 1983. *Simulations*. NY: Semiotext.

Bennet, Lance and Martha Feldman. 1981. *Reconstructing Reality in the Courtroom*. New Brunswick, NJ: Rutgers University Press.

Berman, Art. 1988. *From the New Criticism to Deconstruction*. Chicago: University of Illinois Press.

Black, Donald. 1976. *The Behavior of Law*. NY: Academic Press.

Bogue, Ronald. 1989. *Deleuze and Guattari*. NY: Routledge.

Cicoux, H. 1981. "Castration or Decapitation" *Signs*, 7,1.

Coombe, Rosemary. 1989. "Room for Manoeuver: Toward a Theory of Practice in Critical Legal Studies." *Law and Social Inquiry* 14: 69-121.

____. 1990. "Postmodernity and the Rumor: Late Capitalism and the Fetishism of the Commodity/Sign." In W. Sterns (ed.). *Baudrillard in the Mountains*. NY: St. Martins Press.

____. 1991. "Contesting the Self: Negotiating Subjectivities in Nineteenth Century Ontario Defamation Trials," (Unpublished manuscript).

Culler, Jonathan. 1979. "Jacques Derrida." In J. Sturrock's (ed.), *Structuralism and Since: From Levi Strauss to Derrida*. NY: Oxford.

Deleuze, Gilles. 1983. *Nietzsche and Philosophy*. NY: Columbia University Press.

____. 1988. *Foucault*. Minneapolis: University of Minnesota Press.

____ and Felix Guattari. 1987. *A Thousand Plateaus*. Minneapolis: University of Minnesota Press.

De Haan, W. 1990. *The Politics of Redress*. Boston: Unwin Hyman.

De Man, P. 1986. *Resistance to Theory*. Minneapolis: University of Minnesota Press.

Derrida, Jacques. 1967. *On Grammatology*. Baltimore: Johns Hopkins University Press. (Trans. G.C. Spivak).

Ellis, John M. 1989. *Is There a Text in This Class?* Cambridge, MA: Harvard University Press.

Fish, S. 1982. "Working on the Chain Gang: Interpretation in Law and Literary Theory," *Critical Inquiry* 9.

____. 1984. "*Fish v. Fiss*," Stanford Law Review 36.

Flax, Jane. 1990. *Thinking Fragments: Psychoanalysis, Feminism and Post-Modernism in the Contemporary West*. Berkeley: University of California Press.

Flynn, Bernard. 1989. "Derrida and Foucault: Madness and Writing." In H.J.Silverman's (ed.), *Derrida and Deconstruction*. London: Routledge.

Foucault, Michel. 1977a. *Language, Counter-Memory, Practice*. D. F. Bouchard (ed.) Ithaca: Cornell University Press.

____. 1977b. *Discipline and Punish*. NY: Pantheon.

____. 1973. *The Birth of the Clinic*. NY: Vintage.

Gilsinan, James. 1982. *Doing Justice -- How the System Works -- As Seen by the Participants*. Englewood Cliffs, NY: Prentice-Hall.

Giroux, Henry. 1983. *Theory and Resistance in Education*. MA: Bergin and Garvey.

____. 1988. *Schooling and the Struggle for Public Life*. Minneapolis: University of Minnesota Press.

Goodrich, Peter. 1984. "Law and Language: An Historical and Critical Introduction." *Journal of Law and Society* 11(2):173-206.

Grosz, Elizabeth. 1990. *Jacques Lacan: A Feminist Introduction*. NY: Routledge.

Groves, W. Byron and M. J. Lynch. 1990. "Reconciling Structural and Subjective Approaches to the Study of Crime." *Journal of Research in Crime and Delinquency* 27(4):348-375.

Heath, Stephen. 1981. *Question of Cinema*. Bloomington, IN: Indiana University Press.

Henry, Stuart and D. Milovanovic. 1991. "Constitutive Criminology." *Criminology* 29(2):293-316.

Irigaray, Luce. 1985a. *Speculum of the Other Women*. Ithaca, NY: Cornell University Press.

____. 1985b. *This Sex Which is not One*. Ithaca, NY: Cornell University Press.

Jackson, Bernard. 1985. *Semiotics and Legal Theory*. NY: Routledge and Kegan Paul.

____. 1988. *Law, Fact, and Narrative Coherence*. Merseyside, U.K.: Deborah Charles Publications.

Katz, Jack. 1989. *Seductions of Crime*. NY: Basic Books.

Kristeva, Julia. 1980. *Desire in Language*. NY: Columbia University.

____. *The Revolution in Poetic Language*. NY: Columbia University Press.

Lacan, Jacques. 1977. *Ecrits*. London: Tavistock.

Laclau, Ernesto and Chantal Mouffe. 1985. *Hegemony and Socialist Strategy*. London. Verso.

Lecercle, Jean-Jacque. 1990. *The Violence of Language*. NY: Routledge.

____. 1985. *Philosophy Through the Looking Glass: Language, Nonsense, Desire*. London: Hutchinson.

Love, Nancy. 1986. *Marx, Nietzsche, and Modernity*. NY: Columbia University Press.

Lynch, M. J. and W. B. Groves. 1989. *Primer in Radical Criminology. 2nd Edition*. NY: Harrow and Heston.

Lyotard, Jean-Francois. 1988. *The Postmodern Condition: A Report on Knowledge*. Minneapolis: University of Minnesota Press.

MacCabe, Colin. 1985. *Tracking the Signifier*. Minneapolis: University of Minnesota Press.

Manning, Peter. 1988. *Symbolic Communication: Signifying Calls and the Police Response*. Cambridge: MIT Press.

____. 1990a. "Critical Semiotics." *The Critical Criminologist* 1(4): 7-8, 16, 18.

____. 1990b. "Critical Semiotics: Part II." *The Critical Criminologist* 2(1): 5-6, 16.

Melichar, Kenneth. 1988. "Deconstruction: Critical Theory or an Ideology of Despair?" *Humanity and Society* 12(4):366-385.

Michalowski, Ray. 1985. *Order, Law and Crime*. NY: Random House.

Mills, C.W. 1959. *The Sociological Imagination*. NY: Oxford.

Milovanovic, Dragan. 1990a. "Critical Criminology and the Challenge of Post Modernism," *The Critical Criminology* 1(4): 9-10, 17.

____. 1990b. "Humanist Sociology and the Chaos Paradigm: A Review Essay of N. Katherine Hayles, Chaos Bound." *Humanity and Society* (In Press).

____. 1991a. "Images of United and Disunity in the Juridic Subject and the Movement Toward the Peacemaking Community," in R. Quinney and H. Pepinsky (eds.) *Criminology as Peacemaking*. Bloomington: Indiana University Press.

____. 1991b. "Rethinking Subjectivity in Law and Ideology: A Semiotic Perspective" in D. Currie and B. MacLean (eds.) *Struggles for Equality*. Toronto: Garamon Press.

____. 1988a. *A Primer in the Sociology of Law*. NY: Harrow and Heston.

____. 1988b. "Jailhouse Lawyers and Jailhouse Lawyering." *International Journal of the Sociology of Law*. 16:455-475.

____. 1986. "Jurdico-Linguistic Communicative Markets: Towards a Semiotic Analysis." *Contemporary Crises* 110:281-304.

____. and Stuart Henry. 1991. "Constitutive Penology." *Social Justice* (In Press).

____. and Jim Thomas. 1989. "Overcoming the Absurd:Prisoner Litigation as Primitive Rebellion." *Social Problems* 36(1): 48-60.

Mitchell, Juliet. 1974. *Psychoanalysis and Feminism*. London: Allen Lane.

____ and Jacqueline Rose. 1982. *Feminine Sexuality: Jacques Lacan and the Ecole Freudienne*. London: MacMillan.

Moi, Toril. 1985. *Sexual/Textual Politics*. London: Metheun.

Muller, John and William Richardson (eds.). 1988. *The Purloined Poe: Lacan, Derrida, and Psychoanalytic Reading*. Baltimore, MD: The Johns Hopkins University Press.

Newman, Graeme. 1985. *The Punishment Response*. NY: Harrow and Heston.

Nietzsche, Friedrich. 1968. *Basic Writings of Nietzsche*. W. Kaufman (ed.). NY: The Modern Library.

Norris, Christopher. 1988. "Law, Deconstruction, and the Resistance to Theory," *Journal of Law and Society* 15.

Pashukanis, Evleny. 1980. "The General Theory of Law and Marxism." In P.

Beirne and R. Sharlet (eds.), *Pashukanis*. NY:Academic Press.

Pecheuz, Michel. 1982. *Language, Semiotics and Ideology*. NY: St. Martin's Press.

Phohl, Stephen and Avery Gordon. 1986. "Criminological Displacements: A Sociological Deconstruction." *Social Problems* 33(6): 94-113.

____ and A. Gordon. 1985. *Criminological Displacements*. Video Text. Boston: Parasite Cafe Productions.

Ragland-Sullivan, Ellie. 1986. *Jacques Lacan and the Philosophy of Language*. Chicago, IL: University of Illinois Press.

Rusche, Georg and Otto Kirchheimer. 1968[1939]. *Punishment and Social Structure*. NY: Russell and Russell.

Ryan, Michael. 1982. *Marxism and Deconstruction*. Baltimore: Johns Hopkins University Press.

Sarup, Madan. 1989. *An Introductory Guide to Post-Structuralism and Postmodernism*. Athens, GA: The University of Georgia Press.

Schwartz, Marty. 1989. "The Undercutting Edge of Criminology." *The Critical Criminologist* 1(2):1-2,5.

Shaw, Peter. 1986. "The Politics of Deconstruction." *Partisan Review* 53:252-262.

Silverman, Kaja. 1983. *The Subject of Semiotics*. NY: Oxford University Press.

Smart, Barry. 1983. "On Discipline and Social Regulation: A Review of Foucault's Geneological Analysis." In D. Garland and P. Young's (eds.), *The Power to Punish*. London: Heinemann Press.

Smith, Paul. 1988. *Discerning the Subject*. Minneapolis: University of Minnesota Press.

Soper, Kate. 1986. *Humanism and Anti-Humanism*. London: Hutchinson.

Thomas, Jim. 1988. *Prisoner Litigation: The Paradox of the Jailhouse Lawyer*. Totowa, NJ: Allen and Littlefield.

____ and Aogan O'Maochatha. 1989. "Reassessing the Critical Metaphor." *Justice Quarterly* 6: 143-172.

____ and Gordon Meyer. 1990. "Joe McCarthy in a Leisure Suit: (Witch)Hunting for the Computer Underground." *The Critical Criminology* 2(3).

Tillich, Paul. 1956. "Existential Aspects of Modern Art." In C. Michaelson's (ed.), *Christianity and the Existentialists*. NY: Scribner.

Volosinov, V.N. 1986. *Marxism and the Philosophy of Language*. Boston: Harvard University Press.

Weber, Max. 1978. *Economy and Society*. Berkeley: University of California Press.

Williamson, Judith. 1987. *Decoding Advertisements: Ideology and Meaning in Advertising*. NY: Marion Books.

Wittgenstein, Ludwig. 1983. *Philosophical Investigations*. Oxford: Oxford University Press.

Zizek, Slavoj. 1989. *The Sublime Object of Ideology*. NY: Verso.

Chapter XI

"GOOD FAITH","BAD FAITH": RHETORIC, IDEOLOGY AND THE UNITED STATES SUPREME COURT*

W. Richard Janikowski**

Polemics have beset the exclusionary rule since its inception. While Justice Douglas believed that the United States Supreme Court's decision in *Mapp v. Ohio* (1961) had ended "the storm of constitutional controversy" (p. 670) engendered by Wolf v. Colorado (1949), the ensuing years have demonstrated that the storm "has not only intensified - but engulfed the fourth amendment exclusionary rule itself." (Kamisar 1983: p. 566). Critics have called for abandonment of the rule (Burger 1964; Wright 1972; Schlesinger 1977; Wilkey 1978) while defenders consider it constitutional or political necessity (Sunderland 1978; Kamisar 1982; Canon 1982). Others suggest a need to limit application of the exclusionary rule to those situations where police have acted willfully, maliciously, in bad faith or without reasonable cause (Coe 1975; Ball 1978; Jensen and Hart 1982; Uviller 1982). Moreover, various members of the Supreme Court at different times have called for re-examination of the scope of the rule: *Stone v. Powell* (1976) (Burger, C.J., concurring, p. 496; White, J., dissenting, p. 536); *Brown v. Illinois* (1975) (Powell, J. concurring in part, pp. 609-612); *Schneckloth v. Bustamonte* (1973) (Powell, J. concurring, pp. 261-271); *California v. Minjares* (1979) (Rehnquist, J., dissenting from denial of stay).

Responding to these criticisms, the Court, since its decision in *Mapp*, has developed numerous exceptions to the exclusionary rule. This process, culminating in the Court's decision in *Leon v. United States* (1984), has substantially diminished the scope of the exclusionary rule. This paper examines the development of the exclusionary rule with particular emphasis on the reasoning used by the Court to justify the rule and the later exceptions. It is suggested that the Court has redirected its analysis of the foundations of the exclusionary since it's decisions in *Weeks* and *Mapp*. Since *United States v. Calandra* (1974), the Court has used a balancing of interests approach, essentially cost-benefit analysis, to determine the appropriateness of the exclusionary remedy in a particular area. This new direction has provided the Court with the opportunity to fashion the various exceptions to the rule. Analysis of the discursive constructions of the various decisions reveals the manner in which the values of various justices influence the outcome of particular cases, and points to the manner in which outcome actually constructs doctrine. As Brion (1994: 22) has noted:

> A salient attribute of the adjudicative process in the United States legal system is its doctrinal dynamism. Indeed, it is something of a misnomer to speak of 'judicial docrtine,' as if dispute resolution proceeded deductively by the application of enduring doctrinal principles to particular facts to yield a result. Rather, particularly at the appellate levels of the adjudicative process, law-as-precedent is being tested as much as the merits of the positions of the contending parties. 'Doctrine' instead is a product of academic legal scholarship, which in major part is synthetic and inferential --deriving from judicial opinions the contours of the doctrine that would generate the results had the courts reached these results deductively. Quite literally, doctrine does not determine the outcome of particular disputes so much as it is that the outcomes of these disputes determine doctrine.

In the area of criminal procedure concerned with the exclusion of illegally obtained evidence the validity of Brion's insight quickly becomes apparent. The recent decisions of a majority of the Supreme Court, which publicly proclaims adherence to a doctrine of 'judicial restraint,' reveal the underlying mechanism for the creation of doctrine.

FORMULATING THE RULE: A CONSTITUTIONAL REQUIREMENT

The United States Supreme Court first addressed the problem of excluding evidence in *Boyd v. United States* (1886). The Court in *Boyd*, finding the Fourth and Fifth Amendments as running "almost into one each other" (p.

630) concluded that the Amendments:

> .... apply to all invasions on the part of the government and its employees of the sanctity of a man's home and the privacies of life. It is not the breaking of his doors, and the rummaging of his drawers, that constitutes the essence of the offense; but it is the invasion of his indefeasible right of personal security, personal liberty and private property.... Breaking into a house and opening boxes and drawers are circumstance of aggravation; but any forcible and compulsory extortion of a man's own testimony or of his private papers to be used as evidence to convict of crime or to forfeit his goods, is within the condemnation.... (*Boyd* at 635.)

Within thirty years, in *Weeks v. United States* (1914), the Court would again be faced with the issue in a case involving the warrantless seizure of letters and articles by U.S. marshals. Finding that the marshals had acted without the "sanction of law" (p. 393) and in a manner that "not even an order of court would have justified" (p. 394), the Court elucidated a philosophical foundation for excluding the evidence that had been used to convict the defendant:

> The effect of the Fourth Amendment is to put the courts of the United States and Federal officials, in the exercise of their power and authority, under limitations and restraints as to the exercise of such power and authority, and to forever secure the people, their persons, houses, papers and effects against all unreasonable searches and seizures under the guise of law. This protection reaches all alike, whether accused of crime or not, and the duty of giving it force and effect is obligatory upon all entrusted under Federal system with the enforcement of the laws. The tendency of those who execute the criminal laws of the country to obtain conviction by means of unlawful seizures and enforced confessions, the latter often obtained after subjecting accused persons to unwarranted practices destructive of rights secured by the Federal Constitution, should find no sanction in the judgments of the courts which are charged at all times with the support of the Constitution... (*Weeks* at 392.)

The Court observed that allowing such evidence to be used in a criminal prosecution would be tantamount to declaring that the Fourth Amendment had no value and that "so far as those thus place and concerned, might as well be stricken from the Constitution." (p. 393). Concluding that punishment of the guilty did not justify sacrificing "those great principles established by years of endeavor and suffering" and embodied in "the fundamental law of the land" (p. 393), the Court stated that "[T]o sanction such proceedings would be to affirm by judicial decision a manifest neglect if not an open defiance of the prohibitions of the Constitution." (p. 394). Clearly the Supreme Court was unwilling to engage in a cost-benefit analysis regarding what it perceived as a fundamental right.

This approach would be reiterated in *Silverthorne Lumber Co. v. United States* (1920). In *Silverthorne* the government made copies of various documents, obtained during the course of a warrantless search, prior to their return to the defendants. The copies became the basis for a subpoena issued to the defendants for the original documents. In reversing a contempt order entered against the defendants for failure to comply with the subpoena, Justice Holmes, writing for the Court, noted that to allow the government to avoid the holding of *Weeks* by use of this type of two step process reduced the Fourth Amendment to a "form of words." (p. 392). Announcing what would later become known as the "fruit of the poisonous tree" doctrine, Holmes suggested that the essence of the Fourth Amendment was not merely that the original evidence was not to be used in court, "but that it shall not be used at all." (p. 392). Essentially for thirty -five years following *Weeks* the Supreme Court rarely addressed the rationale of the exclusionary rule and never compared the relative merits of the exclusionary rule to alternative methods of enforcing the fourth amendment. (Kamisar 1983)

Then in 1949 the Court in *Wolf v. Colorado* appeared to retreat from its prior position. Using a fundamental rights approach, the *Wolf* Court, while finding "no hesitation in saying that were a State affirmatively to sanction such police incursion into privacy it would run counter to the guaranty of the Fourth Amendment" (p. 28), declined to impose the *Weeks* rule upon the states. The majority found that the *Weeks* doctrine "was not derived from the explicit requirements of the Fourth Amendment" but was "a matter of judicial implication." (p. 28). As such the Court believed it could not "brush aside the experience of States which deem the incidence of such conduct by the police too slight" to require imposition of an exclusionary remedy. The Court concluded that the states had not left the right of privacy unprotected but had, and would in the future, develop alternative remedies. While not explicitly addressing the efficacy of the exclusionary rule as a remedy, the majority's focus on alternative remedies suggests the beginning of a cost-benefit analysis.

This interpretation is reinforced by the Court approvingly quoting from Justice (then Judge) Cardozo's opinion in *People v. Defore* (1926):

> The question is whether protection for the individual would not be gained at a disproportionate loss of protection for society. On the one side is the social need that crime shall be repressed. On the other, the social need that law shall not be flouted by the insolence of office. There are dangers in any choice. The rule of the *Adams* case [176 N.Y. 351, 68 N.E. 636] strikes a balance between opposing interests. (Wolf at 32, fn. 2.)

Within twelve years, in *Mapp v. Ohio* (1961) the Court would reverse itself. Holding that evidence obtained in violation of the Fourth Amendment was inadmissible in state criminal proceedings, the Court stated:

> Since the Fourth Amendment's right of privacy has been declared enforceable against the States through the Due Process Clause of the Fourteenth, it is enforceable against them by the same sanction of exclusion as is used against the Federal Government. Were it otherwise, then just as without the *Weeks* rule the assurances against unreasonable federal searches and seizures would be a " form of words", valueless and undeserving of mention in a perpetual charter of inestimable human liberties, so too, without that rule the freedom from state invasions of privacy would be ephemeral and so neatly severed from its conceptual nexus with the freedom from all brutish means of coercing evidence as not to merit this Court's high regard as a freedom "implicit in the 'concept of ordered liberty'". (*Mapp* at 655).

The Court appeared to base its decision in part on a finding that the experience of the states with alternative remedies had been "worthless and futile". (p. 652). Additionally though, the Court recognized another imperative, judicial integrity, for its decision. Justice Clark observed that while some critics had suggested that "[t]he criminal is to go free because the constable has blundered", it is "the law that sets him free." (p. 659). He reminded critics that "[N]othing can destroy a government more quickly than its failure to observe its own laws, or worse, its disregard of the character of its own existence" (p. 659), and directed their attention to Justice Brandeis' dissent in *Olmstead v. United States* (1928):

> Our government is the potent, the omnipresent teacher. For good or for ill, it teaches the whole people by its example.... If the government becomes a lawbreaker, it breeds contempt for law; it invites every man to become a law unto himself; it invites anarchy. (*Olmstead* at 485).

While some critics (Schrock and Welsh 1974) have suggested that it is not clear from the opinion whether the exclusionary rule is constitutionally required because of its deterrent intention, or because it actually works as a deterrent, Kamisar (1983) has cogently pointed out that when taken in its totality the opinion is fairly clear. It can be understood to say:

> We reaffirm the "original understanding" of the exclusionary rule, as explained in *Weeks* and its progeny, that (anything to the contrary in *Wolf* notwithstanding) it is a constitutionally required rule, although not explicitly provided for in the text of the fourth amendment- and moreover (again, anything to the contrary in *Wolf* notwithstanding), it is the most effective (or the only presently available effective) means of deterring police conduct. (p. 623)

It therefore appeared that the basis for the exclusionary rule was an understanding that it was constitutionally required by the Fourth Amendment. In Professor Allen's (1961) words, "the exclusionary rule is part of the Fourth Amendment; the Fourth Amendment is part of the Fourteenth; therefore, the exclusionary rule is part of the Fourteenth." (p. 26).

REFORMULATING THE RULE: DETERRENCE

By 1974 this formulation of the rationale for the exclusionary rule began to be undermined. Beginning with *United States v. Calandra* (1974), the Court in a series of decisions reconsidered the basis upon which the exclusionary rule rested. Now the Court would balance the deterrent effect of the rule against the cost to the government and society of excluding evidence (Whitebread and Slogin 1986).

In *Calandra*, the Court found the exclusionary rule's primary purpose was "to deter future unlawful police conduct and thereby effectuate the guarantee of the Fourth Amendment against unreasonable searches and seizures." (*Calandra* at 348). Therefore the Court concluded that the rule was a judicially created remedy "designed to safeguard Fourth Amendment rights generally through its deterrent effect, rather than a personal constitutional right of the party aggrieved." (*Calandra* at 348). Accepting this formulation of the rationale for the exclusionary rule the court determined that extension of the rule to grand jury proceedings would depend on the costs of such action as compared to any accrued benefits. Applying the test, the court found that any incremental benefit was uncertain at best and therefore refused to extend the scope of the exclusionary to grand jury proceedings.

Utilizing the *Calandra* balancing approach, the Court developed the "dissipation of taint" concept in *Brown v. Illinois* (1975) reasoning that at some point "the detrimental consequences of illegal police action become so attenuated that the deterrent effect of the exclusionary rule no longer justifies its costs." This analysis allowed the Court in *Stone v. Powell* (1976) held that a state prisoner who has been afforded a full and fair opportunity to litigate a Fourth Amendment claim may not obtain federal habeas relief on the ground that unlawfully obtained evidence had been introduced at trial. In reaching this conclusion the Court emphasized the social costs of the exclusionary rule and concluded that limiting the circumstances under which Fourth Amendment claims could be raised in federal habeas corpus proceedings would not reduce the rule's deterrent effect.

Thus in *Rakas v. Illinois* (1978) the Court limited standing to challenge admission of the fruits of an illegal search and seizure to the actual victim of the police misconduct, having previously found in *Harris v. New York* (1971) that even a defendant with standing could not prevent admission of such evidence for purposes of impeachment. In both cases the Court found that any incremental furthering of the exclusionary rule was outweighed by resulting costs.

Similarly, in *Michigan v. DeFillippo* (1979), the Court refused to suppress evidence obtained by police officers relying in good faith on a criminal statute subsequently declared unconstitutional. Finally, in *United States v. Leon* (1984) the Court announced a "good faith" exception to the exclusionary rule judging that "the marginal or non-existent benefits produced by suppressing evidence obtained in objectively reasonable reliance on a subsequently invalidated search warrant cannot justify the substantial costs of exclusion." (922). In essence the Court concluded that the exclusionary rule could not, and should not, be used to deter objectively reasonable police activity.

The Court's conclusion in *Leon* comes after an extensive review of the decisions involving the exclusionary rule. The Court's analysis appears to indicate that a balancing approach has always been the focus of any test determining application of the exclusionary rule. Thus the *Leon* Court found that "the balancing approach that has evolved during the years of experience with the rule provides strong support for the modification currently urged upon us" (*Leon* at p.913). Further the Court concluded that "the question whether the use of illegally obtained evidence in judicial proceedings represents judicial participation in a Fourth Amendment violation and offends the integrity of the courts 'is essentially the same as the inquiry into whether exclusion would serve a deterrent purpose'" (*Leon* at p.920, fn.22). *Leon* therefore stands for the proposition that the fundamental purpose of the exclusionary rule is deterrence of unreasonable police conduct. Utilization of this standard combined with the "good faith" analysis found in *Leon* may well have set the stage for the Court to take a new direction in further developing the exclusionary rule.

A NEW DIRECTION: BAD FAITH?

This new direction in analyzing exclusionary rule cases may have been revealed by the Court's recent decision in *Arizona v. Youngblood* (1988). In *Youngblood* the Court considered whether police must preserve evidence that if scientifically tested might produce results exonerating a defendant. Revisiting "the area of constitutionally-guaranteed access to evidence" (p. 287), the Court held that, absent a showing of bad faith on the part of the police, no due process violation occurs from a police failure to preserve evidence of questionable evidentiary for possible use by the defendant.

The Court's decision reversed an Arizona Court of Appeals[1] ruling that the officer's failure to preserve and test samples of seminal fluid on the clothing of a sodomy victim violated the defendant's due process rights. Police had taken possession of the underwear and T-shirt worn by the victim, a young boy, but did not refrigerate or freeze the clothing. Samples were also taken from the victim's body soon after the crime but were at first only examined for a determination of whether sexual contact had occurred. A police criminologist determined that contact had occurred but performed no further tests. He also did not examine the clothing. The criminologist testified that tests to identify blood group substances were not routinely conducted during the initial examination of a sexual assault kit, and even later, in only about half of all cases. Later the prosecution requested that a blood group test be performed in an attempt to ascertain the blood type of the victim's assailant. This test failed to detect any blood group substances in a rectal swab sample.

More than a year later, a police criminologist attempted a blood type analysis, using an ABO blood type group test and a P-30 protein molecule test, on semen stains found on the clothing. These tests failed to reveal any information regarding the perpetrator's identity.

At trial the defendant's principal defense was that the victim erred in identifying the defendant as the perpetrator of the crime in a photographic line-up. Both a criminologist for the state and an expert witness for the defense testified as to what might have been shown by tests performed on the samples shortly after they were gathered or, by later tests performed on samples from the boy's clothing had they been properly refrigerated.

The jury found the defendant guilty, but the Arizona Court of Appeals reversed the conviction finding that "when identity is an issue at trial and the police permit the destruction of evidence that could eliminate the defendant as the perpetrator, such loss is material to the defense and is a denial of due process" (153 Ariz. 50 at p. 54). The Court of Appeals concluded, without implying any bad faith on the
part of the state, that expert testimony at trial demonstrated that timely performance of tests with properly preserved semen samples could have produced results that might have completely exonerated the defendant.

Chief Justice Rehnquist, writing for a five-member majority, began the Court's opinion by distinguishing the case from prior access-to-evidence decisions. Previously in *Brady v. Maryland* (1963) the Court had held "that suppression by the prosecution of evidence favorable to the accused upon request violates due process where the evidence is material to guilt or to punishment, irrespective of the good faith or bad faith of the prosecution" 373 U.S. at p. 87). Then in *United States v. Agurs* (1976) the Court found that the prosecution had a duty to disclose some evidence of this type even absent a defense request. However, the Court rejected the notion that the prosecutor had a constitutional duty to "routinely deliver his entire file to the defense" (427 U.S. at p.111). Previously in Moore v. Illinois (1972), the Court had observed that there was no constitutional requirement for the prosecution to "make a complete and detailed accounting to the defense of all police investigatory work on a case (408 U.S. at p.786).

The Chief Justice found that the prosecution had complied with the requirements of *Brady* and *Agurs*. The prosecution had disclosed relevant police reports, revealed the existence of the samples and clothing, and given the defendant's expert access to the samples and clothing. Therefore, the majority concluded that for the defendant to prevail on federal constitutional grounds there must exist some constitutional duty over and above that imposed in *Brady* and *Agurs*.

In an effort to determine whether such a duty existed, the Court turned to a review of *California v. Trombetta* (1984). In *Trombetta* defendants attempted to suppress breath test results in a drunk driving prosecution on the grounds that the prosecution had failed top preserve the breath samples used in the test. The Court, finding no due process violation, had rejected the defendant's argument for several reasons:

> .... first, "the officers here were acting in 'good faith and in accord with their normal practices,'" ....second, in light of the procedures actually used the chances that preserved samples would have exculpated the defendants were slim, ... and, third, even if the samples might have shown inaccuracy in the tests, the defendants had "alternative means of demonstrating their innocence." (*Youngblood* at p.288).

The Chief Justice noted that while the evidence in *Youngblood* had a greater likelihood of enabling the defendant to exonerate himself, the prosecution, unlike in *Trombetta*, had made no attempt to use the materials in its own case-in- chief. Further, *Trombetta* had established a standard of constitutional materiality that required evidence to have "apparent" exculpatory value "*before* the evidence was destroyed" (emphasis in original) (Youngblood at p. 288). The Chief Justice observed that the possibility that the semen sample, if preserved or tested, could have exonerated the defendant failed to meet the *Trombetta* standard. Further, the defendant failed to demonstrate that the police knew that the semen samples would have exculpated him when they failed to perform certain tests or preserve the clothing by proper refrigeration. The Court concluded that the "presence or absence of bad faith by the police for purposes of the Due Process clause must necessarily turn on the police's knowledge of the exculpatory value of the evidence at the time it was lost or destroyed" (*Youngblood* at p. 288- 89). This was particularly important, the majority observed, since prior decisions in related areas concerning loss of evidence had stressed the importance for constitutional purposes of good faith or bad faith on the part of the government.

This reasoning led the Chief Justice to draw a distinction between the holding in *Brady*, making good faith or bad faith irrelevant where the prosecution fails to disclose material exculpatory evidence, and such cases as *Trombetta* which deal with "the failure of the State to preserve evidentiary material of which no more can be said than that it could have been subjected to tests, the results of which might have exonerated the defendant" (*Youngblood* at p. 289). In the latter type of case the Court found that good faith assumed paramount importance because of two considerations. First, the value of the unpreserved evidence is unknown. Second, the Court indicated an unwillingness to

> impose on the police an absolute duty to preserve all material which might conceivably have some evidentiary significance in a particular prosecution.
>
> We think that requiring a defendant to show bad faith on the part of the police both limits the extent of the police's obligation to preserve evidence to reasonable bounds and confines it to that class of cases where the interests of justice most clearly require it, i.e., those cases in which the police themselves by their conduct indicate that the evidence could form a basis for exonerating the defendant. We therefore hold that unless a criminal defendant can show bad faith on the part of the police, failure to preserve potentially useful evidence does not constitute a denial of due process of law.

Justice Stevens, concurring in the judgment, rejected the new rule as announced by the Court as being too broad. In his opinion, cases might exist in which the defendant was unable to prove that the police acted in bad faith but in which the loss or destruction of critical evidence might make a criminal trial fundamentally unfair.

Justice Blackmun, joined by Justices Brennan and Marshall, argued in dissent that police should be required to preserve evidence which might exonerate a defendant where no comparable evidence is available. The dissenters argued that *Trombetta*'s mention of "good faith" had been wrenched out of context by the majority since in that decision the Court had merely observed that the police had followed their usual practice. In the present case, the dissenting Justices observed, there was no suggestion that police were following general practices when they failed to prevent deterioration of the evidence.

Most importantly though, according to Justice Blackmun, the issue of good faith is merely preliminary to the primary inquiry of the "constitutional materiality" of the evidence. In this inquiry it "makes no sense to ignore the fact that a defendant has been denied a fair trial because the State allowed evidence that was material to the defense to deteriorate beyond the point of usefulness, simply because the police were inept rather than malicious" (*Youngblood* at p.295). Further the dissent argued that apart from the inherent difficulty a defendant would have in proving bad faith, significant ambiguity remains regarding the differences between "bad faith" and "good faith". Therefore, Justice Blackmun noted, the decision did not provide the type of "bright line" test desired by the majority but only succeeded in moving the line "so as to provide fewer protections for criminal defendants" (*Youngblood* at p. 295). Instead the dissent suggested that such cases be evaluated by focusing on

.... on the type of evidence, the possibility it might prove exculpatory, and the existence of other evidence going to the same point of contention in determining whether the failure to preserve the evidence violated due process. (p.297)

THE FUTURE OF THE EXCLUSIONARY RULE

The impact of the decision was apparent almost immediately. Later in the term the Court, acting on a suggestion by the federal government in an amicus brief, remanded for reconsideration in light of *Youngblood* a case involving prosecutorial delay. According to the government's brief in *Michigan v. Leigh* (1989)

> "If, as the Court held in *Youngblood*, the intentional or negligent destruction of potentially useful evidence does not violate due process unless it is done in bad faith, there is no justification for a different rule when delay in bringing charges is held to be prejudicial because it has exactly the same result - the loss of potentially useful evidence. (*Criminal Law Reporter* 1989, p. 4110).

The Court's decision in *Youngblood*, and the willingness to remand for reconsideration in *Leigh*, has ominous implications for the future of the exclusionary rule.[2] Chief Justice Rehnquist's willingness to wrench the language of *Trombetta* out of context to arrive at a desired result may signal a new willingness to adopt a result-oriented jurisprudence. This analysis is supported by the majority's willingness to find a bad faith exception to *Brady*, a decision going to the fundamental fairness of a criminal trial. As Justice Blackmun noted, *Brady* and it's progeny "in no way require that government actions that deny a defendant access to material evidence be taken in bad faith in order to violate due process" (*Youngblood* at p.292). Instead the Chief Justice engages in a sleight of hand to discover a bad faith exception to *Brady*; a torturous and incorrect reading of other cases. In effect the majority translates "good faith" in other cases to mean "bad faith" in *Youngblood*.

This willingness to twist language and reread cases in new light, often out of context, may in the future provide the basis for further distinguishing of the exclusionary rule. It would not be difficult for the Court to find that goal of deterring "unreasonable" police conduct while minimizing the social costs of exclusion can best be met by adoption of a "bad faith" standard. This is especially true if the Court is willing to engage in the type of analysis found in *Youngblood*, where "good faith" can be translated to mean "bad faith". An analysis of this type would allow the Court to take the position that prior exclusionary cases were not being overruled, merely distinguished. Thus a new doctrine is formulated, not based on logic, precedent, or deduction, but on linguistic and discursive constructions designed to justify a particular outcome in the case before the Court. The Court's decisions decisions reveal the tension between the Court's proclaimed doctrine of 'judicial restraint' based on adherence to precedent and doctrine, and the actual manner in which decisions are made by judicial bodies.

CONCLUSION

A careful review of the development of the exclusionary rule demonstrates, Justice Harlan's dissent in *Mapp* notwithstanding, that it was the *Wolf* and *Calandra* Courts which had "forgotten the sense of judicial restraint." (*Mapp* at 672.) These decisions, and those subsequent to *Calandra*, involved a marked departure from the constitutional understanding of the Court in *Weeks* regarding the Fourth Amendment. This departure is most evident in the Court's decision in *Leon* creating the "good faith" exception. The development of the deterrence rationale in exclusionary rules decisions has produced an approach destructive to the American constitutional tradition; an analysis that reduces the Constitution to the status of a mere legislative enactment.

The Court may well be on the verge of doing further damage to the constitutional tradition in future decisions. The possibility of the Court announcing a "bad faith" standard in exclusionary rule cases appears to be hovering above the horizon. The *Youngblood* decision possibly indicates the mechanism by which the Court may develop a "bad faith" standard in exclusion cases. To avoid this result the Court needs to refocus its analysis from the current deterrence rationale, which involves a cost-benefit analysis, to a conceptual framework of constitutional philosophy. A return to the reasoning of *Weeks* within a framework of philosophical integrity can repair the damage done to the Constitution in the past two decades.

* *This chapter is a revision of paper presented at the Annual Meeting of the*

** *W. Richard Janikowski is Associate Professor of Criminology and Criminal Justice at the University of Memphis.*

NOTES

1. On remand the Arizona Court of Appeals reversed the conviction and dismissed the charges. Finding that the Due Process Clause of the Arizona Constitution provides greater protection than its federal counterpart, the Arizona court rejected application of the *Youngblood* standard in state criminal proceedings. (46 CrL 1337 (1990)).

2. These decisions and the governments position obviously also have implications for other areas of criminal procedure. For example, application of this standard to the emerging field of DNA fingerprint evidence might well prevent defendants from effectively being able to contest alleged "scientific" evidence of guilt.

REFERENCES

Allen, F. 1981. "Federalism and the Fourth Amendment: A Requiem for Wolf." *Supreme Court Review* 1961:1-48.

Ball, E.F. 1978. "Good Faith and the Fourth Amendment: The 'Reasonable' Exception to the Exclusionary Rule." *Journal of Criminal Law and Criminology* 69:635-657

Burger, W. E. 1964. "Who Will Watch the Watchman?" *American University Law Review* 14:1-23.

Canon, B. C. 1982. "Ideology and Reality in the Debate Over the Exclusionary Rule: A Conservative Argument for Its Retention." *South Texas Law Journal* 23:559-582.

Coe, P. S. 1975. "The ALI Substantiality Test: A Flexible Approach to the Exclusionary Sanction." *Georgia Law Review* 10:1-51.

Jensen, D. L. and R. Hart. 1987 "The Good Faith Restatement of the Exclusionary Rule." *Journal of Criminal Law and Criminology* 73:916-938.

Kamisar, Y. 1982. "How We Got the Fourth Amendment Exclusionary Rule and Why We Need It." *Criminal Justice Ethics* 1:3-

___. 1983. "Does (Did) (Should) the Exclusionary Rule Rest on a 'Principled Basis' Rather than an 'Empirical Proposition'." *Creighton Law Review* 16:565-667.

Schlesinger, S. R. 1977. *Exclusionary Injustice*. New York: M. Dekker.

Schrock, T. S. and R. C. Welsh. 1974. "Up from Calandra: The Exclusionary Rule as a Constitutional Requirement." *Minnesota Law Review* 59:251-383.

Sunderland, L. V. 1978. "The Exclusionary Rule: A Requirement of Constitutional Principle." *Journal of Criminal Law and Criminology* 69:141-159.

Uviller, H. R. 1978. "The Acquisition of Evidence for Criminal Prosecutions: Some Constitutional Premises and Practices in Transition." *Vanderbilt Law Review* 35:501- 526.

"The U.S. Supreme Court 1988-89 Term". (1989, August 16). *The Criminal Law Reporter*. 45: 4109-4110.

Whitebread, C. and C. Slobogin. 1986. *Criminal Procedure: An Analysis of Cases and Concepts, 2nd ed*. Mineola, New York:Foundation Press, Inc.

Wilkey, M. R. 1978. "The Exclusionary Rule: Why Suppress Valid Evidence?" *Judicature* 62:215-232.

Wright, C. A. 1972. "Must the Criminal Go Free If the Constable Blunders." *Texas Law Review* 50:736-745.

CASES CITED

Arizona v. Youngblood, 102 L. Ed. 2d. 281 (1988)

Boyd v. United States, 116 U.S. 616 (1886)

Brady v. Maryland, 373 U.S. 83 (1963)

Brown v. Illinois, 422 U.S. 590 (1975)

California v. Minjares, 443 U.S. 916 (1979)

California v. Trombetta, 467 U.S. 479 (1984)

Harris v. New York, 401 U.S. 222 (1971)

Leon v. United States, 486 U.S. 847 (1984)

Mapp v. Ohio, 367 U.S. 643 (1961)

Michigan v. DeFillippo, 443 U.S. 31 (1979)

Michigan v. Leigh, No. 88-557, 104 L. Ed. 2d. 150 (1989)

Moore v. Illinois, 408 U.S. 786 (1972)

Olmstead v. United States, 277 U.S. 438 (1928)

People v. DeFore, 242 N.Y. 13 (1926)

Rakas v. Illinois, 439 U.S. 128 (1978)

Schneckloth v. Bustamonte, 412 U.S. 218 (1973)

Silverthorne Lumber Co. v. United States, 251 U.S. 385 (1920)

Stone v. Powell, 428 U.S. 465 (1976)

United States v. Agurs, 427 U.S. 97 (1976)

United States v. Calandra, 414 U.S. 338 (1974)

Weeks v. United States, 232 U.S. 383 (1914)

Wolf v. Colorado, 338 U.S. 25 (1949)

Chapter XII

MORAL PHILOSOPHY, SOCIAL JUSTICE AND THE QUESTION OF PUNISHMENT IN A JUST SOCIETY*

Dragan Milovanovic**

Establishing first principles to a just social order has been the focal point of a number of prominent treatises. In this article the moral philosophical positions of Rawls (1971), Gewrith (1978), Phillips (1986), Habermas (1976), and more recently Reiman (1990) will be briefly presented and critiqued. I will then present the postmodernist challenge, resting specifically on Lacan's psychoanalytic semiotics and on the recently emerging notions of chaos theory and its central idea of orderly disorder. A constitutive approach to establishing moral first principles will be offered as a necessary beginning point in the transformation from the "is" to the "ought" in social theory. We will conclude by specifying some elements of a just political economic order. Necessarily we will separate two stages: a more static stage where some just ideals have already been instituted along with the distributive principles that are in accord, and a more dynamic stage where injustices are in need of correction by some re-distributive schema (Phillips, 1986: 317-318, 341; Reiman, 1990). The question of punishment and sanction, we will show, is an historical question that has everything to do with political economic structures.

ESTABLISHING FIRST PRINCIPLES

We begin with the idea that human beings live within specific orders. These provide regularities, uniformities, and patterns within which reciprocally presumptive orientations can take place. Hence a degree of stability may be maintained within which coordinated action may develop (Weber, 1978; Phillips, 1986: 3). Thus, social structure has potentially an infinite form within which human beings may live. Social structure provides differential life chances. The question now becomes: is there any set of first principles of justice that we can specify for a just order?

In order to answer this question we must, as Phillips has quite correctly argued, specify the difference between the "is" and the "ought." Whereas the positivistic sciences delude themselves with the ideals of the "is," ostensibly attempting to pay exclusive attention to the descriptive and analytic devoid, so it is claimed, of value-taking positions, the moral philosophers state that a truly humanistic science must also consider the "ought," that is, specifying some principles by which institutions and social relationships should be guided.

Many within humanistic oriented sociology, which I define as a science combing the "is" and the "ought," have been guided by Marx. Marx, especially in *The Critique of the Gotha Program*, had clearly specified three principles of justice. In capitalism the principle is one of formal equality. In socialism, people will be rewarded according to their contribution. In the "higher forms," communism, the principle would be "from each according to his[her] ability, to each according to his[her] needs," -- the needs principle. Although a worthy starting point, this does not take us far. It is time to move on. In this section we would want to briefly present some of the most prominent rational moral philosophers (Rawls, 1971; Gewirth, 1978; Phillips, 1986) including Reiman's recent statement (1990). We would also want to consider Habermas's discourse ethics rooted in a practical discourse as a basis of establishing first principles of a just order. We are especially concerned with the contrast of deductive and inductive processes as well as with deontologically and teleologically oriented approaches.

Rawls

Rawls' book, *A Theory of Justice* (1971), has been the center of much debate. It certainly has been one of the most controversial books on moral philosophy. Let us briefly present the core argument.

Rawls is concerned with establishing a rationally justified set of first principles that could be the basis of a just order. His starting point is some mythical "original position" within which women and men meet to form the primordial social contract and its underlying set of moral first principles that ought to exist. In order to assure that each does not merely reflect her/his ontological status, and that none will argue from differentially situated positions of inequality, a "veil of ignorance" should prevail, according to Rawls. All that must be assumed is that persons are rational and desire to advance their interests. Since no one begins from an unfair bargaining position the principles arrived at would be fair. According to Rawls two principles of justice would indeed be agreed upon (1971: 302):

> *First Principle*
> Each person is to have an equal right to the most extensive total system of equal basic liberties compatible with a similar system of liberty for all.
>
> *Second Principle*
> Social and economic inequalities are to be arranged so that they are both:
> (a) to the greatest benefit of the least advantaged, consistent with the just savings principle, and
> (b) attached to offices and positions open to all under conditions of fair equality of opportunity.

By "basic liberties" Rawls includes the right to vote; to be eligible for holding public office; to have freedom of speech, assembly, and thought; the right of holding private property; and the freedom against arbitrary seizure and arrest (1971: 61). The second principle states that positions and offices in organizations must be equally open to all persons, and that social and economic inequality is permissible only to the extent that the least advantaged member of the group does not suffer (ibid.). Furthermore, there exists a serial ordering where the first principle has priority over the second. In other words, basic liberties can not be infringed by the offered justification of greater social and economic gains. Critical in Rawls' formulation is the "difference principle" inherent in the Second Principle: in other words, that economic and social inequalities can only be justified where they offer the greatest benefit to the least advantaged. Said in yet another way, economic and social inequalities ought to be arranged in such a way that they offer the greatest benefit to the least advantaged.

Criticisms have been offered, most importantly from Phillips (1986); that his principle assumes that we can distinguish morally right from morally wrong principles; that his "difference principle" is insensitive to those who are seriously handicapped or sick (ibid.: 350, 354) and hence not at all really concerned with the truly worst-off; that desert for efforts is incapable of being measured and in fact, an extreme interpretation has it that "no one deserves anything" (ibid.: 359-60); and that his "original position" and "veil of ignorance" can only be attained by denying the complexities of being human, by denying the plurality of choosing agents -- rendering persons a rational standing but one devoid of context, of ontological being -- and hence Rawls' subjects do not really exercise "choice" at all: they have been denied their differential standing and hence possible grounds for being human, in fact, only one homogeneous subject is the deciding entity (ibid.: 60-66).

Gewrith/Phillips

Gewrith (1978) and Phillips (1986) have much in similarity. However, Phillips does improve on Gewirth's fundamental position.

Alan Gewirth, in his classic *Reason and Morality* (1978), does not ground his moral first principles in any original position, but rather he claims, they can be logically derived from the very dynamics of human action. A rational subject he defines as a person who is guided by inductive and deductive logic (1978:22). It is the power of reason itself that will be the basis of logically derived first principles (ibid.). Even when one attempts to attack reason itself, one must, in the process, rely on reason (ibid.: 23).

More specifically, Gewirth argues that the "necessary content of morality is to be found in action and its generic features" (ibid.: 25). Gewirth's notion of action, having much similarity with Weber's notion of an orientation (Phillips, 1986: 90), has it that "the intention of the persons who set them forth is to guide, advise, or urge the persons to whom they are directed so that these latter persons will more or less reflectively fashion their behavior along the lines indicated in the precepts" (ibid.: 26-27).

It follows, argues Gewrith, that action then has two "generic features": "voluntariness or freedom and purposiveness or intentionality" (ibid.:27). From this it follows that first principles of justice must include the right to freedom and well-being as generic rights (ibid.: 64; see also Phillips, 1986: 95). This is so because only by each persons claiming that s/he has these rights each must acknowledge these rights in others that are similar to him/her that are rational agents (Gewirth, 109). When a rational agent acknowledges a right to freedom and well-being in her/himself, s/he must also acknowledge the same in the other, otherwise it would go against logic and be contradictory. Hence, Gewirth concludes with his *Principle of Generic Consistency* (PGC): "*Act in accord with generic rights of your recipients as well as of yourself*" (ibid.: 135). Again, for Gewirth, this is a derived principle from the peculiarities of action itself, specifically with its necessarily embedded right to freedom and well-being. It is only with these rights that action itself can take place; hence, the supreme first principle should acknowledge, for Gewrith, these constitutive elements. We ought not to unduly interfere with other person's right to freedom and well-being.

Phillips, in his book *Toward a Just Social Order* (1986), builds on Gewirth's ideas. In fact he states that "In my view Gewirth has provided all that is required in the way of a rational justification for the rights to freedom and well-being" (1986: 114). He has also stated that deontological theories are preferred over teleological ones; that is, moral first principles that are universalizable are preferred to ones with only local applicability, and that a substantive moral principle based on human action itself is best (Phillips, 1986: 114). Thus for Phillips, Gewirth's two principles, the right to freedom and the right to well-being are first principles for a just order.

It is at this point that Phillips improves on Gewirth's view. First, Phillips emphatically argues that the right to well-being is prior to any other right. Unless a person has a "basic right to subsistence and security" [by the former meaning necessary food, clothing, shelter, and health care; by the latter, security against violence and invasion of privacy]... "they cannot meaningfully exercise their right to freedom" (1986: 115). Since these principles can be established on pure logical reasoning, they should be seen as first principles of a just order. Hence, the generic rights to freedom and well-being and the Principles of Generic Consistency are the justification principles, rationally derived, that are also relevant to law-making and law-finding practices (ibid.: 327).

Phillips also indicates that two phases must be considered when discussing the development of first principles: the static and dynamic phase (1986: 341). Assumed in the static phase is the wide-spread acceptability and applicability of generic rights. Assumed in the dynamic phase, however, are inequalities in well-being and freedom. Necessary, in the latter, then, is a just redistributive schema. But the Generic right to well-being has preference over freedom (ibid.: 342). Going beyond Rawls' "difference principle" which, according to Phillips, is not truly concerned with the worst-off such as the seriously handicapped or sick, Phillips suggest that the principle of well-being necessitates establishing some social minimum in its distributive schema (ibid.: 351-342) by way of transfers. This social minimum can be established only through considering the limits or possible adverse effects on efficiency (ibid.: 352). And this is where Gewirth's argument does not go far enough, according to Phillips (ibid.: 354).

Neither Rawls nor Gewirth are sufficient in providing the grounds for the exercise of people's right to well-being. Gewirth in fact revives a desert's principle arguing that those who work more should receive more (Gewirth, 1978: 313; Phillips, 1986: 354-55) and it is to this, according to Gewirth, that Rawls is insensitive. This is consistent with Gewirth's high emphasis on people's voluntary efforts; desert logically follows rather quickly. Phillips, on the other hand, quite convincingly shows that Rawls must logically find himself in an infinite regress when explaining desert; desert can always be pushed further back to some unknown beginning point; hence, according to Phillips, "Rawls's argument that no one deserves anything is so totally deterministic as to leave no room at all for the exercise of individual initiative, control, and responsibility" (ibid.: 360; Gewirth, 1978: 331). So both Gewirth and Phillips, guided by their rational man constructs and generic principles rooted in action must also accept the notion of desert. The only question becomes one of the appropriate limitation. Although Phillips does present a better argument that could in many ways be seen as apologetic to Gewirth's position it is only Reiman's recent treatise (1990) that saves the day for the rational moral philosophers. The only saving position Phillips presents is that societal income differences ought to be reduced to perhaps a ratio of five-to-one and the surplus should be used for providing for a social minimum. This reduced ratio would not undermine incentives for filling necessary positions in society according to Phillips who provides evidence for this being so (1986: 372, 378). It remains an empirical question for Phillips as to how much further this ratio of income differentials could be reduced to still assure efficiency, investment, and continued interest in accepting diverse jobs. At best, with a decreased ratio, a higher social minimum will be established (ibid.: 378).

Reiman

Jeffrey Reiman's recent book, *Justice and Modern Moral Philosophy* (1990), has overcome many of the shortcomings of Phillips, although, as we will show, he still clings to a rational model of man/woman as do the other rational moral philosophers presented above. We need not, however, disregard the whole theory; each of the rational moral philosophers, including Reiman, certainly do provide important first principles that ought to be considered when envisioning the just order. In this section we will briefly present Reiman's main ideas particularly his novel idea of a "labor theory of moral value" that would be in force during the dynamic stage. We will then present Habermas' open-ended discourse ethics and the idea of a practical discourse within which first principles could arise.

Reiman's deontologically-based first principles are logically derived by reason. Reason demands maintenance of non-subjugating relationships. It is reason itself that provides rational beings a legitimate justification for his first principles. By "reason" Reiman means "the capacity to make correct inferences from propositions" (1990). And "subjugation" means "when a person exercises free will to reach a judgment about how to act but is denied, without true justification, the freedom of action to execute that judgment" (ibid.: 10).

Just as Phillips was to rescue Gewirth from some of his critics, so too Reiman was to rescue Rawls from his critics. Reiman claims that his theory of justice provide Rawls's approach with a "necessary foundation" (ibid.: 21) that overcomes some of Rawls's intuitively formulated theory (ibid.: 230). Reiman's asserts that his own "difference principle" can be derived deductively (ibid.). With this in mind he provides his two summary principles of justice:

> 1. *Whether or not* people *cooperate* to produce benefits, they owe each other noninterference, easy rescue, respect for natural ownership, trustworthiness, intergenerational solicitude, and punishment no greater than lex talionis and deterrence require -- and these are owed to everyone equally.
>
> 2. Where people *do cooperate* to produce benefits, they owe each other distribution of the benefits and efforts that went into producing them according to the difference principle -- that inequalities must work to maximize the share of everyone in society starting from the worst-off individual (1990: 2-3).

The first principle is required by "natural justice"; the second by social justice. Most important is where Rawls and Reiman contrast as to the difference principle. Whereas Rawls's difference principle focuses on how goods ought to be distributed, Reiman's focuses on how proportions are determined. Thus Reiman's claim is that his difference principle is primarily directed at the protection against subjugation and only secondarily at distributing goods (ibid.: 3). In fact, Reiman's position on a difference principle, in our view, is much superior to Rawls's or Phillip's in that it provides an answer to the question of just deserts (his "labor theory of moral values") as well as to how a solidarity discourse might take form (a discourse of "mutual benefit"). Let's see why.

Reiman's starting position is an ongoing social structure which he defines as characteristically a forced system of labor (ibid.: 213, 223); that is, behavioral patterns have become crystallized that can no longer be viewed as genuinely voluntary. Along with this, life chances are structurally limited (ibid.: 221, 232). He also assumes that agents understand their mortality and that each person is driven by self-interest (ibid.: 15). Given this, a rational justification for non-subjugation must exist. Reason must offer benefits that outweigh the forced nature of the social structure. For Reiman "the social contract is reason's answer to subjugation by the social structure" (ibid.: 229).

Against this backdrop Reiman develops his two principles of justice during the dynamic phase. To this end he derives his difference principle which he calls a "labor theory of moral value" (ibid.: 244). Rather than focusing on distribution of goods, what his principle advocates is the distribution of labor that is inherent in the good's production. Labor he defines as "a definite quantity of time and energy from the finite sum of time and energy available to an individual over the course of his life" (ibid.). So the central measure will be time labored. Thus for Reiman, if the difference principle allows inequalities and at the same time is to make room for incentives for greater labor it must work at two fronts: (1) the worst-off must, during the dynamic stage where a re-distributive schema is a requisite for change, be provided with a principle where they simultaneously benefit by the actions of the better-off and are also provided an incentive schema, and (2) the better-off's gained inequality must at the same time benefit the worst-off, but this re-distributive schema must not be a dis-incentive for increased work and benefit for the better-off. Reiman's difference principle as was the case with Rawls does allow for inequality, differential benefits, and just deserts but only where the worst-off gain also. To pass the test of non-subjugation, the principle must overcome a system of forced labor that is inherent in a social structure (ibid.: 273). To do this, Reiman has devised an ingenious formulation that indeed overcomes the limitations of Rawls' theory, particularly as it deals with the difference principle. Consider the following (from Reiman, 1990: 279-280):

1. **Equal distribution**

	A		B
measured in labor time:	8 hours	<-->	8 hours
measure in goods:	8 loaves	<-->	8 cups

2. **Lowest minimum incentive**

measured in labor time:	8 hours	<-->	12 hours
measured in goods:	16 loaves	<-->	12 cups

3. **Highest minimum incentive**

measured in labor time:	8 hours	<-->	16 hours
measured in goods:	24 loaves	<-->	16 cups

4. **Free market range**

measured in labor time:	8 hours	<-->	16-23 hours
measure in goods:	24 loaves	<-->	16-23 cups

In line number one, A exchanges 8 loaves of bread which took him/her 8 hours to make, with B for 8 cups (of whatever), which took B 8 hours to make. This would be the traditional capitalist mode of just desert. Reiman's difference principle, however, would work in such a way as to provide an incentive for B, the worse-off, to produce more by the fact that in doing so, s/he receives an additional incremental increase from A. Thus in line number 2, by B working 4 more hours s/he will produce 4 more cups, but in the exchange with A, will receive 8 more loaves rather than 4 more (= the incremental increase as the incentive). A, on the other hand, in working in the same time it took him/her to produce 8 loaves and because of her/his greater capabilities and incentives, may now produce 16 loaves, twice as much as before, and will receive 4 more cups (rather than 8 more) from B. In other words, A, working the same time and producing more, will get more goods.

In line number 3, the highest minimum incentive is presented. In line number 4, the full range of permissible differentials is depicted. Here, if A has the capacity to produce 24 loaves in 8 hours and if B, the less-talented (and worst-off) can produce 16-23 cups in 16-23 hours, benefits will still accrue to both A *and* B in an exchange. Hence, A exercising his/her talents in 8 hours could receive 16-23 cups; whereas B, in working 16-23 hours could still receive a disproportionally greater return with the effort expended. This, then, would support Reiman's "principle of mutual benefit" (ibid.: 282-284), or "principle of reciprocal advantage" (ibid.: 289). Here "each benefit conferred by one person on another is matched by a reciprocating benefit" (ibid.: 276). It is this, Reiman, tells us, that overcomes the suspicion of subjugation; reason itself demands it.

Reiman tells us that during the dynamic (transitional) stage the redistributive schema would also need further political intervention in the form of redistributive taxation and welfare programs (ibid.: 286). But the upshot of Reiman's proposal is that it is perfectly conceivable within the capitalist mode of production, and can, under the appropriate circumstance lead to the distributive schemas associated with socialism and to that of communism (ibid.: 286). He tells us that at that point where an incentive schema is no longer necessary (i.e., scarcity is overcome and desire to labor itself becomes an incentive) his difference principle would no longer allow inequalities in the distributive schema (ibid.). Here, for example, Marx's principle under socialism would provide the standard for the just distribution (ibid.). Reiman's difference principle not only answers the call for the need for differential incentives required by prevailing differentials in labor during the dynamic stage where a re-distributive schema must be at work, but it also provides the potential for the development of a solidarity discourse rooted on a mutual benefits ethics.

Habermas

The final moral philosophy we will briefly present and discuss is Habermas's discourse ethics that would be established in practical discourse. This approach has evolved over a number of years in Habermas's writings (Habermas, 1976, 1984, 1987, 1988). Briefly, Habermas distinguishes between a "practical" and a "technical-instrumental" discourse. The former can only be realized in the sphere of human interactions, in concrete, practical settings; here, establishing knowledge and understanding is a collective undertaking. In the latter, bureaucracies, work places, schools, prisons/jails and mental health institutions, and science favor rational discussion concerning means and ends. In his two volume set, The *Theory of Communicative Action* (1984, 1987), he has traced the rationalization of the "life world" in which technical-rational discourse has increasingly prevailed over practical discourse. For Habermas the question of appropriate principles of justice abruptly arrives during legitimation crises. This underscores the idea that for Habermas legitimate authority is one that is justifiable, or one that is willingly accepted. However, genuine first principles are not established through a unilateral rational discourse by philosophers: they must await situations of practical discourse within which persons provide competing validity claims. Discourse ethics, therefore is context specific. Developing substantive principles is therefore an open enterprise and is subject to the limitations of language and communication in practical discourse.

Habermas's starting point in establishing possible grounds for the development of first principles is the much heralded "ideal speech situation" (1976: 107-108). Here interlocutors present criticizable validity claims within an unrestricted setting. "No force except that of the better argument" is the one that will prevail. The task is to establish a consensual understanding. Assumed, of course, is the ideal community of equal interlocutors; that is, the symmetry principle that underlies the ideal speech situation. It should be stated that this has been presented as an ideal, not really attainable in interactions. As Phillips states, Habermas is offering not a substantive principle but a methodology in arriving at a practical consensus (1986: 81). Whereas for Rawls, agents establish their first principles in the "original position" behind a "veil of ignorance," for Habermas, agents establish their principles in the ideal speech situation (ibid.). In a very true sense, then, the ideal first principles could only be reached in this setting. Since the latter remains only an ideal, then, universalizable first principles are, too, only an ideal.

Phillips's attempt to undermine Habermas's point, stating that the symmetry principle could never be attained (1986: 84), misses the point, as does his view that perhaps an individual, thinking alone, could arrive at the higher principle (ibid.: 85). The first is too restrictive, the second too generous. However, Phillips is correct in stating that since establishing substantive first principles, for Habermas, is an open-ended process, then he is incapable of providing, from this starting point, a grounded, universal position of the just order (ibid.: 87). The very real possibility exists, argues Phillips who draws some inspiration from Phillip Pettit, that if an ideal speech situation is in fact reached a *number* of principles of justice might materialize and leave the order beyond a grounded basis of criticism (ibid.: 88). In many ways, then, Habermas has reached the impasse that has been levied against Derrida's anti-foundational position. If everything is criticizable, always remaining open to change, then a relativistic point might be accepted, and in the case of repressed groups, no grounded basis might then justifiably exist for revolt. Alan Hunt has well stated the point:

> If "one opinion is as good as another" the project of scholarship itself seems to be doomed if the opinion of the fool is as valuable as that resulting from painstaking study. If "anything goes" it becomes impossible to distinguish between a moral judgement and self-interest. If there is no means to construct an argument which makes it "better" or "stronger" than another then all judgements, whether legal, political or moral, are arbitrary, and arbitrariness is a step along the road to either anarchy or tyranny (1990: 524).

In sum, we accept Habermas's thrust concerning the ideal speech situation in a qualified way. Without more, it is, ironically, potentially nihilistic. Its main improvement on Rawls, Gewirth, Phillips, Reiman and other rational moral philosophers is that it dismisses any unilaterally and abstractly dictated set of first principles that do not recognize the communicatively and linguistically established reality construction processes of pragmatic encounters.

Critique and the Question of Punishment in a Just Order

Having examined some of the key contemporary statements on moral principles in a just order, we have located a methodological thrust predicated on some notion of an original position, with Rawls's seeing it being combined with a veil of ignorance out of which rationally justified first principles could develop, with Gewirth's and Phillips's beginning point on the constitutive elements of action itself, with Reiman's starting point on an ongoing social structure of forced labor, and finally with Habermas's ideal speech situation within which substantive principles could arise. These could be based on formal rationality (Rawls, Gewirth, Phillips, Reiman) as opposed to a substantive rationality (Habermas); on deontological justifications (principles-based theories such as Rawls, Gewirth, Phillips, Reiman) as opposed to teleological (focused on desired end states, for example see Alasdair MacIntyre's *After Virtue*, 1981) -- Reiman, too, does seem to acknowledge a component of the teleological justification when he advocates punishment in a just society which looks toward future good consequences particularly when he talks about general deterrent effects (1990: 198); on notions of deserts, with Rawls questioning its precise determinability, Gewirth and Phillips in praising it as a natural consequence of rational action by agents in control, with Reiman noting its necessarily divisible quality, and with Habermas ostensibly arguing that it too is a principle that arises in practical discourse of the ideal speech situation; on the question of how to devise a redistributive schema during the dynamic stage that benefits the truly disadvantaged (handicapped, sick, elderly, etc.), with Rawls providing little guidance, but with Phillips pointing the way to assuring some social minimum, with Reiman offering the notion of "easy rescue," and with Habermas standing somewhat embarrassingly moot. Having said all this we now turn to the question of punishment in a just society.

For Gewirth and Phillips, punishment is permissible in the just society. Since the state in a just order reflects the generic rights of rational individuals, coercion may be necessitated where some do not stay within the contractual terms. Those punished are not denied their generic rights, for the state too finds itself justified by the generic principle of consistency (Phillips, 1986: 101).

Thus for Gewirth and Phillips, coercion and pain inflicted on those who do not comport with generic rights is perfectly justified in a just society.

Rawls' position on punishment is contradictory. Accepting the idea that defining just deserts accurately is impossible (1971: 103-105) or "impracticable" (ibid.: 312), he nevertheless defends a system of punishment, at times erroneously equating a more coercive form (punishment) with a more symbolic form (penal sanction) (ibid.: 240-241; 314-315). If desert cannot be justified in the positive direction, it surely cannot be defended in a negative direction as well.

Reiman, in his more recent statement, justifies punishment in the just order. In less evolved societies natural justice demands retribution along the lines of *lex talionis* (1990: 187); in more developed societies marked by a social structure, just punishment would be more in terms of "proportional retributivism" (ibid.). Having much in similarity with Gewirth (1978: 294-295, 297), Reiman seems to oppose restitution for it simply returns the previous situation of status quo and it overlooks the fact that the victim has not contributed to the disturbance in the first place whereas the offender has. Retribution, on the other hand, "involves imposing a loss on the offender that reduces him below the status quo ante" (ibid.: 188). So for Reiman, "taking enough from the thief so that what he is left with is less than what he had before the offense is retribution, since this is what he did to his victim" (ibid.). *Lex talionis*, for Reiman, re-establishes a situation of "mutual respect," of equality (ibid.: 194). Reason, he tells us, demands this.

Before moving onto Habermas's position, it is worth while to go over a recent commentary by Willem de Haan on conceptual distinctions (1990: 111-112). In his book *The Politics of Redress: Crime, Punishment and Penal Abolition*, de Haan, an abolitionist, distinguishes between penal punishment and penal sanction. The latter stands for particular rules prohibiting certain actions and for the necessary consequence with their violation, the former provides specific painful penalties if the rule is found to be broken (see also Hirst, 1986: 142-59). Penal punishment usually stands for coercion, infliction of pain and loss, and suffering. As de Haan's analysis indicates, punishment can be traced to the idea of being treated like a slave (1990: 112). On the other hand, Freiberg has defined sanction as an "intentional manipulation of values" (cited in de Haan, 1990: 112), and that combining punishment and sanction is "conceptually, heuristically, and semiotically unfortunate" (ibid.). Working it from another direction, Hirst (1986) has shown that under socialist legality, where punishment has disappeared, does not also necessarily equate with its coercive forms disappearing (ibid.). In other words, outwardly one may stipulate a system of pure sanction, but still have coercion, pain, loss and suffering being inflicted. De Haan's conclusion, and we agree, is that there is no intrinsic connection between punishment and sanction (ibid.). Having rectified that, we can now turn to Habermas's contribution to the debate. We are especially persuaded with de Haan's integrative work here (1990: Chapter 6, 8) and therefore will follow it.

De Haan's main criticism of Gewirth's and Phillips justifications of punishment in a just order is that for them the notion of punishment is non-problematic; they do not undertake an examination of the deeper significance of sanction as a response to transgressions (1990: 116) and hence punishment is seen only as a necessary evil. Phillips does attempt to also argue for the need for more internalization of guilt mechanisms during socialization (1986: 210-241) and hence for redress, reparation, and atonement, but does not draw out how this is specifically different from punishment (de Haan, 1990: 118-19) and in actuality is better seen as one of a number of possible responses to problematic behavior. More consistent with the abolitionist movement is Habermas's discourse ethics.

Whereas Rawls, Gewirth, Phillips, and Reiman provide substantive first principles generated by reason and logic, for Habermas these can only be established at a more local level in practical discourses of concrete situations. Substantive rationality, then, can only be grounded by way of discourse and communication in on-going social activities. Here, criticizable validity-claims are being offered on an on-going basis which are resolved only in context. In fact, de Haan rightfully argues against the rational moral philosophers in that defining rationality, universalistically, in terms of acceptance of deduction and induction is too rigid and does not conform to the frailties of the human condition (1990: 124). Rather, discourse found in normal everyday encounters is more open-ended and loose (ibid.: 124; Billig, 1987).

Contrary to the rigid logical requirements established by Aristotle, Billig has argued that arguments more often make use of "enthymemes" which are made up of a "statement together with a justification," and therefore "real arguments always burst around its edges" (1987: 102). This is so because the starting point of any argument may entail the choice of diverse premises and therefore the subsequent syllogisms may vary diversely too (ibid.). Thus for Billig, logic and syllogistic reasoning produces "certainties," whereas enthymemes produce "probabilities" (ibid.). The incontrovertible fact of enthymemes is that they must be supported by another enthymeme which in turn, for justification purposes, must be supported by another, ad infinitum (ibid.).

Having said this Habermas's thesis of a practical discourse seems rather well suited with the workings of everyday normative structures. It offers an open-ended framework for arriving at consensus, and hence provides by way of induction the possibility of substantive moral first principles. It also provides the grounds for rethinking sanction rather than penal punishment. As opposed to Gewirth and Phillip who are arguing for an increase of pain and suffering, Habermas offers a potential development of the ideal of removing harm, pain, and suffering wherever possible (see also de Haan, 1990: 128-29).

De Haan's very valuable contribution to the question of punishment in a just society is his offering of the notion of "redress" (1990: chapter 8) which relies very heavily on Habermas's discourse ethics. He advocates the implementation of a practical discourse model in law-finding practices. Especially compelling is the support he derives from much of the feminist writings concerning women's experiences. In other words, women's real experiences of oppression in context can be the source of more universalistic principles. In addition a "caring" model is being offered, one based on maintaining qualitative relations, an inductive model, and a compelling challenging model to the phallocentrically dominated notions of justice, order, and punishment (ibid.: 155). His notion of redress can be stated:

> a) 'Redress' includes almost every conceivable reaction to an event - individual, collective, structural, material, or immaterial.
> b) It implies that response is mandatory, without pre-defining the event as a crime, an illness, or anything else.
> c) It invites analysis of the event before deciding or choosing a proper response.
> d) As a concept with ancient origins, it invokes the consideration of historical and anthropological forms of dispute settlement and conflict resolution for possible clues to rational forms of response (ibid.: 158).

De Haan advocates that these notions be introduced in our law-finding practices. In other words, practical discourse should be introduced in conflict situations that are being resolved formally before some adjudicatory forum. Importantly, the central concern will be with *context* (ibid.: 159-60). Necessarily, a wide range of meaning constructs in the form of narratives will be presented, debated, and some sense of the "what happened?" will surely begin to materialize. Here, more formal and abstract concepts such as responsibility, accountability, intentionality, necessary care, and guilt could be debated *in context* (ibid.).

Two outstanding problems with de Haan's position remain however. First, as he himself shows to be problematic, how is some type of closure arrived at? Can there ever be complete agreement? (Note the Clarence Thomas nomination proceedings for the Supreme Court Justiceship and the challenge posed by Anita Hill). Second, he claims that the practical discourse he advocates would be aimed at developing "generalizable and principled conclusions" that transcend the concrete context, group, and/or community (ibid.: 159). One wonders, however, how this could be so. What underlies this position is that it is not a pure inductive model that he advocates, but rather a model that looks toward reciprocal interactions between loose deductive and inductive processes. It seems that his view could be better developed into a constitutive model of establishing moral first principles that would be neither static nor totally open-ended. We shall return to this point in the next two sections.

Having said that, however, there does seem some room to integrate some aspects of action theory of Phillips with Habermas's notion of the ideal speech situation. In other words, agents do in fact enter ongoing encounters which are structured normatively. A constitutive approach, for example, would recognize that agents are both constructors and constructed entities. Pragmatic encounter provide not only a context, but also discursive subject-positions. Add to this that each interlocutor brings with him/her a unique self-text and desires that need to undergo translation as they seek expression in one context, discursive subject-position, and discourse rather than another, and we have inherently destabilizing tendencies within any unfolding textual production of an encounter, even in spite of being an ideal speech situation. But this leads us into our next section of the postmodern challenge.

THE POSTMODERNIST CHALLENGE

The most important critique of rational moral philosophy has to do with its rational man/woman construct. Rawls, Gewirth, Phillips and Reiman all assume the centered subject in control. Postmodernism challenges this central presupposition. Here we want to briefly introduce one prominent alternative construct of the subject and an alternative spatiotemporal portrayal, and then move onto how Habermas's thrust of a practical discourse offers one potential element in the construction of substantive first principles. In the final section we sketch a possible alternative transformative politics. We offer the idea that rather than a deductive model or an inductive model we need a constitutive model in the specification of first principles in a just order.

The most prominent alternative construct of the subject is Lacan's psychoanalytic semiotic model (1977). He drew inspiration from the early Freud, particularly *The Interpretation of Dreams*; Levi-Straus's analysis of the Symbolic order; Benveniste's insightful presentation of the nature of personnel pronouns; Jakobson's specification of the two semiotic axes that order discursive production -- metaphor/metonymy, paradigm/syntagm and Hegel/Kojeve's analysis of the nature of desire. His composite statement introduces a novel conception of the decentered subject, a subject more determined by discourse than its producer.

Lacan's subject can be presented in its static and dynamic form. the static form, his Schema L, can be pictured:

Figure 1
Schema L

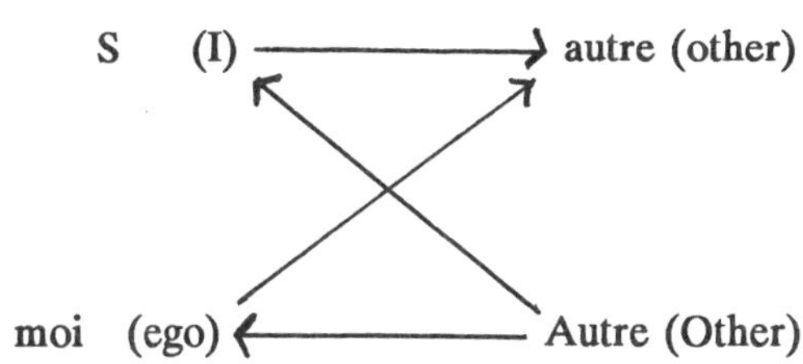

Briefly, Lacan's decentered subject is "stretched out over all four corners" of this schema. The *Other* stands for the unconscious, language and culture -- the locus of the Symbolic order; it is populated by floating signifiers. The *S*, more often presented with a slash through it, the slashed subject, is the subject of speech; it is the position, the grammatical I, taken up by the subject of desire in discursive/narrative constructions. It is the entity that momentary stabilizes the moi and its sliding identifications; these are momentary, fleeting, and fictional images of unity of the subject. The *other* stands for the objects of the egos' desires, what gives the ego its momentary sense of fulfillment. Desire is what materializes as a response to "lack," a "manque-a-être." What follows is a search for objects of desire, *objets petit* a (this includes signifiers) which offer the potential for fulfillment, for *jouissance*. The subject attempts to stitch over, *suture*, gaps in its being by embodying *objets petit* a with desire.

Lacan's subject has an inter-subjective dimension, the moi-other axis, and an intra-subjective dimension, the I-Other axis. These interact in discursive production to produce meaning at different levels: conventional discourse is predominantly guided by the paradigm/syntagm semiotic axis, which coordinates narratively coherent story production; the more hidden level of textual production, guided by the metaphor/metonymy semiotic axis remains fluid and produces de-stabilizing effects; and finally the domain of primordial desire is embodied by the condensation/displacement semiotic axis through the process of figuration. Hence meaning production results from the interaction of all three levels (Milovanovic, 1992). We can depict this as:

Figure 2
Semiotic Axes and Discursive Production

paradigm ↑ metaphor ↑ condensation

syntagm ↑ metonymy ↑ displacement

Lacan's more dynamic model of the psychic apparatus can also be pictured, his "completed graph" of desire (I have omitted the other three):

Figure 3
Completed Graph of Desire
(J. Lacan, *Ecrits*, p.315)

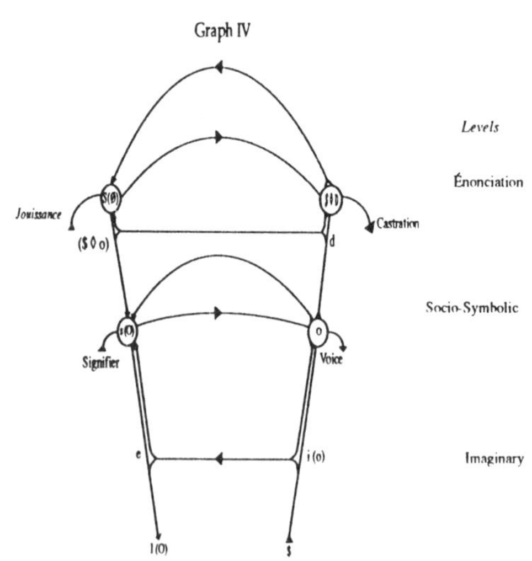

What this complex diagram indicates is precisely how discursive production takes place. Let me provide the short explanation. At the lower right we see the slashed subject. We move upward and come upon the first level, the interaction between the e and i(o), the level of imaginary identifications; that is, the interaction between the fictional identifications of the e, the moi, and its imaginary other, i(o). Next, we come across the Other, the locus of unconscious sliding signifiers. As the subject attempts to suture gaps, that is as desire is mobilized and the search for *objets petit* a gets underway, signifiers are sought that would embody desire. The Other, structured like a language, coordinated by the metaphor-metonymy semiotic axis, provides the material out of which discursive production takes place.

The movement and embodiment of desire can be traced: it begins its journey at the deep structure and undergoes "figuration" by way of the tropes of displacement and condensation; the emerging form is then subject to the psychic work of metaphor and metonymy; and finally it is embodied within signifiers that float within particular discourses (i.e., juridic, scientific, oppositional, etc.) which are structured by the tropes of paradigm and syntagm and which await temporary residence by subjects. We begin with an utterance and anticipate other words. Words, or signifiers, are anchored to some signifieds, in a linear sequence guided by syntax and grammatical codes. It is only with the completion of the utterance, the punctuation, that we return to the beginning of the utterance and fill-in the meaning of each signifier within the syntactical chain of signifiers which then provides us with the meaning of the whole utterance. Meaning is deferred until the punctuation point and the retroactive glance. Hence s(O) stands for the punctuation, the point at which sliding signifiers are given specific anchoring, *point de capiton*, to particular signifieds. The top half of the diagram indicates the internal processes in which *d*, desire, is given embodiment, $\$\Diamond$a (read: slashed subject, signa, *objet petit a*). The final point is I(O), the ego-ideal, a symbolic identification of the subject. It stands for the other identification of the subject with some trait (I) of the *Other* (Zizek, 1990: 104). For example, the juridic subject in law is one such source of identification; the media provides many others in its manipulation of desire and the creation of the consumer it needs.

Chaos Theory

The second major contemporary strand in a postmodernist science that undermines the rational moral philosophers' enterprise is chaos theory (Mandelbrot, 1977; Gleick, 1987; Prigogine and Stengers, 1984; Briggs and Peat, 1989; Young, 1991a, 1991b, 1991c; see also Pepinsky's application to an understanding of violence, 1991). What is offered is an alternative epistemology and space-time mapping. Briefly, chaos theory posits:

(1) *Non-linearity*. Rather than accepting the idea that some incremental increase in some factor(s) produces a proportional increase in some outcome(s), chaos theory provides much evidence that some minor increase in an input value may produce vast disproportional effects in some outcome. A butterfly flapping its wings in Southeast Asia could produce a hurricane in Florida. Applying these findings to argumentation, what is called into question here is the linear logic inherent in deductive syllogism. Rather, as Billig (1987) and de Haan (1990) have pointed out, argumentation is much more open-ended than those rational philosopher reviewed above are willing to admit.

(2) *Fractal nature of space*. Traditionally post-renaissance sciences have been caught up in the use of whole integers in explaining space. For chaos theory, however, space can be of a fractional nature. Thus we have spaces of 2 1/2, 1 3/4, etc. dimensions. Similarly, as T.R.Young has pointed out (1991c), that although the Newtonian paradigm may perceive truth values as having values of either a zero or a plus one, chaos theory implies that truth values may take on fractal values, that is the truth value may take a value of anywhere between 0.0 and 1.0. We have seen recently in the much televised Hill-Thomas confrontation that all involved parties were very much into a notion of a zero or plus-one truth claim (Who is lying? Who is telling the truth?), where in fact, we would suggest the "truth" really takes on a fractal value. Thus the binary Aristotelian logic incorporated in law as well as in law-finding practices generally are suspect.

(3) *Attractors*. Chaos theorists offer an alternative methodology of mapping dynamic systems (Gleick, 1987: 119-153; for an application to deviance theorizing, see Young, 1991a; Pepinsky, 1991: 44-47). Attractors are those trajectories and cumulative patterns that are drawn in "phase space" that map these dynamic movements over time. An attractor is that point toward which a system in movement tends. Some maps depicts linear movements, others, however, portray non-linear movements that often take on complex figures, such as the "butterfly attractor." The latter have been referred to as "strange attractors." These attractors behave in ways contrary to Newtonian physics. They represent both order and disorder: globally a pattern indeed emerges; locally, however, variation and indeterminability exists.

(4) *Self-similarity*. Chaos theorists note that behavior at the local and global levels may have much in similarity as to internal structures. Likewise

the day-to-day behavior of subjects. But in both cases, no precise fit exists. Part of the reason is because of *iteration*. Because we can never be precise, in chaos' conceptualizations (as in quantum mechanics') of original positions, then subsequent iterations can produce disproportionate effects after several of these iterations. Thus cycles can best be represented by a torus (Young, 1991a, 1991b, 1991c). Only approximations exist. Thus, for example, in lawyers preparing briefs with their interpretation of some rule, law, and principle, they are more often varying somewhat from each others' interpretations. Below we depict one interpreter, "a," compared to several interpreters of say the applicability of certain syllogistic reasoning to a "fact" situation; in "b" we have several interpretations; and in "c" interpretations of "n" lawyers doing interpretive work.

Figure 4
Self-Similarity and the Interpretive Torus
(from T.R. Young, 1991d, "Deviance and Chaos Theory: Postmodern Understanding of Social Disorder")

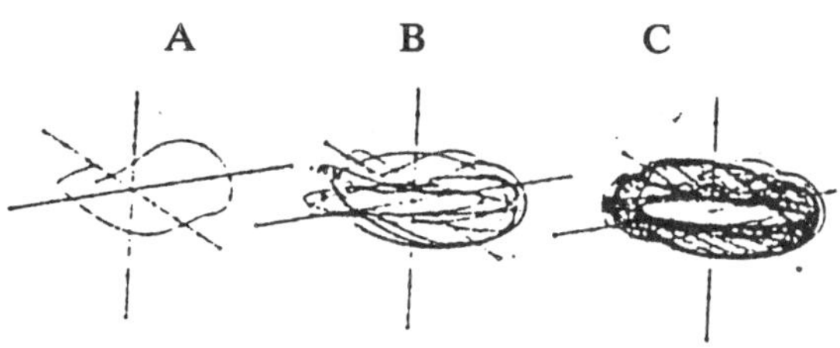

Now, we can take a time-slice from this torus, what is referred to as a Poincaré section, which would then represent in two dimensions, the normative interpretative practices at one time interval. But this time-slice may vary over time. And in fact overall variation may transform into qualitatively different patterns, even into chaotic ones, referred to as "butterfly attractors" (Young, 1991d). Thus, with an introduction of one variable, be it an even small one, it could transform the otherwise stable torus into two or even more toruses, one of which might take the form, again, of the butterfly attractor. (ibid.).

(5) *Bifurcations*. This stands for the process of splitting of some parameter. Interestingly, chaos theorists have found that after about 3.6 bifurcations, chaotic behavior emerges. Significant too, that chaos theorists such as Prigogine and Stengers (1984) have shown that out of this disorder,

order will emerge *spontaneously*; a "something-out-of-nothing" thesis. Prigogine received a Nobel prize for this discovery. Implied here is something of profound proportions: any well conceived and rationally constructed order will no doubt encounter bifurcation points; since we cannot be precise as to original conditions, and since iterations are continuous, at some point unpredictable events will take place approaching chaos, but out of which spontaneously based order will materialize. In anticipation of the next section, it is this idea that Habermas' thrust of a practical discourse as the starting point of substantive moral first principles is given credence; we need not devalue spontaneous results of practical discourse in the ideal speech situation; in fact, this offers the potential of a new (orderly) basis of understanding.

(6) *Dissipative structures*. The notion of a dissipative structure has it that structures continuously break down but are spontaneously reconstructed anew. The critical generating factor is a "far-from-equilibrium condition" (Prigogine and Stengers, 1984: 12-14; Briggs and peat, 1989). In other words, the concept of a dissipative structure combines the notion of order and disorder. The development of a new responsive and relatively stable order necessitates the far-from-equilibrium situation. This concept is well assimilable to the model we will develop in our final section. Our integration of Unger's transformative politics with his criticizable institutional structures is well in accord with the notion offered here. Indeed, structure is necessary for human action to take place.

POLITICAL ECONOMY AND PRINCIPLES OF JUSTICE IN A JUST ORDER

We are now ready to return to the question of establishing first principles of justice in a just order. Of course it is important to keep in mind the distinction between the static and dynamic phase. During the static phase, it will be recalled, it is assumed that a just order has been attained. During the dynamic phase gross inequalities exist and the ability to exercise first principles of justice is curtailed. This necessitates some form of a corrective re-distributive schema in ameliorating existing injustices. We now develop some preliminary analysis for developing just first principles. Our starting point is an ongoing hierarchical system of gross inequalities and an acceptance of the idea of a decentered subject. Although the rational moral philosophers begin with the incorrect framework of subjectivity we need not dismiss all that they have developed. Accordingly, we draw from Phillips and Unger in the analysis of possible political economic structures, from psychoanalytic semiotics and chaos theory for more fruitful lines of inquiry concerning subjectivity and change, and from Habermas and de Haan the inspiration for alternatives to penal punishment.

Prolegomenon to the Question of Punishment in a Just Order

Sanction and penal punishment, we have previously argued, have been incorrectly conflated as concepts (de Haan, 1990; Hirst, 1986: 144-147). Punishment, as one means of sanctioning, implies harm, loss, or suffering. Sanction is simply a response to norm violating behavior (Hirst: 1986: 144-145); it could include restitution, fines, community-service, mediation, etc. Gewirth and Phillips, as de Haan has pointed out, miss this distinction (1990: 111-112), and hence must fall back to the idea of punishment being a necessary evil. Thus, for instance, de Haan has questioned why restitution and compensation could not restore social equilibrium, that is the re-establishment of generic rights (1990: 115), to which, it might be added, Reiman has responded rather forcefully, that justice demands that the response to the violator be somewhat more punitive because the violator has caused the victim to be less than s/he was before the violation and thus the violator should suffer the same consequence (1990: 188). What is being missed is the distinction between sanction and penal punishment by the rational moral philosophers. We thus need a starting point. Hirst has provided a worthwhile one (1986).

Hirst has provided important connections between a socio-political order and its implemented punishment schemas. He has stated that:

> means of punishment are *artefacts of social organization*, the products of definite institutional, technical and discursive conditions....[a]rtefacts can be explained not be their individual "purpose" alone but by the ensemble of conditions under which such constructions or forms become possible...forms of punishment [therefore] are related to conditions of social and political organization (1986: 152).

Means of punishment imply a particular construction of the subject and this construction ("interprellation") creates the necessary objects of a rational punishment schema (ibid.: 155-156). We are now in a better position for stating a case for a constitutive approach to the generation of first principles of a just order.

Constitutive Theory

A constitutive theory is well suited in explaining not only the decentered subject, but how moral first principles in a just order may develop. The constitutive approach argues for a model of overdetermination of interpenetrating effects (Hunt, 1986: 1990: 538-39; 1991: 50-52; Klare, 1979; Harrington and Yngvesson, 1990; Fitzpatrick, 1984; Henry and Milovanovic, 1991; Douzinas, Warrington, and McVeigh, 1990: 119-120). This approach goes beyond the linear dynamics of mono-causal economistic theories -- of the instrumental marxist variety for example, or the working out of the Absolute Spirit as in the case of Hegel -- and beyond a structural determination view that argues for the investigation of relatively independent and stable spheres of influence -- economic, political, ideological, juridical, where the economic only exerts its influence "in the last instance." For constitutive theorizing, legal and social relations mutually constitute each other and "directionality is a matter of specific historical conditions" (Hunt, 1991: 51). Rather than arguing for whether legitimation is procured by consent or coercion, constitutive theory argues that subjects are "normalized" (constituted, interpellated) in a diversity of sites -- the workplace, the family, the prison, mental health and welfare arenas, the school, the informal economy -- and thus consent is always already "pre-shaped to conform to extant structures of domination" (Fitzpatrick, 1984: 130). This is a "contemporaneous" dynamic; "consenting persons are constituted in and by these social forms, which interact concurrently with-in law and so operate to constitute law" (ibid.). Hence, we agree with Hunt (1990: 539) that discourse and practice must be understood as the key determinants of structure and agency.

The constitutive theses follows Hirst's observation that each mode of production tends to discover the principles of punishment it needs. To various degrees, Gewirth, Phillips, Rawls, and Reiman provide principles of justice well-in accord with the maintenance of capitalism. Phillips and Reiman do, however, point to an alternative direction that necessitates a transitional stage, the dynamic phase where a redistributive schema would exist.

Criticizable Validity Claims

A number of criticizable validity claims can now be posed that integrates much of our work here. Each point provides one of the elements of a more holistic approach in establishing more just principles in a just order.

However, these are somewhat preliminary and hence subject to debate.

(1) *Prior to the possible exercise of substantive first principles basic goods such as adequate food, housing, clothing, medical care, security, and education must be provided to all.*

Commentary: Phillips has made a very clear case that before subjects can truly exercise generic rights they must be afforded some minimal level of basic goods and care (1986: chapter eight). Gewirth falls short of this requirement, as does Rawls, for they both fail to specify how truly worst-off (the handicapped, seriously sick) are to be taken care of. Phillip's answer is some "social minimum" to be established without adverse effects on savings or efficiency (1986: 352). Reiman's minimalist answer is his principle of "easy rescue" (1990: 161), the "duty to assist seriously endangered others when one could do so with little risk or loss to oneself."

(2) *Until that time where labor itself is a source of inspiration some system of incentives will be necessitated.*

Commentary: The moral philosophers as well as Reiman's more critical view argue that incentives are necessary in society. Although Rawls has claimed that just "deserts" cannot be accurately measured (and hence the extreme interpretation that no one deserves anything, Phillips, 1986: 360), and Gewirth has argued that those contributing more are deserving of higher rewards, Phillips and Reiman place restrictions. Phillips makes a good case that reducing the ratio of the top layered compared to the bottom layered income levels to a 5 to 1 ratio would still assure that incentives would exist for education, production, efficiency and order. Reiman has also provided a redistributive schema, his *labor theory of moral values* that assures an incentive schema during the dynamic phase. For Reiman, if that stage is reached where an incentive schema is no longer necessary, justice would demand a distributive schema (1990: 285-288).

(3) *A "Program of Empowered Democracy" has found important elements at the political economic level, in Unger (1987) and Phillips (1986) and at the agency level in the psychoanalytic semiotic perspective.*

Commentary:

(a) Roberto Unger in his monumental *False Necessity* (1987) has provided a *tour de force* in the analysis of alternative structures to current hierarchical forms of domination. Identifying the tendency of bureaucracies to ossify, he lays out a framework by which we may maintain open and criticizable institutions (ibid.: chapter five).

The core of his ideas rests with the notion of a "central capital fund." A first tier of this social investment fund would fall under the control of a representative body and executive. The second tier would consist of diverse investment funds established by tier one. The third, would consist of "capital takers": temporary funds would be made available to small teams of workers and entrepreneurs. Each team is free to make its own decisions on penalties and rewards within the limits established by tier two. Hereditary transmission of large sums would be abolished, and each subject would be provided minimal welfare guarantees. A system of rights would protect the citizenry. This would include: (1) market rights -- teams of workers, technicians, and entrepreneurs would have available to them some portion of a social capital. The small interest collected would go back into the social capital fund; (2) immunity rights -- these would assure the subjects the possibility of active disagreement, and would assure unrestrained access to input in criticizing institutions without prejudice; it would also provide some minimal welfare entitlements; (3) destabilizing rights -- these would include all rights to question any ossifying tendency and power concentrations in a society; they assure some source of conflict which undermines the tendency of institutions becoming unresponsive; and finally (4) solidarity rights -- these would give idealized legal expression to "social relations of reliance and trust," which ideally would be enforced by mediation mechanisms.

Consistent with these would be cultural changes. Unger describes how institutional roles themselves would become more open. He advocates "role defiance" and "role jumbling" (1987: 564). The incongruous nature of social experience, he tells us, would be a source of celebration not repression; it would be one method of more genuinely educating the passions. Accordingly, what is advocated is a permanent loosening "between the subjective experience of personal encounters and its symbolic representation" (ibid.: 565). In short, Ungers' proposals assure the maximal amount of innovation and experimentation in a social order. He advocates the logic of difference rather than a logic of equivalence.

All this of course would increase the points of differences; conflict, therefore would no doubt increase. But the means of conflict regulation would now be central. Here sanction in the form of mediation, restitution, and apology would have central significance. And so too would Habermas' discourse ethics generated in concrete encounters. It is here, too that de Haan's notion of "redress" would make sense.

(b) Phillips has also provided many ideas that seem to be in accord with Unger's (see particularly Phillips, 1986: chapter nine). He identifies three ideal requirements of a productive system: [1] "a just distribution of social and economic benefits, [2] a high degree of efficiency and economic growth, [3] and conditions of work that foster people's identity formation and autonomous development." The first principle we have developed earlier. The second and third have much similarity with Unger. He acknowledges that large-scale state institutions/corporations must exist. But moderate-scale enterprises which would be most dominant in his envisioned socialist economy, would be organized around the notions of self-management. He does make a distinction here between workers participating in overall policy which entail value judgments as opposed to the technical which necessitates professional judgments. Some coordinating hierarchy would still be necessary, but no power hierarchy, he claims, would develop (ibid.: 394-395). In addition to the large and moderate scale firms, he would also allow for small-scale private businesses (ibid.: 397).

According to Phillips, certain social minimums will be established for well-being, but no coercive attempts would exist in dictating the benefit to the needy; the best society can do is to use educative means for those who would want to make use of their social minimum in ways harmful to themselves or other (ibid.: 414). Finally, Phillips advocates reducing the ratio of income differentials of the more privileged to the less to 5-to-one. Drawing data from other industrialized democracies he convincingly argues that incentives for attaining higher education and for the fulfilling of diverse jobs would not be jeopardized.

(c) In terms of the decentered subject and an alternative replacement discourse and its attendant discursive subject-positions, we argue that the empowered democracy that we have traced out would present a discourse with forms (signifiers) that would more genuinely embody desire (*objet petit a*); that would offer the opportunity for the subject to take up temporary residence in varied discursive subject-positions none of which would identify completely her/his essential being; that the subject of symbolic identification, the ego-ideal [*I(O)*], would not identify with fetishistic traits such as the juridic subject, phallocentric identities, or media induced identifications but rather with authentic I-thou relationships and a discourse of mutual benefit; and that the subject would break the bonds of alienative production by embodying his/her objects of production with desire which reflectively, as the *other*, would now provide images of unity, completeness, and connectedness.

To make use of chaos's conceptualizations, what subjectivity could trace out over time is a strange attractor rather than limit cycles. In far-from-equilibrium conditions, bifurcation points would undoubtedly be negotiated frequently; but the call would be a full exploration of being human, not repetition and the maintenance of the status quo (see also Pepinsky, 1991).

(4) *The nature of the decentered subject and the recent findings of chaos theory point to the need for a re-evaluation of the nature of responsibility, guilt, accountability and blame.*

Commentary: The postmodern sciences has introduced challenging conceptualizations to our inherited post-renaissance thought. The notion of the decentered subject challenges repressive formalistic renditions of the nature of the human being. The logic of "equivalence" found in a material form in the notion of the juridic subject, the reasonable man/woman in law, and in such legal notions as formal equality do a disservice to the complexities of the human condition. In fact, interpellation is a continuous process, and the legal rational subject is constructed in a multitude of settings. Consent-versus-coercion, therefore, is a dichotomy that has outlived its usefulness. Rather, we find, following a constitutive approach, that subjectivity is created anew in diverse settings and these settings are in turn actively created by the subject. Discourse analysis provides a crucial element in the understanding of how subjectivity is constructed and how desire attains or is denied expression.

Chaos theory with its core concepts of non-linearity, fractal dimensional space, attractors, self-similarity, iteration, bifurcation, and dissipative structures provides alternative conceptualizations that allows liberating lines of analysis that may give freer expression of desire. We no longer can assume that one's input, no matter how small, makes no difference; that truth statements have a yes or no nature but rather that they can range; that even though patterns emerge in a subject's or an organization's activities, no precise matching occurs, only approximations; that iteration inevitably produces unpredictable states because of the impossibility of defining with precision original conditions; that after approximately 3.6 bifurcations chaos conditions are manifest; and that out of disorder, spontaneous order has been shown to develop particularly in the form of dissipative structures.

Our presentation of the decentered subject as well as the core tenants of chaos theory are particularly well in accord with the thrust of Unger's as well as Phillip's more macro-level theorizing of a just order. In other words, consistent with constitutive theorizing, far-from-equilibrium conditions at all levels of the social formation provide a necessary element for change, creativity, greater responsiveness, and transcendence which in turn provide the context out of which subjectivity and desire become manifest.

(5) *A solidarity ethics and discourse, and substantive first principles must begin with an ongoing practical discourse. The question of penal punishment and sanction, too, must begin with ongoing practical discourses.*

Commentary: Finally, we turn to the question of punishment in a just order. The much superior starting point is Reiman's. His beginning point is an ongoing social structure where forced labor and the perception of subjugation exists. From there, we have found out, he derives a labor theory of moral value which attempts to develop a redistributive schema that reduces subjugation. His labor theory of moral value is also a principle of mutual benefit (1990: 276, 282); in fact, it values the idea of reciprocal benefits, and hence a solidaristic discourse. Since his labor theory would directly affect productive and distributive schema the generated discourse would also reach diverse levels.

Rather than the logic of equivalence being efficacious, Reiman's labor theory of moral value could be the primordial point for the development of humanistic idealized expressions of difference: *I* and *thou* would increasingly find in the other a source of support, recognition, identification, but also inherent differences. These are indeed bonds of solidarity not separateness. In combination with Unger's and Phillip's modest proposals for more participatory productive spheres and more open, criticizable structures and institutions, Reiman's model would provide the direction for a less subjugating social formation. Habermas' *ideal speech situation* could begin to become more realistic. With de Haan's thoughtful integration of practical discourse, with his notion of "redress," substantive first principles could arise from bottom up, an inductive model. This would all be in accord with a constitutive model that argues for the idea of multi-causal interpenetration which results in quasi-stable dissipative structures, which would be open, criticizable, and always subject to change. Since subjects would begin to participate in multiple discursive subject-positions greater insecurity and conflict no doubt will result. But de Haan's sanction model centered on the notion of *redress* would be particularly well in accord with the requirements of a just order.

During the dynamic phase, penal punishment based on principles of just deserts, along the lines laid out by Reiman but qualified by limitations based on a least harm principle (see also Knopp, 1991: 186) would seem consistent with the internal dynamics of a hierarchical, exploitive order where subjugation is the norm. We are in agreement here with a feminist/abolitionist view (Knopp, 1991;Knopp et al, 1976). "Places of restraint," for such repetitive sexual violent acts such as rape, in the short run at least, are needed (Knopp et al, 1976: 15-151). A feminist/abolitionist position spelled out by Knopp would seem to admit to the need of "restraint of the few" (1991: 185) even in the long run. Of course, this could only be answered more definitively in historical context.

De Haan has a strong argument for an alternative sanctioning schema, but this can only occur during the more static phase (and we read "static" to incorporate pervasive "far-from-equilibrium" conditions spelled out above); during the dynamic phase one could seriously consider exclusive use of restitution and compensation as relevant responses. But, given some imprisonment, or "places of restraint" as a form of sanction during the dynamic phase, additional harm and suffering need not follow. (For a good clear-headed starting point of reducing places of restraint and for the development of a caring community spelled out in four strategies -- a moratorium of further prison construction, decarceration, excarceration, and restraint of the few, see Knopp, 1991: 184-185.) Some amount of imprisonment given our socio-political and economic structure is a necessary evil and only with the arrival of a just order will the question of the necessity of places of restraint find answers; but we can also make minimum use of it; we can provide due process safeguards and meaningful redress; we can eliminate many of the degrading, dehumanizing, mortifying, and disrespectful conditions; we can provide meaningful prison employment, education, and vocational training; we can add restitutive dimensions to the sentence; and we can provide better transitions on release.

Again, we are one with de Haan's integration of Habermas's ideal of the necessity of developing genuine substantive moral first principles from concrete practical discourses. With the elements we have presented for a just order, greater concern will exist for the presentation of diverse validity claims whether in face-to-face interactions, or whether in the form of a challenge to some ossifying bureaucratic organization. Deductive and inductive logic, so central to the legal method in arriving at "truth," would be discarded for a looser form of argumentation. We say looser not fuzzier or indifferent. Billig has well made the point that concrete argumentation takes more of the form of rhetoric than logic. As he tells us "whereas logical syllogisms produced deductions which were certainties, enthymemes [an enthymeme is a statement together with its justification] dealt with probabilities" (1987: 102). Thus Billig argues that subjects enter encounters with different starting points, different premises, and hence each presents, in his/her own way compelling syllogisms. Each enthymeme in turn can be open to criticism, which could be answered by an explanatory enthymeme, which in turn can be criticized and answered by another enthymeme, and so forth. Of course it is the nature of legal reasoning that all this is circumscribed by formalistic deductive logic and syllogistic reasoning. Here an argument "comes to a full stop, once the premises have delivered up their unsurprising conclusion" (ibid.: 102). Given the decentered subject's need to give expression to desire, it would seem that the enthymemic form provides the possibility of more concrete expression, more "jouissance." We need not be imprisoned in a dominant discourse and its internal rational forms.

In short, de Haan's synthesis of Habermas's notion of practical discourse and its open-ended nature in arguing issues provides an alternative starting point in developing substantive moral first principles in a just order. It would provide an opportunity for considering diverse contexts and meaning constructions in complex orders (de Haan, 1990: 160). De Haan also mentions four points for "practical learning" and the possibility of social change: (1) there must exist the possibility of becoming aware of asymmetrical communicative forms and relations within institutional structures; (2) there should be possibilities of giving verbal form to concrete experiences which criticize institutions and their offered justifications; (3) these experiences and their expression should be entertainable in some forum; and (4) experimentation should be possible with alternative dispute-regulating forums and alternative orders as a challenge to conventionally accepted normative frameworks (ibid.: 165-166). Use of force would be reduced, and the consensus arrived at in an ideal speech situation would coordinate action. As to the appropriate response to problematic behavior, center stage would be the notion of sanction and only secondarily punishment. As a just order approaches and these ideals are instituted there should be very few instances of penal punishment and instead the principle of least harm should prevail. Left for another day is how to develop forums in which practical discourse could take place and some form of closure could be agreed upon.

CONCLUSION

This article has been an exercise in self-clarification of developing substantive first principles and in determining the justification of punishment in a just order. Rational moral philosophers were investigated. Reiman's recent model was seen as far superior. It provided an adequate operationalization of the difference principle in that subjugation was reduced. It also provided the beginning point of a solidarity discourse. Habermas's notion of a practical discourse with its further adaptation by de Haan in his notion of "redress" offered an additional examination of discourse ethics well-suited to Reiman's model. We also investigated Unger's and Phillips's model of a just model of society as well as ideas offered by the postmodern sciences, particularly by chaos theory and psychoanalytic semiotics. We concluded with positing our own criticizable validity claims and noted that much good analysis remains, but these focal points offer much worthwhile notions in developing less harmful responses to problematic behavior and more liberating structures for desire to speak. The final judge of our efforts is history and we still need to learn from the revolutions and experiments of the past especially those of well-intended movements and charismatic figures (Beirne, 1990).

* *An earlier version of this paper was presented at the Annual meeting of the Association for Humanist Sociology, October, 1991.*

** *Dragan Milovanovic is Professor of Criminal Justice at Northeastern Illinois University.*

REFERENCES

Beirne, P. (ed.) (1990), *Revolution in Law: Contributions to the Development of Soviet Legal Theory, 1917-1938*. New York: M.E. Sharpe, Inc.

Billig, M. (1987), *Arguing and Thinking: A Rhetorical Approach to Social Psychology*. New York: Cambridge University Press.

Briggs, J. and F.D. Peat (1989), *Turbulent Mirror*. New York: Harper and Row.

de Haan, W. (1990), *The Politics of Redress: Crime, Punishment and Penal Reform*. Winchester, Mass.: Unwin Hyman Inc.

Douzinas, C. R. Warrington, and S. McVeign (1990), *Postmodern*

Jurisprudence. New York: Routledge.

Fitzpatrick, P. (1984), "Law and Societies," *Osgoode Hall Law Journal* 22: 115.

Freiberg, A. (1987), "Reconceptualizing Sanctions," *Criminology* 25: 223-256).

Gewirth, A. (1978), *Reason and Morality*. Chicago: Chicago University Press.

Gleick, J. (1987), *Chaos: Making a New Science*. New York: Viking Penguin.

Habermas, J. (1976), *Legitimation Crisis*. London: Heinemann.

_____. (1979), *Theory and Practice*. London: Heinemann.

_____. (1984), *The Theory of Communicative Action, Vol 1 Reason and Rationalization of Society*. Boston: Beacon.

Harrington, C. and B. Yngvesson (1990), "Interpretive Sociolegal Research," *Law and Social Inquiry* 15(1): 135-148.

Henry, S. and D. Milovanovic (1991), "Constitutive Criminology," *Criminology* 29(2): 293-316).

Hirst, P. (1986), *Law and Socialism and Democracy*. Winchester, Mass.: Allen and Unwin.

Hunt, A. (1986), "The Theory of Critical Legal Studies," *Oxford Journal of Legal Studies*, 6 (1).

____. (1990), "The Big Fear: Law Confronts Postmodernism," *McGill Law Journal*, 35(3): 507-540).

____. (1991), "Why Did Foucault Get Law So Wrong? Reflections on Law, Power and Sovereignty," (unpublished manuscript).

Klare, K. (1979), "Law-Making as Praxis," *Telos* 40: 123.

Knopp, F.H. (1991), "Community Solutions to Sexual Violence: Feminist/Abolitionist Perspectives," in H. Pepinsky and R. Quinney (eds.) *Criminology as Peacemaking*. Bloomington: Indiana University Press.

_____. et al (1976), *Instead of Prisons: A Handbook for Abolitionists*. Orwell, Vt: Safer Society Program.

Lacan, J. (1977), *Ecrits*. Norton.

Mandelbrot, B. (1983), *The Fractal Geometry of Nature*. New York: W.H.Freeman.

Milovanovic, D. (1992). *Postmodern Law and Disorder: Psychoanalytic Semiotics, Chaos and Juridic Exegeses*. Merseyside, U.K.: Deborah Charles Pub., 1992.

Pepinsky, H. (1991), *The Geometry of Violence and Democracy*. Bloomington: Indiana University Press.

Phillips, D. (1986), *Toward a Just Order*. Princeton, New Jersey: Princeton University Press.

Prigogine, I. and I. Stengers (1984), *Order Out of Chaos*. New York: Bantam Books.

Rawls, J. (1971), *A Theory of Justice*. Cambridge, Mass.: Harvard University Press.

Reiman, J. (1990), *Justice and Modern Moral Philosophy*. New Haven: Yale University Press.

Unger, R. (1987), *False Necessity*. New York: Cambridge University Press.

Young, T.R. (1991a), "Chaos and Crime: Nonlinear and Fractal Forms of Crime," *The Critical Criminologist* 3(2): 3-4, 10-11.

____. (1991b), "The ABC of Crime: Attractors, Bifurcations, Basins, and Chaos," *The Critical Criminologist* (forthcoming).

____. (1991c), "Paradigm Theory: Foundations of Postmodern Sciences" (Unpublished).

Zizek, S. (1989), *The Sublime Object of Ideology*. New York: Verso.

INDEX